"I Will Shoot Them from My Loving Heart"

"I Will Shoot Them from My Loving Heart"

Memoir of a South Korean Officer in the Korean War

WON MOO HURH

McFarland & Company, Inc., Publishers
Jefferson, North Carolina, and London

LIBRARY OF CONGRESS CATALOGUING-IN-PUBLICATION DATA

Hurh, Won Moo.
 "I will shoot them from my loving heart" : memoir of a South Korean officer in the Korean War / Won Moo Hurh.
  p.   cm.
 Includes bibliographical references and index.

 ISBN 978-0-7864-6503-3
 softcover : 50# alkaline paper ∞

 1. Korea (South). Yukkun — Officers — Biography. 2. Korean War, 1950–1953 — Personal narratives, Korean. 3. Korean War, 1950–1953 — Artillery operations. 4. Soldiers — Korea — Biography. 5. Korea (South) — Armed Forces — Military life. I. Title.
 II. Title: Memoir of a South Korean officer in the Korean War
 U55.K343H87   2012
 951.904'242 — dc23
 [B]   2011039159

BRITISH LIBRARY CATALOGUING DATA ARE AVAILABLE

© 2012 Won Moo Hurh. All rights reserved

No part of this book may be reproduced or transmitted in any form or by any means, electronic or mechanical, including photocopying or recording, or by any information storage and retrieval system, without permission in writing from the publisher.

Front cover: Won Moo Hurh, 1951; background © 2012 Shutterstock

Manufactured in the United States of America

McFarland & Company, Inc., Publishers
 Box 611, Jefferson, North Carolina 28640
  www.mcfarlandpub.com

To my ROK and U.S. Army buddies
at the Kumsong Front June–July 1953

Contents

A Note on the Title viii
Acknowledgments ix
Abbreviations xi
Preface 1

1. Chances of Life 3
2. My First Life-Chance 12
3. Memories from the Early Years 20
4. The War and My Shattered Life Course 35
5. Officer Candidate School 55
6. The Frontline and Fort Sill 65
7. Teaching at the ROK Artillery School 101
8. Back to the Front 114
9. Antiaircraft Artillery and Fort Bliss 145
10. Serving the Top Brass 161

Epilogue 171
Appendix: ROK Infantry and Artillery (1950–53) 179
References 181
Index 183

A Note on the Title

THE INHUMANITY AND ABSURDITY of war is contained in the short phrase "I will shoot them from my loving heart," the title of this memoir. I was required to recite this phrase every day as part of my officer training. The quote is taken from the Republic of Korea Army's Combat Code (*Jeonhun*) that went into effect on July 26, 1950. This Combat Code was repealed on July 1, 1951. The complete sentence from which the quote is taken reads:

> *While engaged in combat I will advance according to the order received, and if I see my comrades or subordinates retreat without permission, I will shoot them from my loving heart of patriotism and friendship.* (Item #2 of the Combat Code. My translation.)

Certainly, I did not hold such a heartless view of killing my fellow soldiers. My personal views on war and killing are expressed in the epilogue to this book.

Acknowledgments

PUBLICATION OF THIS VOLUME would have been impossible without the labor of love contributed by my family. My wife, Gloria, and our son Paul (a communication instructor and an English professor, respectively) reviewed every page of my manuscript with patience and care. Patrick, our other son (a mechanical engineer), drew a map of the Korean peninsula to show the location of the places mentioned in the book. And as always our daughter Tracy's cheerful encouragement has been a great help. I am forever grateful for the loving support of my family. My hearty thanks are also due to retired Brigadier General Jung Kyun Shin and retired Lieutenant Ung Jai Lee with whom I consulted on the details of the Kumsong battlefront in June–July 1953. I am deeply grateful to my fellow soldiers both from the ROK and the UN forces, particularly the American soldiers and officers who fought with me at the Kumsong front. Without the help of the U.S. Armed Forces, the ROK Armed Forces would not have survived the Korean War at all.

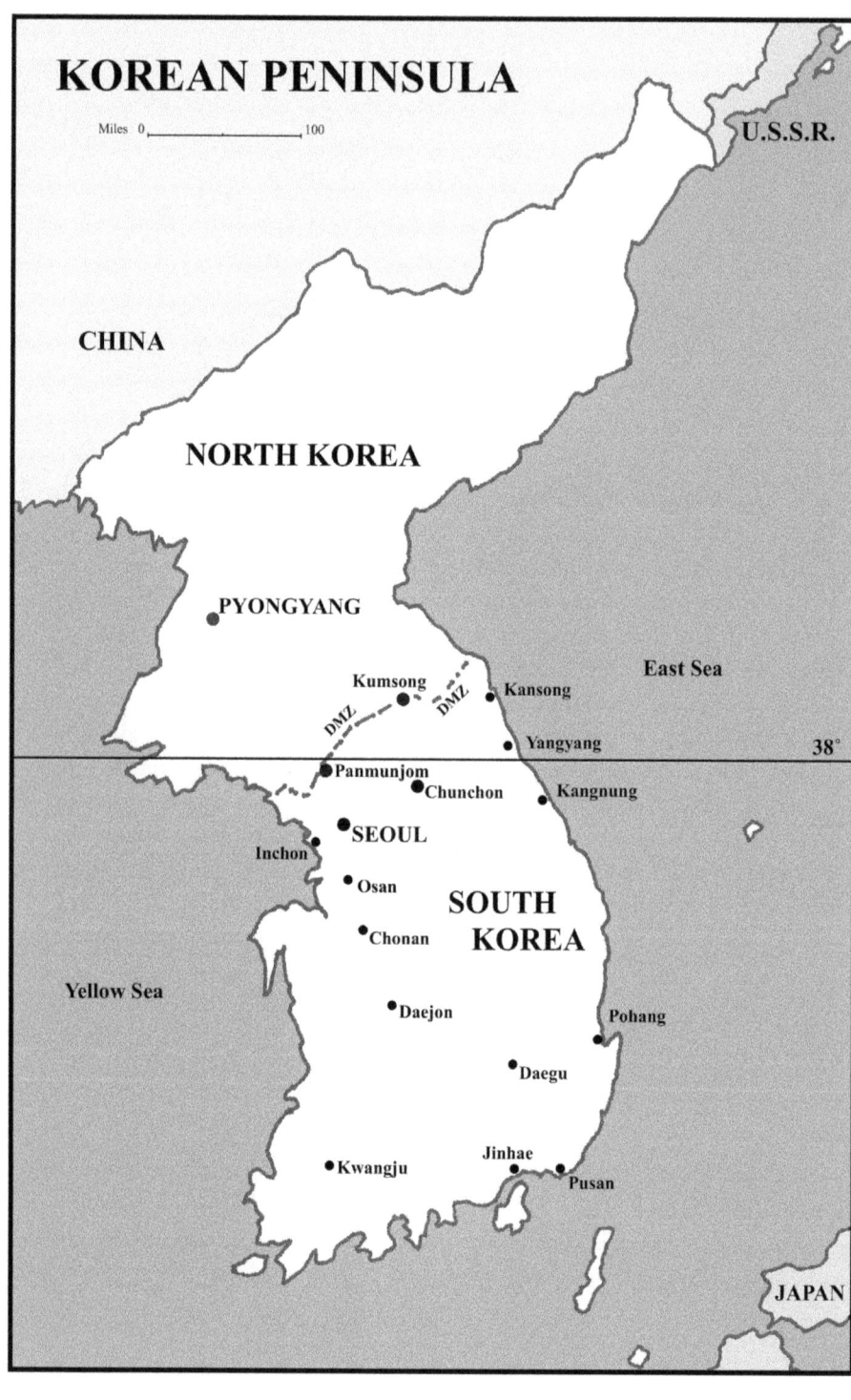

Abbreviations

AAA	Antiaircraft Artillery
CCF	Chinese Communist Forces
CP	Command Post
DPRK	Democratic People's Republic of Korea (North Korea)
DMZ	Demilitarized Zone
FDC	Fire Direction Center
FOB	Forward Observer
HQ	Headquarters
KAMAG	Korean Military Advisory Group (U.S.)
LST	Landing Ship Tank
MP	Military Police
NKPA	North Korean People's Army
OP	Observation Post
OCS	Officer Candidate School
ROK	Republic of Korea (South Korea)
S-2	Staff 2, Intelligence Section of Artillery Battalion HQ
S-3	Staff 3, Operation and Training Section of Artillery Battalion HQ
SGS	Secretary to the General Staff, ROK Army
TOT	Time on Target
UN	United Nations
WAC	Woman's Army Corps

Opposite: Map of the Korean Peninsula showing locations mentioned in the book. Drawing by Patrick Hurh.

Preface

Stories about the Korean War have been published in many languages since 16 nations participated in the war under the United Nations Command. Close to a thousand of books have been published on the Korean War in English in the United States. However, Americans authored most of these and only a few were written by Korean soldiers in English. Moreover, these few stories generally described only the events of the war with little in-depth reflection on the soldiers' subjective feelings about the war itself and their existential conditions in the battlefield.

In my view, a memoir can be written in a number of ways: (1) describe merely the factual events of one's life; (2) add to the factual account one's feelings about events; and (3) reflect upon (1) and (2) in their historical and existential contexts so that the readers can place themselves in the author's shoes for an empathetic understanding of the author's intended message. In this book, I have tried my best to attain all of the above.

Some of the information in this book is based on my occasional field notes, but most comes from my recollected experiences. My story in this book is based on what I perceived, felt, and thought to be true about the things that I experienced more than a half a century go.

A technical note to the reader: the transcription of Korean names in this book is done in the Western way — the first name first and the surname last in order to avoid unnecessary confusion, except for well-known historical figures, such as Kim Il-sung, whose name has always been printed in the Korean way, i.e. the surname first.

At times I have chosen a writing style that reconstructs the verbal dialogue between myself and others through the use of direct quotations. These are, naturally, based on my recollections of the actual words spoken so many years ago. In addition, this dialogue was originally in the Korean language, which means the English words used in the dialogue are actually translations. I also was sensitive to conveying the cultural nuances inherent in any language so as to overcome any "lost in translation" problems that can so easily occur. Nevertheless, in all instances I have attempted to accurately reflect the substance and emotions contained in the direct quotations.

1

Chances of Life

THE QUESTION OF HOW chance rules one's life — one's life-chance — has always been a mystery to me. Some people die and some live — even under similar life circumstances. Since early childhood, there have been several occasions when I could have died. I wonder why God saved my life. I am not just talking about physical illness, although I had a close call according to my mother when I had an infection in the peritoneum (*bogmang-nyum*) at the age of two. I was taken to the hospital emergency room. My abdomen was swollen like a balloon, and I was running a high fever, but Western medicine did not help. I was fighting for my life. As a last resort, my grandfather took me to a Chinese herbalist doctor. Following the Chinese doctor's suggestion, I ate boiled chestnuts every day for ten months. Grandfather personally fed me three bowls of the boiled chestnuts religiously every day. Fortunately, I have no recollection of eating chestnut gruel (*bahmjuk*) for almost a year. My mother strongly believed that the chestnuts saved my life.

* * *

Most of my near-death experiences, however, are not attributable to illness. The first one I vividly remember was a train accident that occurred in the early morning of a foggy spring day in 1941. I was in the third grade and commuting to school by a local train with other students from different neighborhoods. My family lived in a suburban area of Seoul near Book Ahyun Dong train station, and I rode my train the five miles to my school (Chang Cheon Gugmin Hakkyo). The school was located midway between two station stops so I could get off at either stop — the first stop (Shinchon) or the second (Sogang) — and then walk about a mile to reach the school. Usually

"I Will Shoot Them from My Loving Heart"

I boarded the train at Book Ahyun Dong and got off at the first stop, Shinchon, in order to save time. On that day, however, I stayed on the train with my close friends because of some argument with another group of students who had gotten off at the first station.

The train started moving toward the next station, Sogang, and I looked out the window at the foggy spring day. Through the dense fog, I could barely see the railroad track and nothing at all of the farmhouses that I usually saw below the railroad bank. The track was elevated on a soil bank about 40 feet above the rice paddies. The train was moving at full steam when the emergency brakes squealed and the train unexpectedly stopped. Everyone stood up and looked out the train windows to see why we had stopped. Nothing seemed unusual at first, but within a few seconds the train started shaking violently. My friends panicked and were screaming and running to the doors to get out. At that instant without thinking, I crawled under the wooden bench seat. At that point, I lost consciousness.

Faintly I thought I heard someone crying. I opened my eyes, but I didn't know where I was — everything was blurry. Slowly my vision became clear. I was lying on the ceiling of the upside-down train littered with broken glass, mangled pieces of train seats, and strangely a lot of white or small light grayish things that looked like popped corn or rice. (Later I was told they were scattered pieces of someone's brain). I tried to get up but couldn't. I felt a sharp pain in my right leg and lower back. I wanted to see what had happened, but I couldn't raise my leg or my upper torso. I began to hear noises — moaning, crying, shouting, and banging. I lost consciousness again. The next time I woke up, I was on a stretcher. Two men were carrying me to the Japanese-run hospital nearby.

The big hall was filled with injured students brought in for emergency treatment. A young Korean doctor examined me and said my injury was very mild — a punctured leg. He dressed the wound that was the size of a dime and said I could go home after they took an X-ray of my back. Towards the evening of that day, my parents came to the hospital. Later I learned that my Dad had warned Mom in the taxicab that she should be prepared to face the eventuality that I might already be dead. My mother was crying with relief to see me alive. I felt lucky after hearing that 17 people had died and 75 had been injured in the train accident. I learned that the midsection of the train, where I was riding, was hit by another train causing my train to roll over twice and land in the ditch.

1. Chances of Life

We came home late in the day, happy and relieved. But trouble began that night. I could not sleep. Nightmares, heart palpitations, and fever occurred. The next morning I was still running a high fever and felt an excruciating pain in the back of my punctured leg. The leg was swollen, and I could not stand or walk. Since we did not have a car, my mother carried me piggyback to a cab that took me to the nearest clinic. The clinic was a private clinic run by my father's friend, Dr. Lee, a kindly, middle-aged man with a distinguished, handlebar mustache. After examining my leg, he told us that the wound was badly infected, and it would take several months to heal. At that time there was no penicillin. His treatment was to stuff an alcohol-soaked piece of gauze about an inch and half into the wound. The same procedure had to be repeated every other day for two months! Mother had the heavy burden of taking me piggyback to the clinic every other day for two months. In the meantime Japanese officers in the Ministry of Railway Transportation visited me, bringing candies, juice, and other sweet stuff. I did not care much about them. I did appreciate, however, their apology for causing the accident. My wound healed eventually. I survived, but others died.

* * *

Six South Korean artillery officers were traveling together toward the north on the east coast of South Korea in the spring of 1951. These officers were young—most of them between the ages of 17 and 19. I was one of them, 17 years old and almost a high school senior when the Korea War started on June 25, 1950. The only 19-year-old officer among us was Lieutenant Han, a college freshman at Seoul National University and a brilliant math major.

A few days earlier, we had been commissioned as second lieutenants after completing six weeks of infantry training at the Army Comprehensive School for Officer Candidates (Yukgun Jonghab Hagkyo) and a month of artillery training at the Army Artillery School (Yukgun Pobyeong Hagkyo). These schools were created in August 1950 to meet the dire need to replenish the ranks of junior officers at the frontlines, such as platoon leaders in the infantry and forward observers in the artillery. Normally army officer candidate training took at least three to four years, but then the Korean War broke out. During the early phase of the war, training was drastically reduced to six or nine weeks because the casualty rate of the junior officers at the frontlines had reached about 60 percent. Usually an infantry company needed four lieutenants for normal operation, but only one or two were now available. Specifically, the casualty rate of the Army Comprehensive School's graduates during 1950–53 was 45.4 percent (3,117 out of 7,004 officers died). Hence, these officers were commonly called "consumptive officers"(*somojangyo*), meaning they were to be consumed at the frontlines soon after their commission.

I was commissioned as a second lieutenant of the ROK (Republic of Korea) Artillery on April 14, 1951, with my classmates. There were 44 of us in the 13th Class of the Artillery OCS (Officer Candidate School). None of us knew anything about these statistics, but we knew that many of us would die soon because we would certainly be assigned to the frontline, mostly as forward observers. Forward observers were the *eyes* of the artillery batteries, conducting the direction of fire. They were usually with the frontline infantry company commanders or platoon leaders.

So here we were, six "baby lieutenants" minted fresh from the artillery school and ordered to report to the commander of the 11th Division of the ROK Army at the eastern front for our first combat duties. According to the order, all of us were assigned to the same unit called the 102nd Independent Artillery Company. That's why we were traveling together, but we were not sure where the hell the division headquarters (HQ) were since they were constantly changing location depending on their battle situations. Roughly, we figured the HQ would be in either Sokcho or Yangyang—about 400 miles northeast from Jin Hae where we started our journey. And, of course, there were no travel guides, transportation arrangements, nor travel allowances. In short, we were on our own but required to report to the HQ on time—within ten days, no matter what! At the Officer Candidate School, we were fed and clothed, but monetary pay was out of the question. In fact, our uniforms and shoes were so worn out that we were ashamed to present ourselves among civilians in cities we were traveling through. Some of us had a little money given to us by relatives, and we shared our resources with others—mostly for food and emergency needs.

Our major means of transportation was hitchhiking. We could not understand why we could not have any access to military transportation for our assignment. Our first ride was with a convoy of trucks transporting civilian volunteer workers (*nomuja*) for the war effort. These *nomuja*s were not exactly "volunteers" but rather laborers drafted without pay to help repair roads, dig trenches, and carry food, ammunition and other army supplies to the frontlines. Their casualty rate was as high as that of infantry soldiers. Most of them were middle-aged peasants or fishermen, and they usually dressed in white Korean work fatigues. It was a rather chilly April morning when we got on the second of these trucks carrying about 15 to 20 *nomuja*s. We were leaving Pohang (a harbor city north of Pusan) on a dusty road that cut through a small mountain. While on the truck I felt sorry for the laborers and for myself — why on earth must we do this senseless traveling? For what purpose in life? Sheer survival? What is the meaning of all this?

At that moment, an enormous explosion took place in front of us. The truck about 50 yards ahead suddenly vanished in a cloud of smoke. Dust and debris covered everyone in our truck, but we managed to get off to assess the situation. No one in our truck was seriously injured, but the truck in front of us had been hit by an anti-tank mine that blew it to pieces along with all the laborers on it. I felt sick to my stomach when I heard this terrible news, but some of my fellow "consumptive" officers thought it was a good opportunity to see what exactly casualties looked like, so that we would be prepared when we really went to the frontline. Reluctantly I joined them, and we started to look around and examine the wounded and dead bodies of the civilian laborers. There were eight dead bodies and about ten injured soldiers with the possibility of more casualties on the mountain slope. That was enough of a frontline lesson for me, but my close colleague, Lieutenant Jeong asked me to go up the mountain slope with him to find the other dead bodies — and we did. One of the dead had his face blown off, and the remaining back of his skull was filled with blood — the blood was steaming in the cool mountain air. I was shocked, sick to my stomach, scared, and depressed. The explosion could have happened to any of us.

* * *

Our second hitchhiking experience that day was with a convoy of army trucks headed for the Engineering Battalion stationed near Yangyang where we were supposed to report. Heading up the convoy was a big American GMC truck carrying a large bulldozer, followed by five brand-new Toyota trucks. A young engineering officer led the convoy and gave us permission to ride as passengers in the trucks. We felt lucky not only to have survived the earlier mine explosion but also to have found such ideal transportation for reaching our destination. However, one unlucky guy would have to ride on the high seat of the bulldozer on top of the GMC truck or in the back of one of the Toyota trucks. So who turned out to be the unlucky guy? Me. I lost the lotto. I climbed up the GMC truck, took the bulldozer seat, and positioned myself at the highest altitude of the convoy.

It was a gorgeous spring day for traveling, especially along the east coast of the Korean peninsula. The view from the bulldozer was simply breathtaking — a beautiful collage of colors of the sea, the sky, the coastal mountains and cliffs. The East Sea (the Japanese called it "the Sea of Japan") was extraordinarily dark blue against the bright April sun in the clear sky, creating an unimaginably good contrast with the green and chocolate colors of the rocky coasts. Looking at the scenery, I felt I was in another world. So beautiful and peaceful — even though an American Navy cruiser on the distant horizon was also a part of the collage. I thought how nice it would be if I could take a boat and sail across the beautiful sea to Japan.

Momentarily, I forgot about the reality of the war, the impending frontline assignment, my possible death or incapacitation, and all the associated absurdities of human destruction and violence. It had already been ten months since the Korean peninsula had become a killing field, not only for North and South Koreans against each other but also for their respective supporters — the Chinese Volunteer Army and the UN Forces. So even before I joined the army, I had already been exposed to an ugly montage of human destruction, misery, and absurdity.

I woke up from my daydreaming when our convoy made a lunch stop in a small village at the foothill of a high mountain range. Over the *bibimbap* lunch (steamed rice mixed with beef, vegetables, fried eggs, and Korean hot sauce) in the village inn, I talked about the spectacular view of the scenery from the bulldozer seat to my fellow officers and bragged, "I'm expecting an even more breathtaking view when we go over the high mountain range ahead." Now everyone wanted to trade his seat in the trucks for my bulldozer seat, particularly Lieutenant Han, the brilliant math major, who begged, "Come on. It's not fair for you to always have the best seat!"

"I won the seat fair and square," I replied. After more pleas, I finally gave up my bulldozer seat to Lieutenant Han but told him it would only be for a short distance. We made the switch and the convoy started again — towards the steep, winding, and unpaved roads of the high mountains. As we went up higher, the roads got narrower and rougher, but the scenery became absolutely breathtaking. I regretted having traded my seat with Lieutenant Han. Now he was enjoying the magnificent view from my bulldozer seat on top of the four-ton GMC truck. He was in ecstasy — singing, yelling, and waving at the rest of the convoy. He looked so happy. The corkscrew mountain road became steeper, and the scenery became more spectacular. The dark blue sea was still there, and the high mountain road opened a new awesome view of deep valleys below. On the left, we had high mountain walls and on the right were deep cliffs — about 200 meters below at times. I was envious of Lieutenant Han who had the best view high above us all.

None of us was prepared for what happened next. As the convoy moved up the winding road, Han's GMC truck took a sharp left turn to follow the mountain road. My truck was following. At the moment the GMC truck turned out of our sight, we heard a loud crashing noise, and a heavy cloud of dust came from the corner of the turn. I could not see anything. The convoy stopped immediately.

All the officers from the convoy ran up to see what had happened. The cloud of dust slowly cleared, but there was no sign of Han's GMC truck on the road ahead. Instinctively, we all looked down the cliff on the right side of the road. The cliff was not as deep as I thought — about 70 yards down on a 45-degree slope, covered with small trees and shrubs, but I could not see either the truck or the bulldozer. I frantically ran down followed by the other officers. We found Lieutenant Han caught under the bulldozer with no visible external injuries, except for the blood coming out of his nostrils. His body was still warm, but there was no sign of breath, heartbeat, or consciousness. After freeing him, we carried him up the slope to the mountain road but didn't know what to do next. Finally, someone suggested that we load him into a truck and go to a nearby town to see if we could find a doctor who might help him.

After an hour of driving down the mountain road, we came upon a small town near the seashore. Thanks to help from a shopkeeper at the entrance to the town, we found a doctor. A silver-haired, elderly man in a white coat received us in his office located on the first floor of a small two-story clinic. The doctor looked surprised to see a group of officers rushing into his clinic. I quickly told him of the accident on the mountain road that had badly injured one of our officers and said, "He's outside in the truck — unconscious. Shall we carry him in?" The doctor looked at us for a second and then he quickly moved into action telling his nurse to get his emergency bag and follow him outside so he could immediately check on the injured soldier.

"I Will Shoot Them from My Loving Heart"

As we hurried out towards our truck parked near the clinic building, the doctor asked me how long ago the accident had happened. When I told him that about an hour had passed since Han was pinned under the bulldozer seat, he said nothing. At the truck, the doctor only took a minute to examine Han and give us his diagnosis. "He's already dead. Nothing I can do. Probably he died instantly when the bulldozer crushed him. I am sorry," and he sighed.

We were frantic—we just could not believe it! We told him we could give him a large sum of money if he could save Han, although we did not have any money. The doctor said, "Money or no money, his life is over."

We were at a loss for a while about what to do next, and then decided to proceed to the 11th Division Headquarters. Two other officers and I accompanied Lieutenant Han's body in the back of the truck. No one talked. We just looked at the remains of Lieutenant Han. What a waste of life—so young, intelligent, and such a good guy to have died in this way. I would have been the one lying dead in the truck bed if I had not traded my seat with him. In fact, it turned out that he had saved my life. What a strange fate! I was sad and depressed again and thought, "To hell with the scenic view! What's the meaning of all of this?" Several hours passed. Lieutenant Han's face looked peaceful but awfully pale. By the time we arrived at the division headquarters in Yangyang, Han's body was cold and stiff. We could not get his left forearm straight.

We reported to the Division G-1 (Personnel Office). The adjutant major looked us over and asked what had happened to Lieutenant Han. I informed him of Han's death in a mountain accident. The major's response was a curt, "Too bad. Where's his body?"

I explained the body was in the engineering truck. With cold efficiency the major said he would take care of it. Then he ordered us to report to our assigned unit, the 102nd Independent Heavy Mortar Company on the front. Transport was immediately provided for us. We never saw Lieutenant Han again. Neither did we know what happened to the young engineering officer and the driver of the GMC truck that had crashed. Later, we learned that they had survived the accident with only minor injuries.

So Lieutenant Han was quietly "consumed" before even reaching the frontline, and nobody seemed to care. War is war. To kill and be killed are usual occurrences. I was reminded of the novel *All Quiet on the Western Front* by Remarque. It was originally written in German (*Im Westen Nichts Neues*) and translated into many languages. I read it in Japanese (*Seibu senseng ijo nashi*) when I was in the sixth grade, not knowing I was going to be in a very similar situation to the German high school students sent to the frontline during World War I. I recalled some fragmented passages in the book:

> We were eighteen and began to love life and the world; and we had to shoot it to pieces. The first bomb, the first explosion, burst in our hearts.... Through the years our business has been killing;— it was our first calling in life. Our knowledge of life is limited to death. What will happen afterwards? And what shall come out of us? [Remarque 1929, 88, 266–267].

Yes, indeed, what will become of us? In fact, none of us had any idea why were we assigned to a "heavy mortar" company because mortars, such as the 60mm and 81mm, were infantry weapons. In the Field Artillery School we were trained with howitzers, such as the 75mm and 105mm, which were the old vintages of World Wars I and II in Europe. Even our assignment orders indicated that we were supposed to report to the 102nd Independent Artillery Battery. "Who cares?" one of my fellow officers shouted. And he was right. It did not matter. I believed we would soon be consumed one way or another. I looked up at the sky. It was getting dark and the flashes of light and the muffled sounds of shells bursting in the distance were becoming more frequent. But also I could see many stars in the night sky. I thought there is always a chance — a chance to live or a chance to die.

2

My First Life-Chance

MY FIRST LIFE-CHANCE was to come into this world. I was born in the early morning of September 24, 1932, in Jochiwon, Chung-Nam Province, South Korea—about one hundred miles south of Seoul. At that time, Jochiwon was a small town of probably not more than ten thousand. I was the second child of five. I had four siblings—an older sister, two younger sisters, and a younger brother. My grandfather, Jun Hurh, owned and operated a milling factory, and his son, my father, Bu Yong, was his business manager. The milling factory cleaned, polished, and milled grains, mostly rice, for local farmers. Every October there was a competition among the milling business owners in the region. The provincial government honored the miller who best husked and cleaned the new crop of rice. My grandfather won the award almost every year ... according to my mother.

My mother, Myung Sum Eum, was born in 1911 in Gaeseong, the capital of the ancient Goryeo Dynasty (A.D. 918–1391). Gaeseong city is located about 60 miles northwest of Seoul and belonged to South Korea before the Korean War, but now, after the 1953 Armistice Agreement, it is in North Korea.

A year before my mother was born, the Korean peninsula became a Japanese colony. Japanese soldiers assassinated the last queen of the Yi Dynasty (Queen Min), and King Kojong was forced to abdicate the throne in 1907. Korea was "annexed" to imperial Japan in 1910. This "annexation" uprooted Korea's national sovereignty, cultural heritage, and economic resources. Under these circumstances, massive migrations ensued as Koreans moved within the peninsula as well as emigrating abroad, leaving in large numbers to go to China, the United States, and even Mexico.

2. My First Life-Chance

The Eums, my mother's family, moved south from Gaeseong for a better business opportunity. They too were in the milling business and thought Chung-Nam Province was a good place, particularly Jochiwon because of its central location between two big cities, Cheongju and Cheonan, and because it was surrounded by rich farmland. So they settled down in Jochiwon when my mother, their first child, was about five years old. In spite of tough business competition, the Hurhs and the Eums got along better than anyone would have suspected. They bonded fictitious kinship (a brotherhood between the heads of the two families) and vowed to each other to become in-laws if possible. At that time my father was nine years old, that is, four years older than my mother. So my mother (Myung Sum) and my father (Bu Yong) grew up together as playmates in the same town. The memories of that time were expressed by my mother, "Your father was learning to ride a bicycle and he needed someone to push the bicycle and wanted me to do it. I tried my best to push it straight, but many times he fell."

Several years passed. The Eum family eventually moved to Cheongju, the capital city of the Chungbuk Province, about 15 miles from Jochiwon. They thought their business would be better there. Plus, their other relatives had begun to settle down in the vicinity of Eum Seong city. At that time my mother was 11. She never had any formal education but took private lessons in a Seodang (a small one-room school for teaching classic Chinese and Korean literature) for several years. At that time very few girls were educated in the public schools in Korea. It is amazing, however, to note that my mother had a better command of Chinese characters than those who had formal schooling. What she lacked, however, was the chance to learn Japanese, math, and some science courses. Being ignorant of the Japanese language really was a problem for her since it eventually became the official language in Korea under Japanese domination.

Most boys in middle-class families went to elementary school and some moved on to high school, but very few had access to a college education. For example, my father was fortunate to graduate from Boseong High school in Seoul and was even sent to Japan to attend Waseda University in Tokyo. I have no idea what his major field was or how long he stayed at Waseda. According to my mother's story, he probably studied for a couple of years at Waseda but had to come home in order to help his father's business and to eventually get married.

At that time marriage by romantic courtship was unheard of in Korea. Parents or other relatives arranged virtually all marriages. The marriage arrangement between the two families—the Hurhs and the Eums—was a *fait accompli* since the heads of the two families had already agreed to become in-laws, even before their children came of age. Interestingly, however, according to my mother, their marriage was not strictly arranged. It was in a way a "romantic" marriage because she knew my father as a playmate and admired him like her own "big brother" while she was growing up—even after the Eums moved out of town when she was 11. Occasionally the distant Eum family visited the Hurhs. When this happened, the young couple had a chance to glimpse each other, but they were not allowed friendly greetings, conversations, or any physical contact once they had come of age according to the Confucian ethical codes. Whenever Myung Sum (my mother) had a chance to glimpse Bu Yong (my father), she always thought he was handsome and adorable. When she turned 18, my paternal grandmother visited the Eums to formally ask for their acceptance of my father's marriage proposal. It was finally a done deal. They married on the 20th of January, 1929.

The next year my older sister In Moo was born, and two years later I came into the world. Three other siblings followed—my second sister, Eui Moo, in 1935, my brother, Yong Moo, in 1940, and my third sister, Bang Ja, in 1943. The Hurh family's genealogy book tells me we are the 35th generation of the Hurh (also spelled as Hur, Huh, or even Ho) family that descended from King Kim Suro 金首露 and Queen Hurh Hwang-ok 許黃玉 of the Gaya (or Kaya, Karak) Kingdom in Korea. Gaya was of one the three kingdoms existing in the southern part of the Korean peninsula during the period of A.D. 42–562 The other two kingdoms were Silla and Baekje. King Kim Suro was the founder of the Gaya Kingdom in the Kim Hae region, about 20 miles northwest of Pusan.

At this point I must clarify the arduous problem of Anglicizing Asian names by the English alphabet. Latin is the root for many languages in the Western world. Likewise, the East Asian languages, particularly written Japanese and Korean words, were largely derived from Chinese pictographic and/or ideographic characters. The same Chinese character has the same meaning across northeast Asia (China, Korea, and Japan), but the spoken pronunciation will vary depending on the national language or even regional dialects. A Chinese character (word) is not a phonetic alphabet representing its *speech sounds* but conveys its meaning by *graphic symbols*. Thus, when a Chinese character (word) is transcribed in English by letters according to its sounds, it may be spelled differently depending on the regional and national differences in its pronunciation. For example, the written Chinese character 孝 is commonly used to mean "filial piety" in all three northeast Asian countries—China, Japan, and Korea; however, it is pronounced differently—"hsiao" in China, "ko" in Japan, and "hyo" in Korea. Similarly, my surname derived from one Chinese character 許 is pronounced in various ways—"Hsu" in Mandarin Chinese, "Kyo" in Japanese, and "Hur" or "Huh" in Korean. I have tried to Anglicize my family name closest to the original Korean pronunciation brought by the first queen of Gaya. I wanted to approximate a "Hur" or "Her" sound without a strong "r" sound in pronunciation. In an effort to achieve the goal, I added an "h" letter after "hur," hoping it would soften the final "r." It did work, but some people repeatedly spell my surname as "Huhr." It could be worse. So I used to ask my American friends if they had ever heard of the movie *Ben Hur*. I would tell them my name is spelled the same but with an additional "h" in the end. Well, that confused them even more. I will return to this translational problem of spelling names later. I hope Queen Hurh of Gaya would not mind that I spelled her name in English the way I did.

According to the 25-volume Hurh family genealogy and the well-known classic book *Samguk Yusa* (*The History of Three Kingdoms*) in Korea, Queen Hurh came from Ayuta or Ayodhya in India to marry King Suro of Gaya on A.D. July 27, 48. From India? I was curious.

Here is the story told by the *Samguk Yusa*: When the king and the queen were finally in the bed chamber for the first night, the queen quietly said, "I am the princess of Ayuta Kingdom. My surname is Hurh and my first name is Hwang Ok (*yellow jade*). I am 16 years old. I was told by my parents that the Heavenly Lord (Sang Jae) appeared in their dreams and said that Kim Suro was chosen to become king of Gaya because Kim Suro was a holy and a saintly man. In governing the new country, he needs a consort (queen) and I urge you to send your princess to marry him"(Lee 1987, 56).

The dream was so vivid and real that the Heavenly Lord's voice was still clearly resonating in the ears of the Ayuta king and his queen even after they woke up. They thought it was providence revealed by the Heavenly Lord and ordered their daughter, Hwang Ok, to leave Ayuta for Gaya at once.

The princess continued to talk with King Suro during their first night: "So heeding a higher call from Heaven I sailed all the way to your shore in search for the sacred fruit of love, and finally I found the *Beondo* (a peach which was supposed to fruit only every three thousand years) after two months of a long treacherous journey on the sea. Now, your majesty, please allow me to be close to your presence." The king responded: "Since my life has uniquely been spiritual from birth, I knew already your coming from afar. Hence I did not follow my ministers' advice that I should allow them to look for my future queen in my realm. Now you came to me of your own will, and I feel indeed very fortunate to have such a most graceful princess as my queen" (my translation of the Korean passages in *Samguk Yusa* [Lee, 1987, 56–57, 59; cf. *Samguk Yusa*, 1997]).

So goes the legend. They married and Queen Hurh bore King Kim Suro ten children. One day after the tenth child was born, the queen said to the king: "I have fulfilled the heaven's providence by leaving my fatherland for your kingdom and to serve your majesty. But I feel sad to see that none of our children will inherit their mother's surname, 'Hurh'. Would it be possible to ask your majesty to give my surname to at least two of our ten children?" The king agreed. The Hurh genealogy (vol. 1) and the inscription on the queen's grave marker indicate that the king chose two sons among their ten children to bear the queen's maiden surname. Some other genealogical records show that the king granted five children the queen's name. Interestingly, today there are five different branches of the Hurh family clan found in Korea: in Kimhae, Hayang, Taein, Hansan, and Yangcheon. Our family stems from the Yangcheon (or Gong-ahm, i.e., the present Kimpo area near Seoul) branch. Probably the legend has a kernel of truth.

In studying anthropology I learned that most of the world's ethnogeneses (the emergence of ethnicity or nationality) are glorified by a foundation myth of various sorts; for example, the Dangun myth in Korea (a legendary figure born of the son of god and a woman from a bear-totem family tribe who established the first kingdom in Korea) or the *Amaterasu* myth in Japan (a sun goddess who descended from heaven and created Japan). Hence the foundation myth of the Gaya Kingdom and Queen Hurh's story are not totally surprising. They are still fascinating, though, because historical facts are intertwined with intriguing legends. For example, *Hulbert's History of Korea*, the first comprehensive book on Korean history in English, contains the following passages:

> Ka-rak [Gaya] had five dependencies, namely the districts known under the common name of Ka-ya.... Tradition says that one day when the chiefs of the nine tribes of Ka-rak were banqueting they saw upon the slope of Sungbong, called Kuyii-bong, a singular cloud. From the sky above it came a voice. They

hastened up the mountain and there found a golden box containing six golden eggs. These opened and disclosed six boys. One of them was Keum [Kim]-Suro who became king of Ka-rak and the other five were made chiefs of the five Ka-ya, subject to Ka-rak [See Weems 1962, 50–51]).

Tradition says that King Kim Suro obtained his queen in the following way. A boat approached the shore bearing a beautiful woman, Queen Ho (Hurh), whose ornamental name was Hwang-ok or "Yellow Jade." She came from the far southern kingdom of A'yu-t'a (Ayodhya, India?), otherwise known as Ch'un-ch'uk. It is said that she lived 157 years and that the king survived her by one year (Weems, 1962, 50).

Historical records show that the Gaya Kingdom lasted for 490 years until it fell to the Silla, a neighboring kingdom, in A.D. 532 The recent archaeological findings in Gimhae (spelled also as Kim Hae, the capital of Gaya) indicate that Gaya developed a highly distinctive culture in the Korean peninsula (e.g., the *gayageum*— a musical instrument which might have been the prototype of the Japanese *koto*). Unfortunately, however, only scanty information is available today on Gaya society and culture.

I still wonder how Queen Hurh communicated with King Suro Kim. Did she speak Korean or did the king know the Ayuta (Indian) language? Moreover, is the queen's surname as written in Chinese character (pronounced as Ho, Hsu, Hur, Hurh, or whatever) really Indian in origin? There are many Chinese in the Beijing area now named Hsu, and others named Ho in Guangdung Province. My guess is that probably the queen's parents were Chinese in origin and lived in the borderland between southwestern China and northern India. Probably the princess Hsu or Ho arrived at the southern port of the Korean peninsula through a sea voyage, a part of the so-called "Silk Road," which stretched from Rome all the way to China, Korea, and to Japan. But of course, no one knows for sure what route the queen took.

When I went to Korea with my wife, Gloria, and our second son, Paul, in 1993, we had a chance to visit the tombs of King Kim Suro and Queen Hurh in Kim Hae, the old capital of Gaya. The king and queen have separate tombs located some miles apart from each other. We were impressed by the well-preserved big tombs consisting of five-meter-high earth mounds and surrounding statuary and grounds. At the king's tomb, a fence blocked tourists from going close to the mound, but Paul insisted that we should enter the compound and pay our respects to the king. I was pleasantly surprised

"I Will Shoot Them from My Loving Heart"

Tomb of Queen Hurh in Kim Hae, Korea.

by Paul's deep interest in his ancestor. Paul found the caretaker, a kindly looking middle-aged man, and asked his permission to enter the tomb for we were the descendants of Queen Hurh and King Kim Suro, and we had come all the way from the United States to pay respect to our ancestors. To our surprise, he not only opened the fence gate to the burial mounds so we could enter the tomb compound, but he also presented me with a book entitled *The Glory of Garak Kingdom* (Lee, 1987) 가락국의영광, which describes in Korean the history of Gaya, particularly Queen Hurh's origin. At the queen's tomb, we saw a stupa that according to legend was brought by the queen from India. A stupa is a pagoda that houses a relic or a sign of the Buddhist tradition. The pagoda, called *basa seoktap,* was made of five layers of strange-looking brownish rocks. Some scholars claim that the *basa seoktap* is the oldest stupa in Korea. Since Buddhism, according to historical records, first entered Korea in A.D. 372, it is certainly probable that the *basa* stupa was the very first Buddhist tradition introduced to the Korean peninsula. At any rate I was very grateful to have had a chance to visit the Gaya tombs in Kim Hae.

No one actually told me about the ancestral origin of the Hurh family.

2. My First Life-Chance

In fact I did not know we had a 25 volume set of the Hurh genealogy until I accidentally discovered them when I was poking around in our dusty attic. At that time I was about 11 years old, and by then my grandfather had already died and my father had begun to suffer from tuberculosis. The Hurh genealogy, *Yang Cheon Hurh Si Saebo,* is printed in Chinese characters on rice paper and bound in a classic format — yellow covers with red strings. Each volume, about 70 pages in length, covers biographical data of four to five generations of the Yang Cheon branch of the Hurh family members. The volumes were produced by the Yang Cheon Hurh Genealogical Society in the year of *Jeong Myo* (the rabbit year, i.e., 1927) but contain no information about the printer or publisher.

My grandfather, who taught me how to read and write Chinese characters, did not tell me about the Hurh genealogy books. When I told my mother about my discovery in the attic, she simply said, "I know. Don't mess around with the genealogy books. Just keep them there safely." She was not impressed by my interest in the Hurh genealogy and didn't want me to waste my time when I should be studying. However, she was very busy taking care of my ailing father. So I learned myself from the genealogy books about the origin of the Hurh family, including the family motto: "From House to House — Loyalty and Filial Piety. From Generation to Generation — Purity and Honesty." 家傳忠孝世守清白

After my father's death in 1946, I kept the genealogy books in a safe place in my study. However, during the Korean War, we had to evacuate from Seoul because of the invasion of the Chinese Army in January 1951. We put the books in a large earthenware jar for safekeeping from possible fire and partially buried the jar underground. But on our return to Seoul we were disappointed to find them badly damaged by water. About one-third of them were barely legible, particularly the first volume, which describes the history of Queen Hurh. Since then many years have passed, and I had forgotten all about the Hurh genealogy books; however, in 1974 my mother brought most of the genealogy volumes salvaged from the Korean War to the United States. They are now in a dry place in my home.

3

Memories from the Early Years

I HAVE NO MEMORIES at all from my early life in Jochiwon, my birthplace. I was told that my family moved out of Jochiwon when I was about three years old. It was the time when the worldwide economic depression set in — the 1930s. My grandfather's business was, however, booming until 1935.

According to my mother, we lived with three generations of Hurhs in my grandfather's huge household and had many servants and maids, such as cooks, nannies, gardeners and so on. However, the global depression eventually hit my grandfather's business. Most of his investments in stocks and bonds fell through, and his business was in trouble. My mother used to say that my grandfather's "gambling" led to our financial ruin. But in my view, he did not "gamble" in the traditional sense. There were no casinos or other gambling places in or around the town. Actually, what my grandfather gambled on was high-risk business ventures. In any case, the family business became nearly bankrupt. Luckily, my father got a job at a Japanese-owned farm-equipment firm in Seoul, and the entire family, including my grandparents, moved to Seoul.

We all lived together under one roof in a small three-bedroom house in the northwest suburbs (Ahyun-Dong) of Seoul. My earliest recollection of this house was my grandparents' room where I spent most of the time with my grandpa. He was a big man with pockmarks on his cheeks. When I was four years old he began teaching me how to read and write Chinese characters. Within a year I had mastered *Choen Ja Mun*, the introductory text for 1,000 Chinese characters. I had to memorize each character in terms of its shape, pronunciation, and meaning. Each Chinese character is not a letter of the phonetic alphabet representing a certain speech sound but a complete word in itself represented by a pictograph (an image of an object) or an ideograph (a graphic symbol of an idea or concept), or both. This writing system originated in the Shang Dynasty (1766–1122 B.C.) in China and spread to Korea, Japan, Taiwan, Mongolia, Vietnam, and Singapore as an integral part of the northern and southern East Asian civilization, similar to the functional equivalent of the Latin alphabet in the European civilization. Japan and Korea eventually developed their own phonetic writing systems — the Japanese *kana* syllabaries in the ninth century and the Korean Hangul alphabet in the 15th century; however, both countries have not been able to completely get rid of the Chinese characters because of the heavy borrowing of vocabulary from Chinese. When I was growing up, an average middle school graduate was expected to master at least 2,000 Chinese characters. So it was quite an accomplishment for me to have memorized 1,000 characters at the age of five. Moreover, my grandfather forced me to practice Chinese calligraphy for one or two hours every day until I was enrolled in elementary school at age seven. I knew he loved me, but at my young age I resented this forced study. Many times I could hear my friends in the neighborhood calling me to come out and play. It was painful, not only mentally but also physically, because whenever I made a mistake in calligraphy my grandfather hit my shoulder with his long bamboo tobacco pipe. I hated his stern discipline, but I had to respect and obey him. In order to have a break, I often excused myself for the bathroom and stayed there for a long time reading comic books. In contrast, my sister, who was two years older than I was, actually wanted to learn Chinese calligraphy, but my grandfather dismissed her request, saying that girls did not need it. In retrospect, I am now grateful for his teaching me the Chinese characters and the art of calligraphy.

In the spring of 1939, I was in the first grade of Ahyun Elementary School. Korean school classes were segregated by gender at that time, so only boys were in my class. The school was only about a mile from home, and I could walk to class. School buses were nonexistent at that time in Korea. My grandfather walked me to the school in the morning and then sat awhile on top of a small knoll that overlooked the schoolyard. He seemed to enjoy watching the children in the playground before they disappeared into the classrooms. Sometimes I was surprised to see him still sitting on the hill during our recess time. I waved at him and he stood up and waved back with a big smile. I wondered why he did not go home. Maybe he was lonely, I thought, and I too missed him. However, I became embarrassed when my friends would ask me who he was and why was he still there watching us. Since I started attending the school, my grandfather seemed to have lost his "job" of teaching me, although he continued to give me calligraphy lessons at least once a week. He often appeared to be tired and was aging gracefully with more tenderness toward family members. He began telling us bedtime stories, mostly from the Chinese classic literature, for example, the legend of the three warring states, called *Sam Gugji or San Kuo Chih Yen-Ie* (*The Romance of the Three Kingdoms*, 403–233 B.C.). I was fascinated by the ancient war strategies and the wisdom of the Chinese kings. My sister and I always looked forward to nighttime stories from our grandpa.

School was quite different because the schools at that time were taught in the Japanese language. All the students and a majority of the teachers were Koreans with only a few Japanese teachers; however, any use of the Korean language was strictly forbidden. The Japanese colonial government in Korea carried out the most notorious colonial policy in the 20th century-uprooting the Korean ethnic culture and ethnic identity, in addition to political oppression and economic exploitation. In every class we were indoctrinated to believe that primordial Korea was actually a part of Japan and Koreans were descended from the same Amaterasu Omikami (the sun goddess), who was believed to be the primeval ancestor of all Japanese by actual bloodline. Under such an intense pressure for assimilation, we were forced to identify ourselves as subjects of the Japanese empire. So we spoke Japanese at school but Korean at home.

One evening my father came home and told us that our family name would be changed to a Japanese name, "Moriyama." We were shocked. My sister and I shouted almost in unison: "What? Why?" Mother was speechless. Dad sighed, and explained in a sad voice that the Japanese colonial government had issued a decree for all Koreans to change their Korean names to Japanese, and the local district office requested my father to register the new Japanese names of our family members by a certain date. Violation of this directive was subject to a severe penalty. So within a couple of weeks everyone in the family had to go through an involuntary metamorphosis of identity — I was transformed to Moriyama Tomoyuki (森山智之／もりやま　ともゆき) from Hurh Won Moo (허　원　무／許元茂). My older sister's name, In Moo, became Hideko, my younger sister Eui Moo became Kinuko, and my brother Yong Moo's name transformed to Tomoharu. I was simply flabbergasted — I asked myself: "Is this a good thing or not?" I was only nine years old.

When I asked my dad where he picked up these names, he said, "From a Japanese fortune teller, damn it!" I could smell rice wine on his breath.

Eventually, the Korean language was totally forbidden in schools, and Japanese history was taught in place of Korean history. Not only the personal names but also the names of places had to be changed into Japanese; for example, Seoul, the capital city of Korea had to be called Keijo. The picture of the Japanese emperor was enshrined in a prominent place in the schoolyard, and all students were required to pay respect by bowing deeply every time they passed the shrine. Many Japanese Shinto temples were also built on Namsan (a mountain in the south side of Seoul), and the annual visitation to these temples became compulsory for all primary school students. Particularly during World War II, Shinto shrines were the focal center for enhancing Japanese nationalism. I vividly recall one spring afternoon participating in a calligraphy contest with other fifth graders in the "sacred chamber" of a Shinto shrine. I was ordered to write on a huge rice paper, 米英撃滅 ("Annihilate America and Britain!"). When I won the competition, I felt elated and went home to tell my grandpa. He said, "That's well done. What did you write?" So I told him, "Annihilate America and Britain." His happy face fell suddenly and with a shake of his head and a clicking of his tongue, "tsk, tsk, tsk," he implied this was shameful.

My calligraphy was placed prominently on the wall of our classroom. Of course, I did not believe the Japanese propaganda, but I didn't have any choice in what I wrote. No one, whether a teacher or a fellow student, ever questioned the Japanese actions during the Pacific War or the Japanese role in building the so-called "Great East Asian Co-Prosperity Sphere (Daitoah Kyoeiken)." Even when my classmate's sister was drafted to Teishintai (translated literally as "Body Dedicating Troop" but now commonly known as the "Comfort Women's Corp"), our teachers told us that it was a patriotic sacrifice of oneself to the Japanese empire—like the *kamikaze* pilots. However, at home my mother said that what happened to the young women was terrible and sad, but she felt utterly helpless to do anything about it. My father and grandpa reacted more or less the same. They commonly told me I was too young to understand and that I should concentrate on my schoolwork. In retrospect, I was indeed too young to understand the dark side of the Japanese colonialism/imperialism and my own spoiled ethnic identity.

Ironically, however, I began to like Japanese culture, such as *samurai* movies, Japanese food, and most of all, I loved to read Japanese novels. Many nights I stayed up late, reading *Miamoto Musashi, Rashomon, I am a cat, Botchang,* and others. I was a big fan of Natzume Soseki, one of the most famous authors in Japan. Amazingly, Japanese publishers also translated most of the European and American classic literature, such as the works of Shakespeare, Tolstoy, Hugo, Dumas, Goethe, Cervantes, Mark Twain, and Defoe. They published a vast series of translated Western literature, including *A Complete Collection of World Literature* (*Sekai Bungaku Jenshu*). In fact, I read as many books as I could get hold of. My favorites were *The Three Musketeers, The Count of Monte Cristo, Robinson Crusoe, The Adventures of Tom Sawyer, Adventures of Huckleberry Finn,* and *Don Quixote*. Much later I was particularly moved by one Tolstoy's short stories, *God Sees the Truth, But Waits*. The story made me furious and sad. Why does God have to wait so long until it is too late to save the innocent? I thought it might be only the Western God who could be so indifferent to the powerless. Where is God's compassion and justice? I was, of course, naïve, but all of my life I have not been able to tolerate injustice.

My family, both on my father's side and my mother's side, did not have any definite and exclusive confession of religious faith. Like many other Koreans at the time who generally called themselves "Confucian," they could also accommodate other beliefs, such as Buddhism, Taoism, and Shamanism, as long as the other beliefs did not oppose Confucian social ethics, particularly its core tenet—filial piety.

My mother assumed I was studying for my classes whenever she saw me reading because she never learned Japanese. She didn't know I was reading only for pleasure. Many nights when I stayed up late reading Japanese books, she thought I was studying too much and urged me to go to bed. Sometimes I read the books under the futon cover by using a flashlight. I was really a bookworm. While I was visiting my maternal grandparents' home in Inchon (a harbor city 25 miles west of Seoul), I was excited to find the Japanese translation of *One Thousand and One Nights* (commonly known as *The Arabian Nights*) on my grandpa's bookshelf. I finished it within a matter of days, and I felt it was the best part of my visit to my grandpa's house.

I visited our maternal grandparent's home almost every summer when I was between the ages of seven and ten. My older sister and I took a short train ride to get there. Usually our mother accompanied us, but she returned to Seoul within one or two days, so after that we were on our own with our gentle and spoiling grandparents. In any case, we enjoyed our freedom — no schoolwork, no nagging parents, and a very generous and loving grandma and grandpa. While there, I did a lot of fascinating reading. My grandpa, who was running a general store, surprisingly had many Japanese books in stock, and I was allowed to read them. He was a very kindly man with many talents. I thought he could fix anything from furniture to radios, bicycles, toys, and kitchen things. He also raised chickens in the backyard and had a special machine in a storage room for making homemade noodles that he would sell in his store.

According to my grandmother, when I was four years old, she overheard me introducing myself to the chickens that roamed about in the yard. I said, "Kokoya, kokoya (meaning chicks), please don't cry! I am Won Moo of the Hurh family from Seoul. What's your name? Why do you cry all the time? If you don't cry, I will give you a noodle from my grandpa's storage room." This story became a family joke for some time. During these visits, I also painfully watched how my grandma prepared an unlucky chicken for cooking. After witnessing the brutal scene, I refused to eat any chicken for the next 20 years of my life.

My favorite food was Japanese *sushi*, particularly *inari maki*, consisting of a core of seasoned fish inside a layer of seasoned rice, and completely wrapped on the outside by a thin fried egg skin. It contained no seaweed. (I haven't found this in the United States.) Every Sunday my father took our family to a fabulous Japanese restaurant in the Hwasin, the most famous department store in downtown Seoul (Keijo). After the lunch we usually went shopping. It was the most enjoyable day of the week. It was not very common for a Korean husband to take his family out for Sunday dinner and shopping every week. My sister and I thought our Dad was the most civilized man in the whole universe!

My third grade photograph wearing the school uniform and cap. Barely visible is the class leader badge pinned on the left side of my uniform, circa 1941.

"I Will Shoot Them from My Loving Heart"

By the time I began the third grade, we moved to a larger house located further out in the northwest suburban area of Seoul (Bukahyun-Dong), and I had to change my school since the township belong to a different school district. It was a brand new school, Chang-Cheon Elementary School, located near the present Ehwa Women's University, so I would become a member of the first graduating class of Chang-Choen. The third grade at Chang-Cheon school had two classes for boys and one class for girls. The landscape of this area was very idyllic with wooded hills and mountains graced with several ancient Buddhist temples and clear streams running through the extraordinarily green valleys. But my new school was about five miles away from home, and I commuted with my classmates by train until the tragic accident happened as mentioned earlier (Chapter 1). After the accident, my parents would not allow me to take the train and made me walk to school with some other children, a long walk for children only nine and ten years old.

However, we found a shortcut—a three-mile path going over the mountain to reach Shinchon railway station, which was less than a mile away from the school. Thus we cut five miles to four miles. Another advantage to the shortcut was the gorgeous view we enjoyed every day from the mountaintop overlooking a vast stretch of farmlands, towns, school buildings, and even a branch of the Han River, Sogang. On spring or fall afternoons, particularly on the way home from school, we helped ourselves to some of the fresh produce from the vegetable farms, such as carrots, radishes, cucumbers, and melons. Sometimes we were discovered by the owner of the farm, and then we ran for our lives and were never caught. This excitement, in addition to our hunger, caused us to continue our plundering. The disadvantage in taking the mountain path was the cold weather and dark evenings when I came home late because of extracurricular activities. Although this did not happen very often, when it did I was scared to death. A wild rumor going around was that *mundungee* (lepers) were looking for children to eat in the mountains in order to cure their disease. My friends said that they didn't believe it, but I wondered: "Who knows? It might be true." And I thought: "These guys might be thinking the same way I am." Then I really got scared.

Ironically, I was the leader of my class at the time—not by election but by appointment. Usually the smartest kid (academically that is) was appointed leader by the homeroom teacher. As the class leader, I did not have much actual power over my classmates except for performing a few ritualistic duties. Each morning after the group exercise in the schoolyard, I

3. Memories from the Early Years

ordered my classmates to line up in two columns and led them to our classroom, like an army sergeant leading a platoon of infantry soldiers. Once everyone was seated in his designated seat, I then ordered in Japanese: "*Kiritsu!*" (Stand up). The chairs scrapped and clattered as the students all rose. "*Sensei ni keirei!*" (Bow to the teacher). Forty heads and backs bent over to about forty-five degree-angles. "*Tyakuseki!*" (Sit down)! All sat down as the teacher took over the classroom. This ritual was repeated at the beginning and at the end of each class. As a class leader, I wore a small metal badge on which two characters, *kyu cho* ("the class head" in Japanese), were inscribed. The title was mainly symbolic, but every guy wanted to be the class leader. Hence I had some rivals or "enemies" as well as friends. There was indeed a tough academic competitor, Keiko Yanagi (Kyung Gap Yang in Korean), who often obtained higher test scores than mine, particularly in math and science. Usually all the test scores were posted by name on the classroom bulletin boards and thus everyone knew how everyone else was doing. Often tensions mounted among students — envy, jealousy, anger, shame, and depression alike. Sometimes physical violence ensued in various forms: the small but smart kids were beaten up by the big, "dumb" guys. Or in many instances, the small, smart boys hired a gang of big, "dumb" boys to protect them. "Hired" did not involve paying money but rather paying them off by other means, such as doing their homework, letting them copy your answers on tests, giving them candy, or perhaps giving them some tasty items from your lunch box. So various cliques developed within the classroom, and sometimes conflicts between the groups occurred.

However, a conflict between different schools was very rare but could happen as shown by the following incident. A rumor began circulating in my classroom that the Ahyun Elementary School boys in the adjacent town were planning an attack against us on the rural hillside path that I used as a shortcut to the school. I discounted the rumor. One afternoon, three of my classmates and I were on the way home from school, walking down the deserted hillside, when we suddenly heard shouts of "you bastards" and other curses. A large group of boys began throwing stones at us. I could see we were outnumbered and yelled to my friends, "Run," and we turned tail and ran away. The next day I told my "big" guys about the attack, and they pledged to protect me and seemed excited about a possible fight. Going home that afternoon, I was accompanied by ten or so of my tough guys, and as expected the Ahyun group attacked. But this time about 15 or 20 guys attacked us with stones. Everyone began yelling their favorite curses and throwing stones — but I was afraid of the big rocks and ran home. About an hour later, a knock came on our door. I opened it to find a messenger from the neighborhood police station asking if I was Hurh, Won Moo (or Moriyama Tomoyuki in Japanese). My heart began to pound with fright as I went with him to the police station. The police asked,

"Where were you during the stone fight?"
I replied, "I ran home."
Then they asked, "Who threw the stones first?"
And I answered, "The Ahyung group."

I was thankful when I was told no charges would be made against me and the police told me to go home. However, the gossip began in the neighborhood that the son of Moriyama (Hurh) was involved in a stone fight. My father heard about it and came to me wanting an explanation. As I related to him the full story, I felt so ashamed to have brought this trouble on my family.

Three years later I reached the sixth grade, and my days and nights became fully occupied with the worrisome task of preparing for the future — the high school entrance examination or job hunting. Entrance into high school was not automatic — one had to pass the rigorous entrance examinations. The better the high school, the tougher the entrance exams became. My father wanted me to enter Kyunggi High School — the top, elite high school in Korea. It was the oldest secondary educational institution in the country having been founded by the royal decree of King Gojong in 1899. The competition for passing the exam was unimaginably high. The rumor was that only one in 2,000 applicants was accepted. Naturally I was terrified, but at the same time I wanted the challenge and to win. My father was worried as well and every evening sent me to a private tutor to prepare for the entrance exams. I was overwhelmed by the heavy workload. I also had served my class as its leader for three years. In retrospect, I feel I always had a strong drive to attain excellence in whatever activities I undertook, although many times such a desire caused anxiety. My parents never forced me to achieve. I just knew what they expected from me and I wanted to please them.

In the mean time, the Pacific War (World War II) was taking an increasingly heavier toll on everyone. Food and all other essential supplies were rationed, and even primary school children were mobilized to help the Imperial Japanese war effort. We were ordered to dig up half of the schoolyard to make a vegetable garden and to collect any metal such as nails, screws, candle stands, steel tools, and kitchen utensils, that could be used for making military weapons. Brass scraps were in the highest demand because the Japanese forces had a dire need of brass for making torpedoes and bombs. Korean people have historically been known to use many more brass items daily in their household than any other country in East Asia. Brass was used for rice and soup bowls, spoons and chopsticks, teapots and washbasins, and even brass chamber pots! Now Koreans use stainless steel, but the common people at that time pervasively used brass items along with some porcelain or silver products. Korean homes were thus "brass mines" for the Japanese military forces. In addition to these chores outside of the campus, my classmates and I were assigned to attach buttons to hundreds of Japanese army jackets and trousers by needle and thread in our classrooms. It was tedious work for ten and eleven-year-old boys, and we felt the assignment was demeaning because sewing was a girl's job. Attracted by the adventure of combat, we actually wished we could go to war rather than collecting scrap materials in the street, plowing the schoolyard, or doing tailoring in the classroom. Worst of all, as their class leader I had to supervise my classmates while also doing the same dull tasks myself. I doubt my leadership skills were very effective in motivating my fellow students to perform these tiresome tasks over the three years or so until our graduation from elementary school.

At the sixth grade graduation ceremony in the early spring of 1945, I received the Kyunggi provincial governor's Award for academic excellence and leadership. It was the highest honor annually bestowed upon the most distinguished student selected from the graduating class of each public school by the Kyunggi Provincial Governor. My father came to the graduation ceremony and delivered an appreciation speech representing the parents of the graduating class. I was so happy that he came, and I thought his speech was perfect, although I don't recall any details of his presentation. I was too excited—not only about the award but also about the other good news I had received.

I had passed the Kyunggi High School entrance exams—I was one of the chosen few! I could hardly believe that within a month I was to start my freshmen life at Kyunggi. At that time Kyunggi High School was actually called Keikki Chugakko in Japanese and had an instructional curriculum of six years (three years of middle school plus three years of high school). That meant I could go to college after six years, hopefully to the law school of Keijo Teikoku Daigaku (Seoul Imperial University, now known as Seoul National University). My life course was all lined up and I was on the right track! I felt truly ecstatic about my good fortune and my future. My father must have felt the same way. To my surprise, he invited my teachers from the Chang-Cheon Elementary School to a dinner at our home — with red wine from Manchuria. I was not invited, as this was their adult party. Later I learned that the wine was sent from my uncle who was running a jewelry store in Harbin, Manchuria. Manchuria at that time was a Japanese occupied territory in northeast China. It was an extravagant night during a time when food was rationed. I suspect that the wine was smuggled from Russia or somewhere in Europe because Manchuria did not produce any red wine made from grapes.

After all this excitement was over, I began attending Kyunggi High School where the majority of the faculty members were Japanese. Interestingly, the school curriculum included beginning English and military training but no classes on Korean history or language. We were taught *kendo* (swordsmanship) and hand-to-hand combat drills by a one-eyed Japanese sergeant who proudly showed us his artificial "imperial eyeball" given to him by the empress in Japan. He had lost his eye while in combat in the Philippines.

The military training and all of our Japanese controlled education ceased on August 15, 1945. On that morning an announcement came over the radio that the Japanese emperor, Hirohito, would be making an important announcement that afternoon. Listening to the radio at school, I heard Hirohito suddenly announce the unconditional surrender of Japan to the Allied forces. This news was a tremendous shock to me and the other young students because we had been indoctrinated to believe that if Japan lost the war then we would be enslaved by the Allied forces. Soon our shock and fear turned into a grand celebration for the anticipated liberation from the 36-year yoke of Japanese colonialism. Rumors spread with an unbelievable but true message — the American troops would liberate the southern half of the Korean peninsula and the Russian troops would do the same in the northern half. Later we were told by the media (the resurrected Korean language newspapers) that the demarcation line for the division was the 38th parallel, a line set up by the four big powers (United States, USSR, Great Britain, and China) in accordance with their Cairo Declaration. Furthermore, each occupational force would rule their divided half of the country by a military government until Koreans could govern themselves by establishing an independent state or states. In this "arrangement" Koreans did not and could not play any role — their fate was decided by the big powers. Korea had *never been an enemy nation* against the Soviet Union nor the United States, but each country began to *occupy* Korea on August 12, 1945, in the north and on September 8, 1945, in the south.

For the first time in my life, I saw hundreds of foreigners in army uniforms on the streets of Seoul. An endless convoy of American soldiers with big noses passed by the Namdaemun (the South Gate), and they all looked alike, except for skin differences — black and white. Also I observed an amazing thing: carried at the back of every jeep in the convoy was a long fishing pole! I thought American soldiers must so dearly love fishing that they carried fishing poles everywhere they went. Later, of course, I learned these were radio antennas. Anyway, I did not know how to make sense out of the situation — should I feel happy about Americans being on the streets of Seoul rather than Russians, British, or Chinese? I wondered why they had to be here at all? Such were my thoughts. I was only 13 then.

School resumed after the jubilation of *haebang* (liberation) and the hope for independence. The Japanese teachers disappeared and a tremendous change in the high school curriculum took place: Korean language, Korean literature, Korean history, advanced English, German, and French, and World History were added to the regular curriculum. I read Shakespeare, Goethe, Hugo, and Toynbee. Most of all, however, we resurrected our Korean names and at last were free to speak our own native tongue anywhere in the entire Korean peninsula! It was, however, a strange feeling to experience a sudden change in my identity and in the official language almost overnight on the school campus. We had to reacquaint ourselves to the "new" Korean names of our teachers and classmates. Moreover, we felt so strange observing our teachers conducting classes in Korean. In sum, everybody needed time for adjustment — whether teachers or students. First of all, we had to relearn our own Korean language.

Then of course, American cultural items began to appear in the market — Lucky Strike and Camel cigarettes, Budweiser beer, Hershey bars, Wrigley chewing gum, Lux soap, Colgate toothpaste, Skin Bracer, and even Kiwi Shoe Polish. Besides the many jeeps, I also saw shiny Buicks and Fords driving down the street of Taipyungro, the busiest boulevard in Seoul. I thought Americans were "a superior race."

In the midst of all this change, my father died after several years of illness, leaving five children with my grieving mother. He had had a lung problem diagnosed by his doctor as pleurisy in the beginning, but it changed into tuberculosis. He managed it for several years with Western and Chinese medicine, but he didn't improve. I still recall a few times when I met him in his store after business hours and helped him to walk to our home since we did not have a car (like any middle-class family at that time). It was a three-mile walk that included going up and down a couple of hills. I helped him by pushing his back as we went up the hills. Often we had to stop so he could recover his breath. Coming down the last hill, he felt so relieved that we were coming near home. Not long after this, he became bedridden and no medicine seemed to help. One day my mother came home looking excited and said she had found a Korean doctor who specialized in Chinese medicine for lung diseases. This doctor guaranteed that with his medicine my father would recover within a week or so. We were all elated. My father was hopeful for this "last chance" medicine and even spoke of where we would take a vacation when he recovered. The next day mother brought home the Chinese medication the doctor had prepared. Unlike Western medicine, it was not unusual for a Korean doctor of Chinese medicine to dispense medication without seeing his patient. Mother was in a very good mood as she prepared the medicine by combining it with water in an earthenware container and letting it simmer over a charcoal fire. My father drank the medicine that night and I recall my parents talking happily to each other. The doctor promised he would feel better the next day.

The next morning my father never woke up. He was still breathing but unconscious. In a panic, my mother cried out. My sister and I ran into the room and found Mom crying over my father. She said to me, "Run and get the doctor. Tell him your father won't wake up." I followed her directions to his shop, which wasn't far away and gave him the message. He came to the house about an hour later and had us get a couple of live ducks. He cut off their necks and drained the blood into a cup for my father to drink. I wasn't in the room with my father so I don't know how they were able to get my father to drink in his condition. The doctor left. Shortly after that my father died. I was so angry and upset I ran to the doctor's shop and yelled, "You killed my father." In a calm voice, the doctor replied, "I'm sorry. Your father's condition was too serious for me to help him."

Walking home, I felt quite depressed. I suspected the doctor had given my father opium. The very dark-colored medicine the doctor prescribed was unusual Chinese medicine, and I had never seen it before. I tasted it by a touch of my finger. It was mildly sweet but had a very strong earthy taste.

3. Memories from the Early Years

My older uncles made the funeral arrangements and coordinated the family rituals of mourning, which included preparing for the three-day wake based on the Confucian text. According to the text, I was supposed to be the chief mourner since I was the eldest son. My duty was to grieve visibly by continuously wailing "Aigo, aigo, aigo..." whenever the visitors arrived. I tried my best but after a few cries my throat got hoarse; my mother was worried and excused me from the wailing duty, but I had to go through all the other rituals — the funeral procession, the burial ceremony, and a prayer service at a Buddhist temple located on a mountain near the cemetery. The grave mound was located on a quiet mountainside overlooking a valley. I was 14 at the time.

Financial problems began to loom for our family as my father's business was taken over by my maternal uncle. Uncle had been employed by my

Hurh family photograph that my mother wanted taken in memory of my father some months after his passing. Seated from the left are my mother, younger sisters Soonja and Eui Moo, and brother Yong Moo. Standing from the left are my older sister, In Moo, and me, Won Moo. 1946.

father and lived with us for a number of years. My mom thought it would be a good idea for him to take over the operation of the store, but the business didn't prosper. My uncle was in charge of the finances and accounts, which meant my mother or I had to go to him to ask for money. I especially disliked having to "beg" for money to cover my school expenses at Kyunggi High School.

Besides the vicissitudes in our family, the country was also experiencing significant change. In 1948, Syngman Rhee was elected the first president of Dehan Minkuk, the Republic of Korea, and Kim Il-Sung became the head of Inmin Konghwakuk, the Democratic People's Republic of Korea. I felt sad. I did not understand the *realpolitik*—the harsh reality of international politics for hegemony. A unified Korea seemed to me just an illusion. But one thing was clear; Korea had already become a victim of the Cold War between the United States and the USSR. Koreans used to say: "While whales fight, shrimps' backs burst" (*kore ssaume saewoodungie teojinda*). As John Toland put it, "Korea had become a pawn in the great chess match between the United States and the USSR" (1991, 17). I wondered why Korea couldn't be independent. Why did Korea always have to be an occupied country? Not only was Korea occupied, but now it was even divided in two!

Sadder yet, only a few years after the end of World War II, military training again became a part of our high school curriculum. A young lieutenant from the ROK (Republic of Korea) Army came to the school to help organize Hakto Hogukdae (the Student National Defense Corps). Ironically, however, our military training did not go beyond marching exercises and troop formation drills. We never learned how to use weapons; in fact, the training was equivalent to another physical education class. Although there was the specter of a civil war because of the gradual withdrawal of American troops, South Koreans in general, and high school students in particular, did not seem to take such a possibility seriously. As a high school senior, I was more concerned about the university entrance exams than anything else in the spring of 1950. My aspiration was to study law at Seoul National University.

4

The War and My Shattered Life Course

ON THE SUNNY, AFTERNOON of Sunday, June 25, 1950, my dreams for the future began to shatter when I saw on the streets of Seoul convoys of South Korean Army troops heading north and watched groups of refugees coming from the north. At the time I thought it was just another border skirmish. However, this was the first time I saw refugees carrying bundles of personal belongings. The next morning, Monday, I went to school as usual, although there were even more refugees fleeing south. Later in my classroom on the second floor, I heard the thunderous sound of exploding bombs. My classmates and I crowded around the school windows where we had a panoramic view of Seoul because of the school's hilltop location. We watched with shock as Soviet-made Yak fighters bombed government buildings, including the Capitol, near our high school. Black smoke rose over the buildings. School was dismissed immediately. We were told to listen to the radio for when school would resume. My classmates and I were surprised by the closure of the school, but we were not in a panic, thinking school would resume in a day or two. Although I did not know it at that time, I would never return to Kyunggi High School.

Hurrying through streets filled with townspeople, refugees, and South Korean soldiers, I sensed an unsettling atmosphere of confusion and urgency. I decided to head for my mother's shop located by Namdaemun (South Gate). At the shop, Mother told me of the rumors that the North Korean Army would soon reach Seoul, but no one had any idea what to do. We returned home where my sisters and brother were waiting, ate our supper, and listened to a radio news report featuring a South Korean government official who assured the citizens of Seoul that our troops would stop the enemy invasion. He told us to remain calm. After that I can't recall receiving any more news reports. It was probably around this time that our electricity went out.

The next night, while we were sleeping or trying to sleep, an earth-shaking explosion woke us up. The Han River bridge (the main bridge connecting the highway and railway between Seoul and the south) had been blown up by the South Korean Army to delay the advance of North Korean troops into the southern part of the country. By the morning of June 28, North Korean soldiers were already passing by Namdaemun in Seoul, just two blocks from my house! I could not believe my eyes, but there they were—with an endless convoy of tanks (T-34s), numerous self-propelled guns, various mortars and heavy machine guns on trucks, motorcycles with sidecars (like the German Nazi motorcycles), and thousands and thousands of soldiers armed with strange looking guns (PPSh-41 submachine guns, commonly known as "Burp Guns" with a 72-round drum magazine). Soon I came to the realization that not only were my dreams for the future shattered, but now my very survival was at stake.

Within a few days, a local, underground group of Communists in Seoul emerged and began an organized hunt for President Syngman Rhee's government officials. Street trials were held for anyone the communists wanted eliminated. A "People's Court" was held in the middle of the street near Namdaemun when I happened to be passing by. A man, a local Communist, was accusing a South Korean police officer of corruption and exploitation of the poor. Around 35 people were watching the "trial," when someone in the crowd shouted, "Death to the accused!" The North Korean army officer in charge asked the rest of the crowd, "What is your verdict?" Everyone was momentarily quiet, but then about half of the crowd yelled, "Guilty!" The North Korean officer pressed the quiet individuals in the crowd, one by one. "How about you?" "Hey, you over there!" Many of them, out of fear, started to murmur, "Guilty." Others began to leave. Not being able to stand this kangaroo court any longer, I sneaked away from the crowd. A minute later I heard a gun shot and felt a chill run through my body. I knew the police officer had been executed on the spot. I ran away in shock without looking back.

Many impromptu People's Courts were held in the streets of Seoul, and hundreds of former South Korean officials, soldiers, rich landlords, and other so called "reactionaries" were sentenced to death or imprisonment. I was

4. THE WAR AND MY SHATTERED LIFE COURSE

scared by the thought that these local Communists might also start drafting South Korean youths for there "People's Volunteer Army" by simply picking them up off the street or hunting for them from house to house! My dreadful thought became a reality much sooner than I imagined. A number of draft stations were set up in Seoul streets to recruit young South Korean men to augment the "People's Army," and house searches for this purpose became frequent. There were more local Communist sympathizers than I could have ever imagined. They were in every block of the city acting as informants for the People's Court and as recruiters for the People's Volunteer Army.

One day the radio announced that classes were resuming at Kyunggi High School. I was skeptical whether the school was really opening and did not go. Later I found out that those students who did return were all taken to North Korea for military training and were eventually sent to the frontline. Some of my classmates were taken. No one ever knew what happened to them to this very day. They simply disappeared forever.

The North Korean People's Army (NKPA–Inmingun) continued their advance by crossing the Han River and moving rapidly to the south — reminiscent of the Nazi German's *blitzkrieg* maneuver in World War II. Large cities, such as Suwon, Cheonan, and Daejon, soon fell (or were "liberated" according to the Communists) into the hands of the NKPA. The Communist locals were now controlling the media outlets, but I was able to tune my radio to some distant South Korean stations. The power supply was often cut off, but I could use my self-made crystal radio that didn't require electric power or batteries. Everything was in short supply, particularly food, water, medicine, electricity, and fuel. Furthermore, the local People's Committees began drafting at least one "voluntary" laborer from each household to help transport NKPA ammunitions over the Han River one night every week. If I volunteered, I would surely be sent to North Korea to join their army. If I didn't, my mother would have to join the "voluntary" laborers for the NKPA since none of my siblings could do the job. I was at a loss as to what to do. Where could I hide? Escaping to the south was impossible because I would have to cross the battlefront.

My friend and neighbor had relatives in a village, Gapyong, located 35 miles northeast of Seoul. He suggested we both go there and hide until the war was over. I was not really enthusiastic, but I had no other plan. My mother at first disagreed with the idea, but later, reluctantly and with tears, she gave in. She thought she might regret her decision later if things turned out badly for me, but felt she did not have much choice. At dawn on a July morning, my friend and I, disguised as farm boys in big straw hats and ragged pants, ventured on our way to Gapyong. We walked through the war-torn streets of Seoul, and as we crossed several bridges in the outskirts of the city, we were overwhelmed by the stench of decaying corpses. The foul odor emanated from the river basins under the bridge where we saw piles of bodies. Some of the dead were soldiers from both sides, but most of the bodies were civilians, including children. It was sickening to think these people had been dumped to rot without any burial. In the scorching July sun, we were gagging and sweating from the heavy air and the terrible stench. Our hearts were also pounding in fear that the local Communists might discover us at anytime.

We regretted our venture as soon as we arrived in the village. My friend's relatives warned us that rather than being safer from Communist detection, we were more conspicuous in their small village where everyone knew each other. We stayed in Gapyong for a week, experiencing acute anxiety and boredom. Our hosts were an older, very friendly couple with no children, but they seemed to worry about their own safety because of our presence. Plus their cooking was so awful that, although we were desperately hungry, we could not eat because of the constant diarrhea their food gave us. We decided to return to Seoul, not just because of the inedible food, but also because we had little chance of avoiding detection by the local Communists. It would be better for us to risk our lives by hiding at home, eating home cooking, rather than being exposed in a small village and suffering the unfamiliar ingredients and dubious preparation of the farm cuisine.

We survived the risky trip back home. Our families were glad to see us, but again they were afraid we'd be discovered. My mother began going around the neighborhood and spreading the story that her son had left Seoul for the south and now she was worried because she hadn't heard from him. So my family acted as though I was lost, but in fact, I was hiding at home. We lived in Soon Wha Dong, located about two blocks from Namdaemun (South Gate) in downtown. The Soon Wha Dong house was actually a temporary house my father bought near his shop to reduce his daily commute from our primary residence in the suburb, Bukahyun Dong. Since my father's death, my maternal uncle's family had been living in our suburban house. We could have moved back to the suburban house, but it was more convenient for us to live downtown.

4. The War and My Shattered Life Course

The Soon Wha Dong downtown house was very small—three bedrooms, a wooden-floored living room (*maru*), a kitchen, and a toilet that was an outhouse in the corner of the courtyard. My problem was to find somewhere in the house I could hide quickly and safely. I removed a couple of floorboards from the living room and dug a hole (five by six feet wide and more than four feet deep) in the crawl space under the living room. The job was not easy, but after about ten nights of digging, the hole looked large enough to serve as an emergency hiding place in case any strangers, particularly the North Korean People's Army recruiters, came knocking on the door. It could also serve as a bomb shelter for the family. Disposing of all the dirt was, however, another problem. Every day at dawn my mother and sisters carried the soil out of the house in small bags. I devised the floorboards so that after entering the hole I could pull the boards back into place quickly by myself. From the outside one could not possibly imagine that there was a five foot hole under the living room floor. We kept all our doors locked, and someone stayed home with me all the time to answer the door. Whenever there was a knock at the door, I fled immediately to my hideout. It was always a nerve-racking moment since I was supposedly not home and no one knew my whereabouts. Luckily, there had been no dangerous visitors for a month. Usually my mother and older sister answered the door. I spent my time reading Japanese books and building amateur radios.

I was thoroughly bored but also afraid. The more I thought about my precarious situation, the more I hated the North Korean Communists. I was determined to fight if they arrested me—I'd rather die than join the NKPA. I sharpened my self-made, eight-inch, steel knife and carried it with me at all times. Childish? Perhaps, but I was dead serious. It was not a personal hatred against the people in North Korea but hatred against the Kim Il-Sung regime, his cronies and his unjust invasion of South Korea. I have never been able to tolerate any kind of injustice since my early childhood.

In the early afternoon of one day in mid–August, I heard a gunshot from our neighbor's house. Like any big city, houses in downtown Seoul were built quite close to each other, so we sometimes overheard our neighbors. After the gunshot, we heard someone shouting, "So where is your son? We'll kill you right now unless you confess!" Silence. There was another shot so close that I could smell the gunpowder. I suspected the NKPA soldiers were searching the house. I frantically rushed to my underground hiding place. Everything was silent for a while, and then another gunshot rang out.

People were shouting, but I couldn't understand their words since I was in the hole. I was scared and warned my mother that they might come to our house next. We waited and waited for almost an hour with unimaginable anxiety. While waiting, all sorts of thoughts raced through my mind: What would I do if they found me? Resist? Comply? Commit suicide? Thankfully, they didn't come to our door. I thought God saved me.

All of these life-threatening events — the invasion by the North Korean Army, the exploding tank and artillery shells, the streams of refugees, the bombing of Seoul city and blowing up of the Han River bridge while hundreds of refugees and vehicles were still on it, the impromptu North Korean "Peoples' Courts" held in the streets of Seoul with the public execution of South Korean officials on the spot, the stench of decomposing corpses everywhere, and my desperate efforts to hide from the North Korean Army recruiters — combined to affect me deeply.

This mental state of acute fear and anxiety continued for several months until the U.S. Marines landed in Inchon on September 15, 1950, and crossed the Han River to Seoul on September 24 — my 18th birthday. I heard on the radio about the Inchon landing of the U.S. Forces under the command of General Douglas MacArthur, but I didn't know exactly when the American Marines would come to liberate the area of Seoul where we lived. Only by the approaching sounds of air attacks, shell bursts, and gunfire, did I know that "liberation" had come at last.

The ensuing urban warfare was actually spectacular to watch. I could see from our house the exchange of machine-gun and artillery fire going from one mountain to another. It looked like the American Marines were trying to occupy Inwangsan, one of the tallest mountains northwest of Seoul — only about two miles from our house. A series of air strikes by American planes was in very close proximity to our neighborhood — thunderous bomb explosions and black smoke were everywhere. Shrapnel was falling into our yard. I told my family to go down to the hideout for protection, but I kept watching the attack through my bedroom window. My mother desperately wanted me to join them in the bomb shelter, but I couldn't stop watching the war going on in front of my eyes. It was like a World War II movie. I was glued to the stark reality of the war drama. I was fascinated to see the strange looking American fighter planes with no propellers and a big hole in the front of the plane. Flying at an exceptionally fast speed, they approached silently but left with a tremendous noise. Later I learned that

4. The War and My Shattered Life Course

these were the first jet fighter planes (F-86 Sabres) ever deployed by the U.S. Air Force in actual combat. I also found out later that the Soviet Union developed and used an even more advanced jet fighter plane, the MiG-15, during the Korean War. Fortunately, the Soviet Union did not supply the MiG-15 fighters to North Korean or Chinese forces until 1951.

The North Korean Air Force did have the Soviet-made Yak-9 propeller fighters, but of course they were no match against F-86 Sabres. The ROK (South Korean) Air Force was even more pitiful: they did not have any fighters or bombers at all but only a few reconnaissance or liaison planes (L-19s) when the war started. I learned later that the ROK Air Force eventually inherited P-51 Mustang fighters from the U.S. Air Force — a World War II–vintage plane. I wondered why the United States had not equipped the South Korean armed forces adequately to defend against a possible invasion by North Korean forces. In contrast, the Russians supplied massive amounts of weapons, ammunitions, and military advisors to the North Korean Army and later to the so-called "Chinese Volunteer People's Army" as well.

Three days later I heard on the radio that in the early afternoon of September 29, 1950, General MacArthur and Syngman Rhee, the president of the Republic of Korea, met together in the smoldering Capitol building in Seoul to celebrate the recapture of Seoul. The tides of war were favoring the ROK and American forces as they moved rapidly northward towards the 38th parallel, the line dividing the Korean peninsula into north and south.

Now the Republic of Korean (ROK) Army was in dire need of soldiers. Every young man in South Korea over the age of 17 was to be drafted. I was one of them. I had just passed my 18th birthday a few days earlier. Since my life course for a normal professional career was already shattered and the country needed my help, I was ready to serve. But I did not want to be drafted as a simple infantry private. One of my Kyunggi classmates told me that the ROK Artillery Command was recruiting officer candidates. I thought it sounded like an ideal mission for which I should apply because I always liked doing something creative and using my brain to figure out new things. I already knew something about artillery from a Japanese book my maternal uncle had given me for my tenth birthday called *Fighting Cannons* (*Tatakau Kaho*), which had sparked my interest in World War II artillery weapons. I imagined that the artillery would be more creative than being in the infantry as I would use my mind to calculate distance, direction, and firing techniques. Wouldn't it be more "artistic" than the infantry? Perhaps most important, however, was the consideration that artillery units were generally located at least two miles behind the infantry lines at the front. Not only was artillery more of a mental challenge, but I thought that it would also be safer. Following this logic, I applied for the exam for the ROK Artillery Officer Candidate School in late October 1951.

The exam was held in Jin Myung Girls High School in Seoul, which was located near my Kyunggi High School. As I walked to the exam I had a fatalistic feeling that perhaps I would fail the test and be drafted, but it was worth taking a chance that I might pass. With that fatalistic view, I didn't feel nervous even though I had no idea what the tests would be like. The tests were conducted in a large gym that had been partitioned by temporary barriers into about five U-shaped sections. Each section contained the examiner's desk and a chair for the applicant. As I was waiting in line with the other applicants to be interviewed, we heard the distant rumbling sounds of explosions. We nervously looked at each other and wondered what was happening, but we all stayed in line. Soon it was my turn. There was no written test. It was more like an interview as the friendly looking, middle-aged artillery colonel asked me various questions and I answered orally. The oral exam included a variety of subjects, such as math, science, and English. I was good at languages and philosophy, but not particularly gifted in science, especially math. In fact, math was my weakest subject in school. However, when the colonel examined me on the math portion of the test, I felt quite at ease because he asked me questions to which I already knew the answers, such as "What is the square root of minus two?" and "What is the purpose of studying trigonometry?" To my surprise, everything went better than I expected as I didn't have to solve any math problems. Walking home I had a good feeling that I might avoid being drafted.

After two weeks, I went to check the exam results that were posted on a board at the ROK Artillery Command in Seoul. I was pleased to find my name listed. I had passed the test and was to report to the ROK Artillery Headquarters in Taegu (spelled now as "Daegu,") about 230 miles south of Seoul on January 29, 1951—a date I remember because of the ensuing events. The ROK Artillery Command in Seoul issued me a card indicating my status as a ROK artillery officer candidate so that I would not be drafted into the infantry as a private first class.

I had not told my mother about my artillery venture as I thought she would be devastated with worry. I did not know how to tell her so I just kept quiet about my artillery deal. One day in November I received a notice in the mail from the local draft board to report to their office at once. I read the note to my mother, and she was utterly panicked as she knew the sons of her friends had all been drafted. To ease her anxiety, I thought this was the right time to tell her. I said, "Wait Mom. I have something to tell you. I will not be drafted."

"What do you mean?" she asked. I explained to her about my commitment to the Artillery Officer Candidate School. She was surprised but still worried since I still had to join the army anyway. However, she did feel somewhat relieved to know that I was not going to leave her until a couple of months later.

Now I felt I was really liberated—I did not have to hide from the NKPA, nor worry about being drafted into the ROK Army Infantry and becoming a private first class. I was free to go around wherever I pleased, at least for a couple of months.

The war situation was not, however, very promising. The massive Chinese Army (the so-called CCF, Chinese Communist Forces) joined the NKPA for a counterattack against the UN forces. After a series of bloody battles, the Communists regained most of North Korea, crossed the 38th parallel again, and were advancing rapidly towards Seoul. By Christmas 1950, streams of refugees from the north again began passing through Seoul all day and night, seemingly reenacting the prologue to the fateful day of June 25. The familiar thunder of shells bursting and bombs exploding began to haunt us again.

Not again! I was furious and depressed. However, my mother was patient and practical. She arranged a getaway plan with a man who had a truck and was supposed to pick up our family on December 29, 1950, and deliver us to the village called Yip-Jang near the city of Cheonan, about 65 miles south of Seoul. In that village, my mother had purchased a small run-down milling factory before the war, hoping to renovate it someday for an additional business. Besides milling machines, the factory also had an office and two living quarters for the workers. Mother thought it would be an ideal place for a temporary refuge for our family and relatives, including my grandpa's and uncle's families. December 29 came and the family was prepared to go south. Our essential living items and clothes were all packed up in various bundles, boxes and suitcases, ready to load on the truck. We waited and waited but the man with the truck never showed up. My mother was at a loss about what to do. I wanted to help and offered to try to find him, but Mom didn't know how to contact him and our telephones weren't working.

Mom wasn't just disappointed over the collapse of her plan to go south, she was furious because she had already paid him a lot of money in advance. I did not know the details about my mother's arrangement with the man. But anyway, what could we do? Toward evening we finally realized he was never going to come. We had to make another getaway plan and make it quickly.

We decided that for the safety, my sisters and brother should be evacuated from Seoul as soon as possible. Also some other members of my mother's family, her father, sister-in-law, and her children, also needed to evacuate. My mother and I would stay behind to close up the business and our home. Without the truck, the evacuation was a problem. Only two options were possible for the thousands of people wanting to leave Seoul: one was to walk on foot to the south and the other was to take a train. But these weren't passenger trains; they were freight trains fully loaded with military equipment. Riders were permitted to climb onto the rooftops of the freight cars, a rather dangerous proposition. However, this was the quickest way to go south, and we decided to risk it.

Early the next morning on a cold and cloudy day, my mother and I took our whole family and the relatives to the freight train — my nine-year-old brother, Yong Moo, and my three sisters, In Moo, Eui Moo, and Bang Ja, ages 19, 15, and 6, respectively. My grandpa was the leader of the group as he was the only adult male. The scene was one of panic and determination as hundreds of people loaded with bundles and bags jammed the train yards hoping for a ride to the south. Families were frantically trying to keep their family members together amid the chaos. A few policemen were attempting to keep order but without much success. People were pushing and shouting, and babies were crying. I saw some men struggling with each other as they competed to load their luggage on top of the freight car. We scanned the tops of the crowded freight cars and found one with some space. Our young family members needed help to climb up to the roof of the car so Mom paid two young men to help us. Once on top of the car, they found a space by an air vent and arranged the heavy suitcases to form a square-shaped barrier. Using a rope, they tied the suitcases to the air vent forming a safe area within which the family could sit and be protected.

Although the train had no schedule, it wasn't long before the whistle sounded signaling its departure. On that morning of December 30, 1950, I felt so sad as Mother and I stayed behind waving our goodbyes as the train slowly chugged its way out of the Seoul station, heading south. It was indeed a scary sight to watch my siblings riding on top of a freight car without any protective railing. I wondered what would happen to the people, particularly the children, when the train passed through tunnels. Mom and I anxiously watched the train until it was out of sight.

My mother insisted that she and I stay behind because she wanted to find out if we could still locate the man with the truck to transport some of our belongings to the south. We could not. The ROK government announced on the radio that all Seoul residents should evacuate to the south as soon as possible. (Later I learned that the South Korean government had moved to Pusan on January 3, 1951, and that the First ROK Division, responsible for the defense of Seoul, had retreated from Seoul on January 4.)

Mother and I closed up everything in the house and planned to evacuate from Seoul on January 2, but without warning I developed an excruciating pain in my abdomen and became immobile. None of the usual home medicinal remedies helped, and no doctors were available nor were any drugstores open. I was screaming from the pain. In desperation, Mother went out to the black market to buy some painkillers. She came back with an injection device filled with GI emergency morphine that she injected into my buttock. I felt better after that shot. (In retrospect, I think I might have had a panic attack.)

The next morning, January 3, 1951, Mother and I left Seoul for the south on foot as no more trains were running. The weather was bitterly cold with snow flurries as we left carrying a duffle bag and some bundles filled with supplies and clothing for the family. We were directed to walk across the frozen Han River because the pontoon bridges were being used solely by the military and were not available for civilians. Approaching the river over the snow-white landscape, I saw an awe-inspiring scene: hundreds and hundreds of refugees were crossing the white frozen Han River on foot — young and old, women, men, and children. All had on heavy winter clothing that was snow covered. Many carried heavy loads of luggage, and some men even carried lightweight furniture on their backs. Everything was strangely quiet, except for the crunching sound of hundreds of footsteps through the snow. And the snow was still falling.

The river was almost a mile wide at the crossing point and covered by several inches of snow. Because no one knew the thickness of the ice, each footstep taken was frightening. I couldn't swim, so I was terrified when I thought about the possibility of stepping on a piece of thin ice and falling into the icy river. We all walked with our heads down watching where we walked.

It seemed to take an eternity to reach the southern bank of the Han River. (I learned later that about 2.2 million refugees crossed the frozen Han River during the Chinese offensive of December 24, 1950, to January 4, 1951.)

On the other side of the river, we had to pass through a checkpoint where the Korean MPs were stopping and lining up all the young men to catch possible draft dodgers. I easily passed through the checkpoint by presenting my Artillery Officer Candidate certificate. My mother, waiting on the side with the other women, was now quite impressed that I had the foresight to become an officer candidate. The next problem was to find transportation to the south. We followed the crowd and found ourselves at the Yeong Dong Po railway station where more than 20 cars of a military freight train were ready to depart for the south. Everyone rushed to climb up to the top of the freight train. Of course, there was no order. The first climber got the best spot on the roof of the freight car — a spot where you could hold on to or lean against something stable, such as an air vent or a ladder fixed to the roof of the train, and then tie your luggage or yourself to it to avoid falling off the train, especially if you fell asleep. We were fortunate to find an air vent to lean against.

The rooftops of the train were full and it was getting dark and cold, but the train was not moving. We were hungry. Interestingly, an impromptu capitalism sprung up in the midst of the refugee crisis. Young women sold Korean seaweed sushi (*gimbop*) on the platform. Since we could not reach them, someone devised a basket on a rope for picking up the *gimbop* and sending down the money. Around ten in the evening, the freight train started to move. We were relieved but still full of anxiety. My mother was in a sour mood and said, "That truck man. He ruined our life. What will happen to us now?" We ate the *gimbop* and washed it down with soda pop.

The train was running at full speed. The tunnels we worried about were not such a danger after all. Everyone kept low, and the smoke from the train engine was bearable. I watched in amazement at how people adapted to such an adverse situation. Men emptied their bladder using tin cans, but I didn't know what the women did. The train moved along but frequently stopped and started. I couldn't see much on that dark night, except the fire and smoke coming out of the train's smokestack. Looking at that smokestack far ahead and listening to the chugging sound of the train, I felt sad and thought, "What will become of us?" I was still depressed when I finally fell asleep atop the train car.

4. The War and My Shattered Life Course

About ten o'clock in the morning, we arrived at Cheonan station. When we climbed down and stood on solid ground again, a tremendous feeling of relief swept over us. A cafe near the train station served us a hot breakfast of soup, rice, and *kimchi* (a spicy pickled cabbage containing lots of garlic, red hot peppers, and green onions) that raised our spirits. Fortified, we began to walk to the Yipjang milling factory, which was more than five miles away. Unlike war-devastated Seoul, the Cheonan suburbs were peaceful and idyllic. We hoped our family could stay in the area until the war was over. We were anxious to see if my brother, sisters, and relatives had safely arrived at the milling factory in Yipjang village, our designated meeting place. We walked on an unpaved country road with frozen rice paddies on each side. It was a cold day, but in the bright sun with no wind, we felt as if an early spring was on the way. I was carrying a medium-sized piece of luggage, and my mother carried a purse and a small bag of personal effects. Beyond the rice paddies we could see in the distance a few farmhouses with straw roofs, but no one was on the road we were traveling. "No refugees here?" Mother said with a surprised look. Reassuringly I said, "Probably they all went further south in case the Communist armies would overrun the country — just like they did a few months ago. They're probably headed to Pusan or at least to Daegu." As I said this I suddenly realized that no refugees got off the train at the Chonan station except us! Why didn't I think of this before?

My mother was quiet for a moment and then told me what was bothering her — she knew I would probably have to leave earlier than planned for Daegu to report to the Artillery Headquarters. She had been hoping we would be together for another two or three weeks. She went on to explain that the family's chance of survival would be much better in the Yipjang area where we still had some relatives living and the milling factory. Although she hadn't seen the milling property for some time, she was hopeful it was still functional — at least some large bags of rice and dried foods should be in storage. Mother reasoned that the family would have at least a place to cook, eat, and sleep. As we walked, Mother explained her determination to stay in Yipjang with our family. But then with tears in her eyes, she said, "I'm scared, Son." After a moment of silence, she wiped her tears and said resolutely, "But worries won't help. We'll just do our best when we get there." She was a strong woman.

We arrived in Yipjang village around three in the afternoon. Our milling factory was located on a sunny knoll in the outskirts of a small village with a dozen farmhouses. As we approached the knoll, Mother pointed out to me the factory building, and we began to walk faster as our anxiety increased over whether the family had made it safely ahead of us. The factory ground looked more spacious than I imagined, but the main building appeared rather run-down with its cinder-block walls and snow-covered tin roof. There was no fence enclosing the factory compound, nor any sign of people — all was quiet on this sunny, cold January afternoon.

As soon as we entered the main building, we were surprised to be greeted by more than 20 people, including my siblings and many of mother's relatives. The ages of these refugees ranged from three to 68. And all were safe and sound! What a God-given occasion to have a big family reunion so near the frontline. A large meal was prepared, and we had a good dinner. After the ride on the roof of the train for 15 hours, it was a feast to me. During our excitement and celebration, we began to hear the familiar thunder of bursting shells in the distance, but we tried to ignore it.

I asked my sister about the family's ride on the freight car roof. She told me that it wasn't easy, especially for the women when they had to go to the toilet. In order to avoid the problem, my sister was told not to eat or drink too much even though she was hungry and thirsty. The most difficult problem for her on the trip was our young brother's constant begging to go home, and he would actually try to get off the train, but she restrained him. She had to keep a close watch over him all the time.

Soon after the feast was over, we heard the rumbling noise of heavy army trucks. Several convoys of American troops with what looked like medium artillery howitzers were passing through Yipjang village. We had no idea where they were going, but they seemed to be headed north. I guessed that they were a reinforcement unit to support the infantry on the frontline. If so, it would mean the frontline was nearer to us than we had imagined. Although I did not know for sure the maximum range of the U.S. medium artillery pieces, I thought it could be no more than 15 or 20 miles. I was scared. However, I would have been even more terrified if I had known the actual range of a 105mm howitzer, the most commonly used U.S. medium artillery weapon during the Korean War. Its maximum range was, in fact, only seven miles!

The happy celebration over the reunion of my relatives that evening gradually changed to an atmosphere of immense worry and an acute sense of hopelessness and helplessness. We feared another attack by the Chinese and North Korean armies that would make us again refugees, but this time we would have no place to go. We hoped that with the support of the U.S. forces, the ROK Army would counterattack or at least contain the Communists north of the Han River. We had lost our trust in the ROK Army, but we could not believe that the U.S. forces were also proving to be so weak in holding back the Communists. We became utterly depressed. Why couldn't we have prevented this disaster from happening? Seoul was lost once in 1950, but to loose it again within six months! Later I learned that during this time (June 1950 to January 1951) 500,000 people perished and more than two million became homeless.

Now our family was homeless and had nowhere to go. The South Korean government fled to Pusan, the southern city on the tip of the Korean peninsula, the last sanctuary. The rich, the powerful, and the famous people had already moved down there, but we did not know anyone in Pusan and had no resources to make such a long journey. Even if we made it to Pusan, the probability of our survival was questionable. Every adult in our group was discouraged and did not know what to do.

The women and children went to bed, but the adult males gathered to discuss how to cope with this crisis. Although on a lot of things they did not agree, one decision was unanimous — the young adult males must evacuate right away because they were in danger from both the ROK/US and the CCF/NKPA. I was devastated and tired. I wondered, "Who cares about anything at all? Who is on the side of people like us? People with no house, no money, no land, and nowhere to go." I went to bed in the midst of their discussion.

In the morning the family "council" decided that the young male adults, my uncle and I, should evacuate to the south immediately. The others — the children, women, and my grandfather — would leave the milling factory as soon as possible. But where to? In the midst of all this confusion, I knew I had to leave for Daegu city very soon so I could report for duty at the ROK Army Artillery Headquarters on January 29, 1951. Daegu was the temporary South Korean capital at that time. Later the capital moved further south to Pusan (now spelled as Busan) as the last resort. My uncle and I began our refugee journey that morning. When we left the milling factory, snow was falling, covering everything with an illusionary white blanket of peaceful beauty. But our spirits were low as we made our sad departure.

When we packed up the night before, I remember my mother saying, "Don't look back! Go on, and we shall meet again if God wills!" Even today, as I write this memoir, I can vividly remember the snowfall and my mother's sad and worried expression on her beautiful face while she bid me goodbye. She was only 39 and I was 18. I could hardly stand it. I said in tears, "I will see you soon!" When I said it, I felt so bad because I knew I was probably seeing her for the last time. My mother, siblings, and other relatives stood on the knoll of the factory, sending us off with hand waves of good-bye. I went down the road a little way and looked back. Mom was still there, waving at me to go on. The snow was now falling heavily — we hardly could see each other.

The city of Daegu was 150 miles away. My travel companion was my uncle, Kimo Lee (my mother's younger sister's husband) who now took charge of my destiny. He was a free-lance businessman working in the milling factory equipment business. A nice guy. I remember he drank a lot, but he had never shown any sign of intoxication. Usually Koreans (for that matter, many northeast Asians) show a flushed face when they drink too much. But he never did. In fact, the more he drank, the paler his face became!

My uncle Kimo and I had backpacks containing items such as dried food, cooking utensils, blankets and a map. But I also had something in my possession that no one knew about — a good sum of cash. Before my departure, my mother made a secret pocket in my boxer shorts and put about $200 worth of Korean money in that pocket.

We walked down the same road that my mother and I had traveled on the previous day from the Chonan railway station. We hoped to catch a freight train, but arriving at the station that evening, we learned that the trains were no longer running. Many refugees were still huddled in and around the station, but a stream of refugees started walking on the railroad tracks toward the south. Since our hope of reaching Daegu by freight train vanished, we began to figure how long it would take for us to walk to Daegu. If we walked an average of 15 or 16 miles a day, we would reach Daegu in ten days.

We walked mostly on the railroad tracks following the footsteps of the other refugees. They seemed to know the shortcuts to take. Except for the occasional sound of a child crying, it was an eerily silent march. No one spoke. I could only hear the footsteps of the refugees trudging through the January snow along the railroad tracks. At that time most of the highways in Korea were not well developed, having many unpaved, narrow stretches. Now the highways were crowded with military vehicles and columns of refugees making them almost impossible to use. So we followed the railroad tracks, even though the tunnels were a problem. We ventured through short tunnels, but avoided the long, dark tunnels because we didn't know if the trains might start running again. We had to take detours around those tunnels by climbing over the mountain or searching for an alternative path — a country road or a main highway. When night fell, we sought out any place that offered some shelter. Sometimes we slept in the kitchen of an abandoned house or under the overhang of a Buddhist temple. Other times we were fortunate to meet some hospitable farmers in small villages who gave us food and shelter.

The pain I experienced as a war refugee was not only physical, such as hunger, fatigue, and chills from the cold weather, but also an overbearing psychological pain caused by a sense of helplessness, hopelessness, and meaninglessness of my existence. In short, I felt as if I had lost the compass of my life and was wandering in a maze trying to find out the bearing of my existence. I thought to myself; suppose I survive this ordeal, and make it to Daegu, successfully finish the Officer Candidate School, become an artillery second lieutenant, and be sent to the frontline as a forward observer. What would the outcome be? My dying for the fatherland? The only meaning I could find for fighting the war was to save my family and possibly my neck as well. I questioned the motivation of those in power who glorified the war in the name of patriotism, national unification, and democracy. Particularly I questioned those leaders who did not go to war themselves nor did their children; however, they compelled the powerless parents to send their loving children to the killing fields. It was certainly a senseless and brutal civil war instigated by Kim Il-sung's regime (the Democratic Peoples' Republic of Korea) in an attempt to attain its ruler's life-long ambition of unifying the two Koreas under the Red Banner. I wondered why the U.S. intelligence systems failed to detect North Korea's many years of elaborate preparations for this *blitzkrieg* attack.

The more I thought about my situation, the more depressed I became. Deeply entrenched in aimless thought, I did not realize we were still walking on the railroad track and that it was getting dark and cold. Time again to search for shelter and food for the night.

My uncle lit a cigarette. It looked warm and comforting. "Can I try?" I asked. Uncle looked at me and said, "No, it's no good for you, plus you're too young to smoke. It's a bad habit." I did not say anything. I never smoked in my life. Why start now? We continued to walk in silence. After a while uncle asked, "Do you still want to try?" I looked at him and said nothing. He took a cigarette from a red pack and gave it to me. The package looked quite different from the Korean cigarette packs I was familiar with. Uncle explained it was a Yankee cigarette called Pall Mall. He had bought a few packs on the black market thinking he could bribe someone to give us a ride to Daegu, but had no luck in that regard.

I lit the cigarette, inhaled, and coughed for a minute. "Yuk, I don't think I like it." Uncle laughed and I grimaced. So that was my first cigarette — Pall Mall. It was not the last, however. I picked up the habit later from my comrades in arms. It took 25 years for me to unlearn the habit.

My uncle and I repeated the same refugee routine for about ten days — walking all day following the railroad tracks and feeling constant fatigue and hunger in the damp, cold weather. We bypassed Taejon (now spelled as Daejon), the capital city of Chung Nam Province, and finally one early morning in mid-January 1951 we arrived near the outskirts of Daegu. The weather in the area was much milder, and there was no snow on the ground. We stood on the bank of the Nakdong River that runs from the north to the south and passes through the west side of Daegu. The Nakdong River was not as wide as the Han River in Seoul, but it had been the last line of defense in July 1950 for the ROK and the U.S. armed forces against the North Korean Army, which had been determined to finish up their task of "liberating" (occupying) the rest of South Korea. In fact, the Communist forces had overrun the entire Korean peninsula except for the tiny southeastern tip that the U.S. and ROK forces called the "Pusan Perimeter."

I was awestruck when I realized we were standing at the very place where fierce fighting had taken place just five months earlier — the northern front of the perimeter. The Pusan Perimeter had encompassed a geographic area of about 50 by 75 miles — the 50 miles made-up the northern front and the 75 miles was the western front and both fronts faced the enemy. To the east and the south was the ocean so the ROK and American forces had nowhere to retreat. They had to either defend the perimeter or attack. If they failed, it would have been the demise of the Republic of Korea and her people as well. The northern front was defended by the ROK army and the western front was the responsibility of the U.S. troops. A decisive, bloody, six-day battle was fought (August 17–23, 1951) to maintain the perimeter. Later, I heard that on the northern front alone about 10, 000 soldiers were killed (3,000 from the ROK and 7,000 from the NKPA). I had no idea about the casualties on the western front. On the western front, the U.S. Air Force carried out massive carpet bombing in support of a counterattack by the UN Forces. Ninety-eight B-29s flying out of Okinawa dropped more than 900 tons of bombs in 26 minutes.

My uncle and I were then witness to the aftermath of that bloody battle. The dead had been removed, but there were many disabled North Korean tanks, broken artillery pieces, burned-out vehicles, and other remnants of the senseless, bloody civil war. The weapons were now rusting and corroding, but what about the souls of all the soldiers who perished, whether Korean or American? While we were looking at the remains of the bloody fight, the Nakdong River flowed quietly before us as if nothing had happened. I wondered — what's the meaning of all this?

We crossed the Nakdong River using a temporary pontoon bridge because all the regular bridges were still being repaired. The scene on the other side of the river was about the same — the bank was littered with the remains of the war. We walked about ten miles and finally reached Daegu city in the late evening. My uncle arranged our stay in Daegu at his friend's house, but he was unsure about the details of our accommodation. His friend, Major Kim, was a military police officer stationed in Daegu who lived in a large apartment in the busy downtown area. Most of the ROK governmental offices were there, and business went on as usual, just like Seoul before the Communists invaded.

We arrived at Major Kim's apartment and were led to the second floor. I suspected that the first floor was for Major Kim's family. As soon as we climbed the stairs, I was shocked to see the situation. Five men were sitting on the wooden floor of a huge room that had no furniture of any sort except for several mattresses. The men were also Major Kim's friends who had fled from Seoul, just like us. They all appeared to be in their 30s, and my uncle seemed to know most of them. Major Kim never showed up. I felt very much out of the place as the only teenager among this group of middle-aged men. I asked myself — what should I do? I still had two more weeks to spend before reporting to the ROK Artillery Command. After some snacks, we all went to bed on the mattresses. I could not sleep very well. I kept wondering what would become of me.

The morning came even in that Godforsaken place. I got up and went to the bathroom. I looked really awful when I saw my reflection in the mirror — dirty, tired, hungry, and bored! I decided to leave this place as soon as possible, but for where? My uncle took me out to a noodle shop for a quick breakfast and told me that he would visit his business colleagues downtown during the day and return to Major Kim's apartment in the evening. I could either join him or I could look around the city and then meet him at night at Major Kim's. I chose to explore the city by myself. Uncle gave me the telephone number of his business colleague where he could be reached during the day. Daegu city was extremely congested with heavy traffic and many displaced people. The weather was cloudy, damp, and cold. After walking aimlessly for a couple of hours, I found an enticing Chinese restaurant and treated myself with *"tangsuyuk"* (sweet and sour pork) using my mother's money still stashed in my boxer shorts.

As I was finishing the delicious meal, someone tapped my shoulder and said, "Taste good, Won Moo?" It was Geon Bae Kim, one of my school classmates! I was overjoyed. I was even more delighted to learn that he was also scheduled to report to the ROK Artillery Command for the Officer Candidate School on the same date I was. He was staying in a farmhouse on the outskirts of Daegu with two other prospective army officer candidates. The kindhearted farm family had given them a large *ondol* (heated floor) room without charge and there they cooked their own food. I asked if I could join him. I was thrilled when the answer was "yes." I called my uncle and told him the story. He was also pleased and told me that my other uncle, Du In (my mother's brother), had come to Daegu also and was going to stay at Major Kim's as well. I felt quite relieved to leave Major Kim's place.

After a five-mile walk, we reached the place where Geon Bae was staying, an old farmhouse with a thatched roof. I met Geon Bae's roommates, and the farmer and his wife — all extremely friendly people. We cooked rice with some side dishes and had a wonderful dinner together. That night I felt so blessed and slept like a log. The next two weeks went by quickly. We talked a lot, explored the countryside, did some reading, and, to my shame, I learned how to smoke. I worried about my family left in Yipjang, but it would be eight months before I would hear from them again.

5

Officer Candidate School

FINALLY THE DATE I was scheduled to report for Officer Candidate School, January 29, 1951, arrived. I checked into the Artillery Command Headquarters in Daegu and was to be transported by truck and train to the Army Comprehensive School of Officer Candidates in Dongnae (about 70 miles south of Teague and ten miles north of Pusan). My uncle Du In came to see me off at the Artillery Command HQ. We had a chance to talk for about ten minutes. He said he was drafted into the army a few weeks earlier but released from basic training camp on the grounds that he was physically unfit to become a soldier. He looked very pale and thin. I noticed his pants looked very ragged and offered to trade my pants with him, assuming that the army would issue me a fresh set of uniforms in Dongnae anyway. We made the trade. I told him about our relatives situation at the Yipjang milling factory. He hoped to go back to Seoul with his family as soon as the UN forces pushed back the enemy to the north. I felt sorry for him, but at least he was saved from the bloody fight on the front as a private first class. He was married and had two young children. I wished him well and departed with no tears but a sad, forced smile.

That evening I, along with 43 other artillery officer candidates, arrived at the Army Comprehensive School of Officer Candidates (Yukgun Jonghab Hagkyo). This school was temporarily created on August 15, 1950, to meet the desperate need to refill junior officer positions on the frontline; casualty rates among this group had reached as high as 60 percent during the first year of the Korean War. The name "Comprehensive School" meant the school for junior officer candidates from all branches of the army, such as the infantry, artillery, engineering corps, signal corps, ordnance, quartermaster, finance, and strangely, from the marine corps as well. The school produced about 7,000 junior officers in one year; however, about half of them perished within three years (1950–53), so they were known as *somo jangyo* ("consumptive officers"). Would I become one of the consumed?

The Combined Officer Candidate School was housed in Dongnae Girls' High School. The main building was occupied by the administration while the classrooms were used as sleeping quarters for the officer candidates. For some unknown reason, the artillery candidates were assigned to sleep in a run-down storage room. Forty-four of us settled in an empty warehouse comparable to the size of a high school classroom. Luckily the storage room, or rather our quarters, had many windows and a wooden floor. An infantry sergeant and two corporals issued us "new secondhand uniforms" supplied mainly by the U.S. Army Surplus Agency. The American uniforms were far too large for most of us. Some of them were even from the U.S. Women's Army Corp (WAC) The shoes we received were also old ones — with worn-out soles, no strings, or occasionally no heels! Each of us was also issued two olive-colored army blankets, a thin mattress, and a cotton cloth bag containing two aluminum bowls (one for rice and the other for soup), a spoon, and a pair of chopsticks. Eleven people were assigned to sleep along each of the four walls of the room, and the middle of the quarters was multifunctional — it was where we ate, studied, lined up for roll call/inspections, and received our orders for the day. There was no indoor bathroom in our warehouse-quarters so we had to use an outdoor communal latrine that consisted simply of rows of holes in the ground. The latrine had no toilet seats, tissues, or roof, but was encircled by rudimentary, straw curtains made of old rice bags. I was shocked. Not to have privacy was one thing, but imagine the exposure of skin during a bitter cold Korean January! And of course there was no running water. We were instructed to use a stream running near the side of our quarters for washing whatever we needed to clean — our bodies, clothes, food bowls, spoons, chopsticks, and so forth. Sometimes the stream was frozen, but we managed to at least wash our faces, and brush our teeth in the morning. I was so happy to have kept a small bar of soap. I don't recall anyone having the privilege of a hot bath while we were in the OCS, except for those who were fortunate enough to have some money for the public bathhouse in town. We just hand washed in the cold water, about once a week. Hence, our multipurpose room smelled all the time of food and body odors. Moreover, there were lice problems, despite the spraying with DDT.

5. Officer Candidate School

One morning I woke up earlier than anyone else in the room and went outside to the stream. I washed my face and looked up at the hill above the stream. Everything was quiet and the sky was slowly opening up with a misty, gray color. I began to wonder about the meaning of my existence. My immediate impulse was to run away. Then I felt an immense pity for myself, my family, the nation, and even the enemy. I said to myself, "Yes, you may run away from the present but to where? There is nowhere to run. You are in an existential limbo. You have a one-way tunnel to go through with no turning back. Someday there may be a light at the end of the tunnel." So life goes.

The typical daily routine was as follows: We woke up to the bugle call at six, washed our faces, lined up for roll call and inspection, ate breakfast (a bowl of rice with soup), and went out to the field for training. Every meal was much the same — plain white rice with fish and seaweed soup. Only rarely did the soup contained pork or beef. No side dishes. No dessert, coffee, or tea. We were perpetually hungry for *kimchi* and meat. After the meals, we washed our own bowls and went out for training. Interestingly, we were seldom trained in the classroom but always went outdoors. Each of us was supplied with a little cushion to sit on that was made out of a hemp-bag stuffed with rice straw. No writing or other supplies were given out. In the cold weather, we sat on the ground to learn how to read maps, use weapons, and how to lead our soldiers (platoon leadership). But we learned very little about army tactics and strategies because we were only junior officers. The cold weather, however, helped us stay awake while we were listening to the instructor. The hemp-bag cushion was a godsend gift. It functioned as a portable chair. Without it, I don't know how we could have survived the infantry training in such cold weather.

The training started with M-1 rifles and proceeded to recoilless rifles, machine guns, hand grenades, infantry mortars and rocket launchers. All of these U.S. weapons were too heavy for most 18-year-old Korean boys. For example, the basic shoulder weapon of the infantry soldiers, an M-1 rifle, weighed 9.5 pounds. I could not even hold the weapon steady. At the firing range, I jammed my thumb in the rifle and the pain was excruciating. The thumbnail turned blue and eventually fell off. Slowly the nail grew back, but even today the nail is deformed. I was a good shooter. I usually hit the bull's-eye three times out of ten.

The biggest problem while we were in the OCS was hunger. The only way to relieve our hunger was to buy something from the *chubo*, an equivalent of the American PX. Literally, *chubo* means "a wine shop," but it was a joke —

there was no wine but rather sundry items, such as rice cakes, crackers, candies, cigarettes, and toothpaste. The most popular item for us starving candidates was, of course, the rice cakes because they would fill our stomachs quickly. Everyone who had money rushed to the *chubo*, which was always crowded, especially in the evening. The hungry crowd behaved like a mob as everyone pushed each other to get close to the store counter. There was no line. I joined the crowd and with my mother's money bought some rice cakes to relieve my hunger pains. I felt so ashamed of myself for devouring the rice cake while standing in the corner of the *chubo*. I really felt like an animal. Later I would be overwhelmed by the sad thought that war was essentially nothing but a dog-eat-dog, kill or be killed, fight. Koreans translate Darwin's famous words "survival of the fittest" as "the strong eat the flesh of the weak" (*Yagyuk Gangsik*). So I thought we are not very different from animals, particularly when we are at war. Where are the morals in this war? Yagyuk Gansik? I was utterly ashamed and depressed but felt helpless to do anything about it.

Good feelings usually come when you have some control over an adverse situation and have a feeling of hope of improving the situation. I had no control over my own situation. And how about patriotism? I used to love my country, Korea, as I loved my parents. But which Korea now? Of course, South Korea (the Republic of Korea) because that's the place I was born and raised. But was I ready to die for it? Yes, but not necessarily for the dictatorial regime of President Rhee — but rather for my family and my future life, if there was one. I hated the North Korean Army's invasion of South Korea, which ruined my dreams and hope for the future. My prime motivation to fight against the North Korean Army was not for ideology or patriotism, but mainly for revenge against what they had done to my family, my country, and me. That was the true purpose and meaning for my participation in the Korean War. The war became very personal to me. I felt we had to win this war, and I was ready to die for my cause — not for an abstract, collective ideology but for my own personal interest. I wanted peace and freedom so that I could get on with my own life. If I died in the process, then so be it.

I was tired of hearing government officials, military leaders, and the news media glorifying the war — usually in the name of the fatherland, democracy, or freedom. I said to myself, "Now what's the meaning of my being here? Not much. I'll finish the training and go to the frontline and do my best. Don't ask me for the meaning of anything. The only thing I know is that war is hell."

5. Officer Candidate School

Eventually the six weeks of infantry basic training for us, the 44 artillery officer candidates, was over, and the next phase of training began. We were transported to the Army Artillery School in Jinhae for four weeks of training in artillery skills. Jinhae is a harbor city about 25 miles west of Pusan. However, the 197 infantry officer candidates who had started basic training with us in the Army Comprehensive Schools were commissioned as second lieutenants two weeks later and directly sent to the frontline as platoon leaders. Every two weeks the Army Comprehensive School pumped out about 200 "consumptive officers." We were in the 25th class of the infantry school.

It was March when we arrived in Jinhae, an absolutely beautiful town covered in early spring cherry blossoms. The Army Artillery School was located on the campus of a local high school. Again classrooms were used for the OCS quarters, but the accommodations in the Artillery School were more civilized than that of the Army Comprehensive School: indoor bathrooms, a dining area, better food with more meat and *kimchi*, and a more comfortable sleeping arrangement with soft mattresses and warm blankets, although we still had to sleep on the floor. As soon as we got up at six in the morning, our first task was to make up our bed by folding the mattress and blanket and piling them neatly against the wall. We then put our helmets and shoes on top of the pile, went to the washroom, got dressed, and stood in front of our bedding for inspection.

There was a senior class of artillery officer candidates also staying in our building—the 12th class who had arrived two weeks before us and were residing in the room next to us. (We were the 13th class of the Artillery School.) One of them was my Kyunggi High School classmate, Myung Sang Lee, an extraordinarily bright fellow. Within two weeks they were commissioned and were all sent to the front as forward observers, except for my friend Myung Sang who became the assistant to the gunnery instructor at the Artillery School. Every two weeks the Artillery School pumped out about 40 forward observers for the ROK Artillery. Each class was taught and supervised by a lieutenant and all were under the command of a captain. We addressed the former as "platoon leader" and the latter, as "company commander." Platoon leaders, First Lieutenant Kim and Second Lieutenant Lee, were very young—maybe only a year or two older than us. Hence, they seemed to understand our needs and problems better than Captain Hong, the company commander. Captain Hong was a seasoned artillery officer with a great deal of combat experience and ambition, but he had no compassion for the plight

"I Will Shoot Them from My Loving Heart"

of his subordinates. We always feared him. He taught the very first day of our class outdoors on a sunny spring day. The topic of his lecture and demonstration was an introduction to the "Aiming Circle," an instrument used for laying a battery of howitzers. The lecture was tedious, we were tired from moving on the previous day, and the warm spring sun was so comfortable that some of us dozed off. He picked up one of sleeping soldiers and started beating him in front of us. (It happened to be Yang Shin Han, the brilliant math major from Seoul National University, mentioned earlier in chapter 1.) Captain Hong slapped and punched his face and did not stop until his nose bled, shouting, "Sleeping in a training session is equivalent to sleeping before the enemy at the front! Do you understand?" We were terrified but wide-awake.

Beating of insubordinate soldiers was an accepted disciplinary measure in the ROK Army at that time. Sometimes it was even encouraged. In fact, at the frontline, a commanding officer was allowed to shoot his subordinates and comrades who disobeyed an order and violated the code of combat. The officer candidates at the Army Comprehensive School were required to recite the Code of Combat every morning and evening after the roll call. The code included the following:

> 2. While engaged in combat I will advance according to the order received, and if I see my comrades or subordinates retreat without permission, I will shoot them from my loving heart of patriotism and friendship.
>
> 3. While engaged in combat I will treasure my weapon, save ammunition whenever possible, and I will not shoot any target that is not certain and not within the effective range unless an order is given by my superior. If I see any of my comrades or subordinates lose or abandon their weapons, I will shoot them [Translated from *The 6–25 Korean War and the Army Comprehensive School*, see Korean War Veterans Association, 1995; in References].

Later I learned that this code of "right and duty" permitting the shooting of insubordinate soldiers at the frontline by a commander (those above the rank of squad leader) was an emergency measure ordered by the ROK Army Headquarters on July 26, 1950, in an effort to reduce the number of deserters during the early stage of the Korean War. Thanks to the pressure of national opinion, this undemocratic code was repealed on July 1, 1951—several months after we were already assigned to the front.

Most of the training at the Artillery School for Officer Candidates focused on how to conduct fire from the observation post by identifying the location and nature of the target and adjusting the fire for the Fire Direction

5. Officer Candidate School

Center (FDC) and the battery. We learned the advanced skills of map reading, usage of binoculars and radios, identification of the enemy target, selection of various ammunition depending on the nature of the target, and the actual practice of conducting fire at the observation posts in the field. We mainly practiced how to conduct fire missions from the observation post (OP). The OP was usually set up on top of a mountain, and the targets were any conspicuous objects visible with binoculars on the slope of another mountain at a distance of about 500–800 yards. The target could be anything — a big rock, a tree, an abandoned house, or even a grave or a monument selected by the training instructor. A grave? Yes, there were many graves on the targeted mountains. Koreans traditionally prefer to bury the dead on the slope of a hill or a mountain not only because farmland is scarce in Korea but also, from a geomantic (Fung-Shui) point of view, a higher place with a good view is preferred. But graves for target practice? I was shocked, but they were selected by the instructor. In fact, many of the graves had already been destroyed due to repeated shelling from previous OCS classes.

A field practice for the forward observer went something like this: "Ok, candidate Hurh! It's your turn. Can you see the grave over there next to a big black rock, almost like a big mound? That's your target. Let's assume this target is an enemy bunker. Now transmit your fire mission to the Fire Direction Center and adjust, so that the target would be destroyed."

I thought it was really a morally reprehensible order. So I asked the instructor: "Sir, can we choose the big black rock instead of the grave?"

The instructor shouted, "You idiot! A 105mm howitzer is not a rifle for sharp shooting. Even if the rock is the target, the shell burst will also destroy the grave since the effective range of destruction is 50 yards in radius! Did you forget? Now go on, idiot! Send fire mission, now!" I felt sad for the dead and their families. I learned again the idiocy of war — shelling the dead to learn how to kill the living. I gave my order, "Hello, FDC? This is Candidate Hurh at OP #3. Fire mission, azimuth 350, distance 800. An enemy bunker. Will adjust." A few moments later the FDC responded, "On the way," and the sound of the incoming shell ended with an explosion on the side of the mountain. It had missed the grave, but it was my job to send an adjustment (either by directing to the right or left, or by adding or dropping range) back to the FDC. One or two more adjustments later and the grave was obliterated. "Good!" my instructor proclaimed admiringly.

In training that was the end of the exercise, but in real combat the forward observer could give one more request: "Fire for effect!" That meant the entire battery (six howitzers) or battalion (18 howitzers) would then fire on the same target and adjust their firing time so that all rounds would hit the target at the same time for a maximum effect. So if an artillery battalion fired ten rounds to its target for effect, it would mean 180 rounds of shells would hit the same target at the same time! And remember, each 105mm shell's effective range of explosive destruction is 50 to 100 yards in diameter. Thanks to the lack of ammunition, we were spared from practicing any "fire for effect" missions while we were in the Artillery School.

In spite of the tough discipline and intensive training, we liked the Artillery School better than the Army Comprehensive School. A number of factors may have contributed to this difference. The atmosphere in the Artillery School was more congenial due to its small size: there were only about 80 candidates at any given time, whereas in the Army Comprehensive School the comparable number was about 500. Moreover, the composition of the candidates at the Artillery School was more homogeneous than that of the Army Comprehensive School because the latter provided the basic infantry training for almost all branches of the ROK army. Also the majority of artillery candidates were high school seniors or college freshmen recruited from metropolitan areas. The composition of the Army Comprehensive School was more diverse in terms of age, education, occupation, and regional variation.

In the Artillery School, I felt like I was home again camping with my school friends. We developed a close comradeship. It was just like a small family in which everyone could relate to one another since we had so much in common, such as age, education, urban background, and military service. We were all destined to become forward observers at the front. The majority of our Artillery OCS classmates came from Seoul, and two of them were my former school classmates (one in elementary school and the other in high school). So we shared everything and helped each other, but sometimes this invited problems. For example, one time my friend, Kwang Jo Chung, received a package of rice cake from home. We were sharing the cake during the afternoon recess between classes even though we knew it was against regulations to eat in our quarters during the recess. The temptation was too great. While we were devouring the rice cake, we heard footsteps in the hallway. For a second we looked at each other, swallowed the cake right away, and looked for a place to hide the remaining cake. Kwang Jo lost his cool

5. Officer Candidate School

ROK Field Artillery Officer Candidates of the 13th Class, commissioned as second lieutenants. Lt. Won Moo Hurh, back row, third from right; Lt. Yang Shin Han, front row, second from right, who was killed in a truck accident on the way to the front; and Lt. Chang Ho Cho, front row, third from right, who was captured by the CCF in 1951 but later escaped in 1994. The three officers seated on the front center bench are from left, Lt. Hyo Suk Lee, Capt. Jong Chul Hong, and Lt. Chang Joon Kim. The building in the background is the ROK Army Artillery School in Jin Hae, Korea. April 14, 1951.

and didn't know what to do. I grabbed the sack of cake and pushed it under my helmet on top of the blankets and mattress that were piled against the wall.

Lieutenant Kim, our platoon leader, walked in. With a surprised look he asked, "What are you doing here? You're not supposed to be here during the recess!" We stood in front of our bedding and I answered, "No, sir! We forgot something."

Lieutenant Kim did not seem to believe me and said, "Candidates Hurh and Chung. Five steps forward." He inspected our beds and said, "Candidate Hurh, turn around 180 degrees and look at your helmet on top of the blanket." I turned and to my shock saw my helmet was tilted about 40 degrees to the left and the sack was exposed to our view. "Explain!" Lieutenant Kim ordered.

I was dumbfounded. The rice cake must have expanded for some reason. How stupid. It was time to confess. The cake was confiscated. Our punishment was to run around the huge school grounds for an hour wearing nothing but army boxer shorts in the chilly evening air of early March. I relearned the principle of *in gwa ung bo*—what you get is a consequence of what you did.

Even though there were other disciplinary infractions, we all graduated from the Artillery School on April 14, 1951. There was no ceremony. Each one of the candidates was commissioned as a Second Lieutenant of the ROK Artillery and given a diploma. I felt a great satisfaction that each of the 44 names of my classmates on the diplomas was inscribed by my calligraphy (Chinese ink-brush writing). Someone must have told Lieutenant Kim that I could do the calligraphy. Ordinarily they hired someone to do the job. They saved money, and I enjoyed doing it. Plus I didn't have to go to the firing range and fire on the innocent graves. I did the calligraphy on a lovely spring day while all of the men and supervisors were out at firing practice. I was alone in the quiet of Lieutenant Kim's office, writing each candidate's name on his diploma. What a pleasure and what serenity! I wondered how my mother and my siblings were doing, but I had no way of contacting them.

So after the four weeks of artillery training, we all departed the school as officers and headed for our destination—the frontlines. As we didn't get any salary or other monetary compensation, we were on our own. There was no military transportation at all that we could utilize. We were in dire need of money just to eat or to buy simple things like soap and toothpaste—not to mention the transportation cost to the front. I really needed a new pair of shoes, and I traded my Seiko watch for a pair of used army boots at the Daegu city market.

At our graduation, the genteel Lieutenant Kim said to us, "You'll really need good luck. A lot of it. I wish you all well." Indeed, his remark was prophetic. As described in chapter 1, the next day one of my comrade officers, Lieutenant Han, was killed in an accident as we traveled together to report to our frontline unit—before even engaging in combat.

So here we were, six new "baby lieutenants" from the artillery school ordered to report to the commander of the 11th Division of the ROK Army at the eastern front for our first combat duties. According to the order, all of us were assigned to the same unit, the 102nd Independent Artillery Company. That's why we were traveling together, but we were not sure where the hell the division headquarters were since they were constantly changing their location depending on their battle situations.

6

The Frontline and Fort Sill

THE EVENING OF THE day Lieutenant Han was killed, I and four other freshly minted second lieutenants arrived at the headquarters of the 102nd Independent Artillery Company located in a small village near Sok Cho near the front. "Where is Lieutenant Han?" asked Captain Park, a soft-spoken man in his late thirties, the company commander. I explained, "He died in a truck accident on the way to the Division HQ, sir."

Captain Park's reaction was impersonal: "That's too bad, but we have our job to do. First of all, I'd like to welcome you to our company. We're so glad to have regular forward observers with officer's rank at last! Welcome! Let's have a party!" We ate amazingly well that night — fresh fish from the East Sea, *bulgogi* (barbecued beef), seaweed soup, rice, *kimchi*, and a lot of rice wine. Moreover, the U.S. Army C-Rations were introduced, and for the first time I smoked a Lucky Strike cigarette and ate a Hershey chocolate bar.

That evening we were surprised to learn that the 102nd Independent Artillery Company was only equipped with 4.2-inch heavy mortars — an infantry weapon used in World War II and not considered an artillery weapon because of its short range. We were expecting our artillery group to have the usual set-up of three 105mm howitzer battalions and one 155mm howitzer battalion. However, due to the ROK's short supply of regular field artillery pieces, such as the howitzers, a number of 4.2-inch mortars were mobilized to form several independent "artillery companies" to supplement the regular division artillery group. Thus, the newly organized 4.2-inch heavy mortar companies were added to the division artillery group, and we, the forward observers, were expected to direct their fire — though we had never fired or trained on a 4.2-inch mortar in our life. Unbelievably, Captain Park told us not to worry because the technique of conducting fire as a forward observer is just the same whether for the 105mm, the 155mm, or the 4.2-inch. Captain Park did not tell us one important fact — the forward observer's position for the 4.2-inch is much closer to the enemy frontline than for the long-range artillery howitzers. The maximum range of a 4.2-inch mortar is less than half that of a 105mm howitzer — 2.6 miles (4,400 yards) versus seven miles (12,000 yards). This was bad news for us. We were assured, however, that the 4.2-inch projectile's destructiveness was greater than that of the 105mm. What an idiotic consolation! Actually, we did not care whether we had 105mm or 4.2-inch artillery. What we cared about most was staying alive.

After that first night's good meal and wine, we each took a couple of blankets and went to bed on the floor of an abandoned farmhouse. We could hear occasional bombshell bursts in the distance and the eerie silence that followed. Our orders were to come in the morning.

During the night I had a dream:

> *My mother was waving goodbye to me. She stood in front of a factory house on a snow-covered knoll in Yipjang village where our family had taken refuge when we were fleeing from North Korean troops in January of 1951. The North Korean Army was rapidly closing in. Snow was falling heavily, but I could see my mother still standing on the hill watching me leaving.*

In the middle of my dream, I was suddenly awakened by the shouts of Lieutenant Kim, the company's executive officer: "Enemy attack at the front!" He ordered me to get ready to go to the observation post (OP) right away. My problem was I didn't know where the OP was. According to the Field Manual, the artillery forward observer's OP is usually with or near the infantry company commander's outpost. So I asked Lieutenant Kim for a map and the location of the infantry company that we were supposed to reinforce. He told me my observation team (made up of an observation corporal, a radio operator, and a sentry/telephone operator) had already been dispatched to the OP near the infantry unit, and observation corporal Lee would show me the way. The corporal supplied me with everything I needed: a map, compass, flashlight, and binoculars — and a couple more needed pieces of equipment, a carbine .30 semiautomatic rifle with an extra magazine and two hand grenades. I was unfamiliar with the carbine .30. The only small arm weapons with which we practiced were M-1 rifles and machine guns. According to the Field Artillery Manual, the forward observer is supposed to be equipped with a Colt .45 pistol, not a carbine.

6. The Frontline and Fort Sill

Well, it did not matter. I was thankful to at least be given a weapon at all. What bothered me, however, was the fact that we five newly arrived officers had not been briefed by the company commander or the operation officer about the status of the frontline nor given our mission assignments until the enemy attack began. Instead, we had been given a party. I found out much later that I was assigned to the Second Platoon of the company as its forward observer. There were three platoons in a heavy mortar company, and each platoon had four 4.2-inch mortars. So three of the new officers, including myself, were ordered to our respective OPs and the remaining two were assigned to other duties — one became an assistant to the Fire Direction Center (FDC) of the company and the other was sent to the Ninth infantry regiment as a liaison officer.

Corporal Lee looked much younger than I — maybe, 17. He welcomed me to the team and explained that he had been acting as the forward observer for the Second Platoon due to the shortage of officer-rank forward observers. He introduced me to the others in the observation team. With him were two more baby-faced soldiers — Private Kim, a radio operator, and Private Cho, a telephone operator. Private Kim had a huge radio (SCR 300) on his back and Cho was carrying the field telephone equipment. All of them looked tired. I spread out the map and asked Corporal Lee, "Do you know where our OP is tonight?"

Lee replied, "Yes, sir. It's the same hill that we climbed yesterday. It's less than two miles from here. You don't need a map. We know the way."

"Well then, let's go!" I ordered.

The night was pitch black, except for an occasional flash of light from behind the mountains in front of us, followed by the distant sound of bursting shells. We made our way on small winding village roads, through rice paddies, and over burnt woody hills with the familiar stench of decomposing human bodies — the most absolutely disgusting and oppressive smell that God has ever allowed to exist. I was familiar with the odor having experienced it before after the North Korean soldiers slaughtered innocent civilians in and around Seoul and left them there in the scorching sun in June 1950. We never spoke a word, but we knew what the smell meant.

We climbed up a small but steep mountain to reach the OP. At the top I expected to see our infantry soldiers, but no one was there. I whispered to Corporal Lee, "Where are they? I mean the infantry!"

Lee said, "Sir, no one's here except us." He reported that the infantry was on the hill to the west of us and that they had known our OP was here for the past week and would communicate with us when they needed our artillery support. He pointed out that the company FDC had designated this place as our OP. I thought it was very strange because I had learned at Officer Candidate School that the OP was always positioned by the infantry platoon leader or the company commander. In this instance, our situation was isolated. I called the FDC. They confirmed our position as the OP for the second platoon (battery).

So here we were alone on top of a Godforsaken mountain in the middle of a pitch-dark night — without any infantry protection. We were supposed to observe the enemy and conduct fire, but how could we see anything except the occasional shell bursts at a distance. There was no moon and very few stars in the sky and absolute quiet between the distant explosions. I thought, "What an absurdity! Do we sit here and keep watch in the darkness until the sunrise? What should we do if the enemy sneaks up on us? Even one guy with a hand grenade or automatic weapon would finish us in seconds." Neither the infantry nor the artillery school told us what to do in this kind of situation.

I was scared. I asked, "Corporal! If this place has been an OP, why didn't you built a bunker or at least dig a trench for protection? What did you do here at night?"

The corporal said, "Each night one of the observation crew stayed in the OP and the rest of us slept in a vacant farmhouse down at the foothill. We took turns every night."

I was stunned. "Did the Company Commander know this?"

The corporal replied, "Yes, sir. He approved because there's been no enemy activity around here for the past several weeks."

I thought I should order my three soldiers to dig a trench right away so that we could be protected from a possible ambush. But then how could we dig anything in pitch darkness? And how about the sound of digging? Better to wait until tomorrow morning, when everything would be different — I would be in charge. I ordered the soldiers, "Spread your positions and guard against a possible ambush. No farmhouse tonight. We'll dig the OP trench tomorrow." Another shell burst was heard — and then an eerie silence.

I looked up at the moonless sky and wondered to myself, "Will I live tomorrow? How about my soldiers? How about my mother and the rest of my family wherever they may be?" Life seemed absurd. But then I thought, there is always hope — hope for God's providence. I recalled reading Leo Tolstoy's essay in my high school English class almost a year earlier: *God Sees the Truth, But Waits*. So I will wait — wait through the night and through tomorrow and forever — for God's providence.

In retrospect, I was going to be in the middle of a series of massive attacks launched by the Chinese Communist Forces (CCF or CPVF that meant euphemistically Chinese People's Volunteer Forces) against the Allied Forces on all fronts in the spring of 1951. The first attack on April 22 was the so-called "First Spring Offensive" and was aimed mainly at the Republic of Korea (ROK) III Corps, which defended the western flank of our ROK I Corps. But the assault soon affected our eastern sector also — this was just about the time we five officers went to bed after the big welcoming party at the 102nd Heavy Motor Company.

My first night at the OP was scary, and the next morning I made my soldiers dig a trench and then conducted a registration fire. A registration fire is when the forward observer selects a base point in the target area from which he can conduct the subsequent fire missions. The base point is fired precisely, and the firing data is recorded for use in any future fire missions, even in the dark of night. We were quite ready to provide our fire support to the infantry, but for some reason there was no serious enemy activity nor any fire mission request from the infantry for a couple of days. Our company FDC told us to stay where we were until further orders were given. So we enjoyed the break. My soldiers hunted a small wild pig and roasted it over an open fire for a meal. What a heavenly treat! The meat melted on my tongue. Heaven at the frontline meant a good meal with your comrades, a good sleep, and knowing you are still alive.

But soon our 11th Division had to retreat to the south because of a massive Chinese attack against our neighbor, the Capital Division. Eventually our neighbor's defense line broke and they started to retreat. Although our division had done no major fighting, we also had to retreat about 15 miles to the south near a fishing town, Dae-Po Ri, located on the coast of the East Sea. It seemed like a perfect setting for a summer resort with the beautiful shoreline, the dark blue sea, the gentle spring breeze, and the wonderful sunshine. However, most of the town's residents had evacuated, leaving it an empty ghost town.

By luck our company was temporarily put on a reserve status, and hence we decided to enjoy the present. I did not have to go to the OP so I took a nap, and when I woke up, there was a commotion announcing that a group of girls had arrived to entertain us. What? Girls at the frontline? I was shocked and amazed. Then I thought it would be like an entertainment show with the girls singing and dancing for the soldiers. I was mistaken. Each officer was given a ticket to see a girl in a specified room. A ticket? At first I did not know what was going on but then I guessed what it was about. I finally knew to my dismay it was prostitution in the army! I could not believe it. But it was. The master sergeant of our company headquarters came to me saying, "Sir, we all may die tomorrow. Please enjoy. It will boost your morale!" I did not know what to make of the situation.

In a large farmhouse, there were about six rooms, and in each room there was a poor girl waiting for her customers. I went into one and found a girl about the age of 17. She looked just like my sister. I told her that I did not want anything from her, and gave her my ticket so that she could redeem it for money. She looked at me as if I were insane. When I came out, there was my comrade, Lieutenant Choi, asking, "How was it?" I said I did not do it. He said, "You fool! You should have given me the ticket, so that I could have a second round. What a waste!" I was dumbfounded. Although it was not comparable to the atrocities the Japanese soldiers committed against the so-called "Comfort Women," who were largely Koreans, Chinese, and Filipinas during World War II; nevertheless, what I was witnessing was the abuse and exploitation of impoverished Korean women by Korean soldiers. I was appalled. Where did the money come from to pay these prostitutes? I felt angry and then painfully sad. God help us. What a splendid irony — death at the front and sex at the rear. So this is war. I thought my existential world was becoming more like a replay of Remarque's *All Quiet on the Western Front*. I hoped my fate would be different. I wanted to live.

It was extremely quiet at Dae-Po Ri for a week — no enemy offensive nor any casualties, except for an accident — a really stupid accident. In spite of being warned, some soldiers went fishing in a boat and dropped hand grenades to catch fish. But we had two kinds of hand grenades at that time — American-made and Korean-made. The former had a safety lever in addition to the safety pin to prevent a premature explosion until you throw it towards your target. So as long as you held the lever of the grenade, it would not explode even though you had already removed the safety pin. The Korean-made grenade had no such safety lever. You had to throw it within five seconds after the removal of the safety pin or the grenade exploded in your hand. That's exactly what happened. The soldier forgot he had a Korean-made hand grenade when he became excited over finding a school of fish. He removed the safety pin but continued looking for the best place to throw the grenade for a big catch. Boom! Fishing with a suicide bomb? How dumb and what a waste of precious life. I blamed the war again.

In the first week of May 1951, our counterattack began. I had to climb up a different mountain and establish a new OP every day. It was very taxing. Some mountains were all burned out, and we hiked through the black ashes and the remains of charred bodies. We could not tell if the bodies were those of our enemy or our fellow soldiers. After we got to the top of the mountain and established an OP, the very next day we had to move again. Within ten days or so we recovered most of the areas we had lost in April. I was glad of our advance but could not make any sense out of this seesaw or yo-yo war. We found what we had lost, but we may lose it again and may find it again. Such is the absurdity of war.

I wondered what was actually happening. I reasoned that both sides were tired out and knew there was no victory for either side — the Communists or the UN Forces. In fact, talks about an armistice started to loom. We had no access to newspapers but did listen to the radio occasionally. Each side wanted to occupy as much land as possible before the armistice. Thus I reasoned more yo-yo warfare would be forthcoming.

I was right. In mid–May, the CCF launched their "Second Spring Offensive" or "May Offensive," largely against the ROK army sectors from the middle to the eastern front. A few days before the attack, our old company commander, Captain Park, was replaced by Captain Keum Yeol Lee, a much younger and a more ambitious, risk-taking commander. He thought our heavy mortar batteries should be deployed as close as possible to the infantry outpost in order to give them maximum fire support. This meant our forward observers would be closer to the front and positioned with the infantry platoon leaders. Thus, he deployed our batteries behind a small hill on the seacoast quite close to the frontline of the infantry outpost. It was actually a dangerous move because the battery site he chose was the foremost northeastern tip of our infantry outpost, 25 miles north of Sorak Mountain and 30 miles north of the 38th parallel. In fact, the famous Diamond Mountain (Keumgangsan) was not far away, and I thought I might even be able to see it from our OP.

The next day I was ordered to establish an OP at the very front of our defense line. On top of a rugged mountain, my usual team (a radio operator, a telephone operator and an observation corporal) set up an OP with the help of the infantry soldiers around us. A young infantry platoon leader, Lieutenant Kim, told me that the CCF may attack at night accompanied by the discordant and shrill sound of gongs and flutes. I often had heard about the utterly demoralizing effect of an attack by Chinese soldiers wildly pounding gongs and blowing flutes. In any case, I conducted a registration fire and calculated data on a few probable targets suggested by Lieutenant Kim. Since you cannot see the enemy at night, the firing data on each possible target (such as Target number 1, number 2, etc.) must be prepared in advance and sent to the Fire Direction Center (FDC).

Night came and we expected the sounds of gongs and flutes, but instead a loud barrage of machine guns, submachine guns (burp guns) and various kinds of rifles broke out. This was the first time in my life that I saw so many traces of live bullets coming at me. They looked like hundreds of beams of light splashing at me. Our infantry soldiers fired back, and I called the battery FDC for our fire mission. Within a minute the selected targets were fired upon, but the subsequent fire adjustment was very difficult since we could not see the target, although we could observe the impact of our projectiles. So I conducted the fire mission based on the infantry platoon and squad leaders' requests. After we conducted massive fire for effect missions on several targets simultaneously, the enemy fire subsided. Our exchange of fire lasted only about an hour, but it seemed an eternity to me. None of our forward observer team was injured, but there were some casualties among the infantry soldiers. We would know about the details the next day. Throughout the night no more attacks occurred, but our batteries conducted "harassment fire" on the enemy territory every two hours or so. "Harassment fire" means random fire against the enemy with the intent of demoralizing the enemy. I wondered why there had been no sound of gongs or flutes, and why the enemy had stopped their attack. Perhaps our enemy might be the NKPA instead of the CCF? The infantry platoon leader did not have any idea either.

Eventually the sun rose even in this Godforsaken war zone. With binoculars I examined the front. On the slope opposite our OP, I could see several bodies of enemy soldiers but could not tell whether they were the CCF or NKPA. The target areas that we fired on the previous night appeared to be devastated and seemed to include enemy trenches, machine-gun posts, and possible artillery bunkers. The number of casualties on our side was fewer

6. The Frontline and Fort Sill

than 50. I do not recall the exact account, but considering the massive fire exchange we had, I felt we were extremely lucky. I called my company commander, Captain Lee, and reported the current status of the front. He encouraged me to carry on.

Since we could not sleep at all the previous night, I ordered my soldiers to rotate turns for taking a nap. I noticed the infantry was doing the same thing. After I ate some C-rations (the classic equivalent of the modern MRE [Meals Ready to Eat]) I dozed off ... *and all of sudden, someone told me that we were enveloped by the CCF. Sure enough I heard the sound of pounding gongs and blowing flutes. Someone said again, "We are finished!" "No, we're not," I shouted. "Counterattack and fight to the last man, you idiot!" But no one moved...*

Waking up, I was relieved that it was only a dream. During the day, we fortified our trenches and were ready for the night. Around seven in the evening, the attack came again without the sounds of gongs or flutes. This time it was gigantic — a shower of bullets from all sorts of small arms mixed with mortar shells. We fired back whatever we had, but the enemy kept coming closer. The maximum firing range for our 4.2-inch heavy mortars was 4,400 yards (2.6 miles) but we started from 2,200 yards (1.3 miles) because our battery was so close to the enemy. Now I was conducting the fire at a range of about 1,000 yards, and kept dropping the range since the enemy was moving closer to our defense line. I kept requesting, "Drop 50! Drop another 50!" and so forth. When the firing range came to about 700 yards, Captain Lee at the FDC yelled on the radio, "What's going on? The firing range is getting too short. We cannot stay here any longer and may have to evacuate our batteries soon. Is the infantry retreating?"

I responded, "Not yet, sir. They're still holding but probably not for long. They need maximum fire support now! Please keep firing as I requested!" The radio went silent, and the firing stopped from our batteries. I wondered if our battery had already pulled out or had been ambushed by the enemy.

The infantry platoon leader was furious. "Where is your fire support?" While I was explaining the situation to him, another wave of attack by the enemy came, and the entire line of infantry defense started to crumble. I did not know what to do at that moment. The artillery forward observer is useless without his battery. Either he may try to join the infantry or try to reestablish radio contact with his FDC/battery. I chose the latter because the artillery forward observers are not trained for infantry combat. We were useless in hand-to-hand combat, and yet I was hesitating what to do. At that point, the infantry platoon leader shouted to me that his group would start pulling back to the rear for regrouping. In a way I was relieved and ordered my team to retreat. The descent down the steep mountain was not easy in the dark — no flashlights could be used. With no clear path to follow, we stumbled around trees, branches, and shrubs, often losing our footing on the loose rocks. At times we could smell the stench of rotting bodies. During this descent, I could not overcome my feeling of defeat and frustration. I wished we had the larger 155mm howitzers. (Not until December 1951, would the ROK Army have 155mm howitzer batteries.)

At dawn we arrived at the foothill of the mountain along the highway. To our surprise, my commander, Captain Lee, was standing on the road in front of his jeep. He was waiting for us. This was totally unexpected and I was speechless. He said nothing but gestured for us to get in the jeep. We climbed up and sat in the back. When the jeep started to move, I thanked Captain Lee for picking us up. He looked back and said, "I'm glad we found you alive. The entire ROK III Corps on our west flank has been enveloped by the CCF and is now on the verge of collapse. Unless we pull out rapidly to the south, we may face a similar fate." Our 11th Division started to evacuate to the Kangnung area. The city of Kangnung is about 56 miles to the south from our last OP, and 20 miles below the 38th parallel. This was a massive retreat.

Later I learned that the ROK III Corps, the west flank of our ROK I Corps, had in fact collapsed under the attack of the CCF. I also heard that one of my artillery school classmates, Chang Ho Cho, whose army serial number was just next to mine, was killed in action in the area of Inje. Inje city was devastated by the CCF. Cho was assigned to the 101st Heavy Mortar Company for the ROK III Corp, as a forward observer like me. But 43 years later, I was astounded to read an article in *Time* magazine of November 7, 1994: "Cho Chang Ho, 63, has been to hell and lived to tell about it. The South Korean army lieutenant was reported killed in action during the Korean War, and he had been forgotten, even by his family. But for all those years Cho was alive in North Korea." He was captured by the CCF in the Inje area in May 1951, spent 12 years in a gulag near Wonsan, North Korea, and later was sent to a coal mine where he worked for 13 years. Eventually he married a North Korean woman and raised two children in a remote village near the Yalu River. On the night of October 3, 1994, however, he managed to escape from North Korea by crossing the Yalu River to China and finally made his way to the harbor of Gunsan in South Korea on October 23, 1994.

So in mid–May of 1951, our massive retreat to Kangnumg began, and I was assigned to the Ninth Infantry Regiment's War Operation Center as an artillery liaison officer. It was a change from the forward observer duty — less physical danger, less taxing mentally, but dull. I knew no one in the infantry regiment. What I did in the operation center was to coordinate the retreat activities between the infantry and artillery units in our division sector. The food in the infantry was also less desirable than in the artillery. I certainly appreciated Corporal Ju Sik Kim who came with me from our 102nd Heavy Mortar Company and functioned as an aide for my general needs. An officer in any army without an aide would be quite miserable. An aide functions almost like a servant at the front. He cooks for you, washes your clothes, makes your bed, cleans, and does other caretaker duties. He was only a few months younger than myself.

By May 20, most of our 11th Division units had made the retreat to Kangnung, and I was pleased to be ordered back to my battery. Kangnung is an historic city where the Korean king's summer resort was once located, the Kyong Po Dae. Most of its facilities were devastated by the war, but it was still beautiful — the lake, the royal gazebo overlooking the gorgeous dark blue sea, and the most elaborate botanical garden, although very few flowers managed to bloom. I was fascinated. I did not want to leave this beautiful, tranquil area. Why this stupid war? Brothers are killing each other and destroying everything. For what purpose?

Three days later the tide of war turned in our favor again. Thanks to the vast reinforcement from the U.S. forces on our west flank, the ROK I Corps launched a massive counterattack northward along the east coast. The battles were often fierce, and it took us about two weeks to recover our lost territory. As usual I climbed up a new mountain almost every other day to conduct numerous fire missions. I still recall the unbearable stench of decomposing bodies coming from the mountain trenches and bunkers.

In early June we set up our Company Fire Direction Center (FDC) in a Buddhist temple compound, and deployed our mortar platoons on the foothill of Keonbongsan, a huge, heavily wooded, beautiful mountain located about 15 miles southeast of the famous Keumgangsan (Diamond Mountain). Luckily, I did not have to climb up the mountain again for the OP since the company commander, Captain Lee, ordered me to lead the Second Mortar Platoon instead. As a platoon leader I was responsible for the lives of 45 men, four 4.2-inch heavy mortars, and other equipment and supplies, including .50-caliber machine guns, small arms, ammunition, a two-and-one-half-ton truck, and so on. Captain Lee wanted to deploy my platoon deep into the valley as close as possible to the western flank of our frontline so that we could give maximum fire support to the infantry, a venture similar to one he once attempted previously near the Koejin outpost in May. After an hour of reconnaissance we found an ideal place to position our mortars — close to the frontline but hidden from the enemy's surveillance. It was a flat surface by a stream in a deep rocky valley, almost a gorge, where we could safely clear the high-angle trajectory of our mortar projectiles but be hidden from view within the surrounding areas. It was isolated but naturally protected and quite scenic. Captain Lee seemed to be fully satisfied with the site and said he would visit us as often as possible. We positioned the mortars, called the OP, and conducted registration fires. For the self-defense of our perimeter, I ordered my sergeant major to deploy two .50-caliber machine guns, position several guards around our battery compound, and pitch small tents using ponchos for the night's sleep. It was a beautiful summer night — stars in the sky, the soft, warm air, the soothing sound of the nearby stream; the summer insects' mating calls; and most of all, no enemy activity. I could not believe I was at the frontline of life and death. I was again searching for the meaning of my precarious existence. What would become of me, my family, and my country?

The morning came. More rounds of registration fire were conducted. Captain Lee came and inspected my platoon. All was quiet. After lunch, I decided to take a nap. I laid down on a huge flat rock near the stream under the shadow of a big tree. And I had a dream or saw an illusion: the image of Christ in a white robe, crucified on the cross with big nails in His feet and hands. He didn't speak but just looked down at me with very sad eyes. I was not a Christian nor did I believe in any religion.

Just like many other young Koreans at that time, my only religious or ritual experience was paying compulsory visits to Japanese Shinto shrines, accompanying my mother to a Buddhist temple when my father died, and visiting ancestral graves on Chusok, the full-moon Thanksgiving celebration day. I heard about Christianity but seldom read the Bible or attended a Christian church. Why, then, did I have this dream or vision of Christ?

6. THE FRONTLINE AND FORT SILL

Like most Koreans at the time, our family was Confucian, but that did not mean we believed in Confucius as a god, but rather we thought of him as a moral teacher or a sage. To believe in Confucius means to adhere to his social ethics, particularly filial piety, but not particularly to worship him as a supernatural entity. Similarly deceased parents and ancestors were revered by their offspring but not worshiped as gods or goddesses. On every Chusok and on the anniversary of a close relative's death, most Koreans visit their ancestor's graves to pay respect by bringing offerings of food and wine. My contact with Christianity was very limited. As mentioned in chapter 3, while I was in elementary school, I was an avid reader of the Japanese-translated *Complete Collection of World Literatures* (*Sekai Bungaku Jenshu*), and I learned the rudimentary history of the life of Jesus, his suffering, crucifixion, and resurrection as reflected in various Western literatures. I was curious to know more about Christianity but was too busy with other things, such as schoolwork and play. At the middle school, one of my friends was a Catholic, and he talked about his obligation to attend the Sunday mass, but I was not interested in knowing why. I presumed that was just their way of life. If there was a heaven, I thought there could be many ways to get there—Christianity, Buddhism, Shintoism, or whatever. My parents never talked about any exclusive religion. For them, a "good" religion must be inclusive, tolerant, and accommodating to everyone. But a stunning event took place two years after my father's funeral. His mother (my grandmother), who was dying from a stroke, asked for us to bring a Catholic priest to administer the final rite. We were absolutely flabbergasted! We never knew she was a Catholic—she never attended a Catholic church or any other Christian church. Through slurred speech, she took pains to tell my mother that she was baptized in Doonpo when she was 12, and her baptismal name was Maria! (Doonpo is her native town in Choong-Nam Province where the French Catholic missionary work started in 1846.) So for the first time in our life, a Korean Catholic priest came to our home and administered the last rites to my grandmother. I was not in her room, but I was told that she passed away in peace two days later.

So why did I see Jesus Christ appearing in my vision or dream at the Godforsaken frontline in the summer of 1951? I had no idea. Nevertheless, I was very much comforted by the vision. Someone was expressing pity for me and for my soldiers. Someone cared. I was overwhelmed by the grace and thanked God.

All was quiet on the eastern front — not even a single gunshot was heard in three days. There was a rumor going around that both sides (the UN command and the CCF/NKPA) were seriously considering a possible armistice, and so there would be no more major offensives. The status quo would be maintained, except for minor sporadic fights to gain better terrain for defensive purposes. The stalemate was a welcome break for us frontline soldiers. Captain Lee occasionally visited my platoon, and we shared lunch together in my tent. Over lunch we talked about the possible armistice and its impact on the future of the two Koreas. The more we talked about the fate of Korea, the more powerless and hopeless we felt. I thought the two Koreas would not be able to determine their fate by themselves, but rather Korea's future would depend on the two big powers — the United States and the People's Republic of China. An armistice is not a peace treaty but a temporary cease-fire, and so I felt this seesaw war was not going to be over but only temporarily postponed. Millions of human lives had been sacrificed, but the border between the two Koreas remained more or less the same as before the war had started.

The realization of the futility of the war depressed us, so we changed the topic of conversation to learning about each other's personal lives. Captain Lee grew up in North Korea and came to South Korea a few years before the Korean War broke out. He joined the ROK Army by enrolling as a cadet in the Military Academy in 1948. The following year he was commissioned as a second lieutenant and the next year began serving in the Korean War. His combat experience was quite impressive. But he did not tell me anything about his family except for the fact that he had never married. I did not press him about this, and instead talked about my family and my ordeal as a refugee evacuating from Seoul to Chonan by riding on the rooftop of a freight train. He was very sympathetic and asked me what had happened to my family since then. "I don't know, sir. I don't know where they are now or if they are alive." I replied almost in tears. Silence followed. Then Captain Lee stood up and said, "I'll see you later. Take care."

The next day, Captain Lee phoned and said, "Every week our trucks go down to Seoul for supplies. Would you like to ride along to Seoul and find out the whereabouts of your mother? I can give you a three day furlough." I was overwhelmed by his kindness and thanked him. However, I was concerned about who would take care of my platoon. He reassured me that under his supervision the sergeant major could carry on for the three

6. THE FRONTLINE AND FORT SILL

days. What an unexpected chance. I was so excited that I could hardly sleep that night. I was immensely thankful to have such a compassionate commander as Captain Lee.

A few days later I headed for Seoul with Corporal Chang, the driver of the truck. He was an older guy, probably five or six years older than me. He had a wife and children in Kongju, not far from Chonan-Ipjang where I had left my mother and the family on that snowy day six months previously. So I told him that we might go down to the south further than Seoul to visit my mother and siblings, if I could find any information about their whereabouts. I was hoping to find more information on the family from Uncle Duin, my mother's younger brother, who might have returned to Seoul from Daegu by that time. Corporal Chang seemed pleasantly surprised and asked me, "Do you mean, sir, that on this trip I could have a chance to see my wife and children in Kongju?" I told him it was a possibility if my family was still in the Chonan area. Kongju is about 30 miles from Chonan. Corporal Chang could hardly conceal his swelling excitement.

We set out on our journey at six in the morning, but it took us more than half a day to reach Seoul from the eastern front. The actual distance was only about 160 miles, but because of the road conditions and many security checkpoints, we traveled at a snail's pace. According to division policy, we were fully armed for the trip with carbine rifles, helmets, and even a couple of hand grenades because of the possibility of guerrilla attacks. At that time all major cities and towns were under marshal law. Well past noon, we pulled up to my uncle's store near the Nam Dae Moon area. I was relieved to see the building was still intact. Moreover, I was overjoyed to see my uncle in the store. Most of the merchandise had been looted, but my uncle was determined to revive the store. He was surprised to see me, and said my mother and the family were evacuated from the milling factory in Ipjang to Onyang, about 12 miles southwest of Chonan. He did not know the specific circumstances of the evacuation, but said my mother and my siblings were surely safe at Onyang.

Corporal Chang and I had no time to waste. We crossed the temporary bridge at the Han River and proceeded to the south. I wondered why the main bridge had not been repaired yet. We were depressed to see that so many places still had not recovered from the severe destruction caused by the Communist invasion. People were suffering everywhere, from hunger, disease, dislocation, alienation, and most of all, a sense of hopelessness. On the dusty roads where we were driving, I could see nothing but despair, could smell nothing but something decomposing, and could almost hear the wailing sound of the millions who had perished since the damn war began. How I hated war, any war!

We arrived in Onyang around four in the afternoon. Corporal Chang dropped me off and headed for a reunion with his family. Before the war, Onyang city had been known as a resort town for its hot springs, but when we got there, it was like a ghost town. As instructed by my uncle, I went to a milling factory near the railway station and asked for Mr. Yoon Seong Hurh, my distant cousin from my father's side. A man in the factory sent a boy to relay the message to my cousin. After waiting about 30 minutes in the hot, humid weather, my cousin showed up. He was a man in his 40s whom I thought I had met many years ago. He poured me some rice wine and said he would take me to my mother's house, which was only about a 30 minute walk away. He told me of Mother's anxiety that I might have died since she hadn't heard a word from me. I explained I had no way of contacting her or the family. Nevertheless, deep inside myself I felt pangs of guilt that I had caused her so much worry. According to Confucian ethics, sons should honor their parents and not cause them any grief. Being impatient to see my mother, I put down the wine cup and stood up. My older cousin understood, and we started off. I hoped my sudden appearance would be a happy surprise for my mother.

Mother's house was located on the outskirts of the town — a small country-style house with a thatched roof. As we approached the house on the dirt road, we could see my mother washing clothes in the courtyard. She looked up at us with a puzzled look. I thought perhaps she couldn't recognize me in my military uniform. Then she came forward with teary eyes and taking hold of my hands said, "Is that you? Won Moo, my son!" We hugged and cried with relief and joy. My sisters and brother came out of the house and joined in our happy reunion. Immediately they began to prepare an elaborate dinner to celebrate my return. That evening we forgot about the war and just enjoyed being together again.

The next morning Mother wanted to know how long I would be staying. She was quiet when I told her only two days and then Corporal Chang would be picking me up. Then she asked if she could ride with us to Seoul, but I explained that it was against army regulations to allow civilians in military trucks. Mom was disappointed but understood. She told me of her plans to go to Seoul soon by whatever means and that the next time I visited her I should look for her there.

Mom was also determined to have a portrait photo taken of me even though I argued against it. She knew I was going back to the frontline and feared we might never see each other again. She made the arrangements at a photo studio in town, and of course, I couldn't disappoint her. For the photo I wore my officer's uniform complete with helmet and two grenades. The photographer posed me in front of a fake city rooftop scene clearly showing some church steeples in the background — a strange combination of war and peace in one photo.

It was good to be home again even for just two days — delicious home-cooked meals, a hot bath, a good rest, and most of all a lot of talking. My older sister told me the story of what had happened to the family at the milling factory after my uncle and I departed for Daegu on the snowy morning of January 5, 1951. Soon after we left, more and more American soldiers moved into the vicinity of the milling factory in Ipjang with jeeps, trucks, and heavy artillery. Several American soldiers approached my grandfather who was the only adult male left in our family. No one in my family could speak English, except for a few words such as "Hello" or "Okay." My sister saw one of the soldiers, who looked liked an officer, asking Grandpa something by pointing around the factory compound. She heard our grandpa saying, "Okay, Okay!" Minutes later, the entire milling compound became an American field-artillery battery position. All of our family members, about 20 of them, including women and children, did not know what to

Photograph taken when visiting my mother during a two-day furlough from the frontline. Notice how heavily I was armed, even with hand grenades — required by the army because of the pervasive enemy guerrilla activities. Ironically, the idyllic background was a painted set. June 1951.

make of the situation as the howitzers, ammunition, trucks, and equipment moved in. Mother kept everyone inside the milling factory, but several American soldiers infiltrated, shouting, "Sexee, Sexee." (The word, "sexee" happened to be in Korean "a bride" or "a young woman.") One of the American soldiers grabbed my older sister In Moo's arms. She was 19 at the time. When my mother noticed what was happening, she grabbed a big rock (about three pounds), raised it above her head, and shouted at the soldier: "You God damn American bastard! Leave my daughter alone or I'll kill you and myself!" Of course, the soldier did not understand Korean, but he was shocked by my mother's frantic reaction. Fortunately he did the right thing and released In Moo.

My sister was saved that evening, but my family worried about what was going to come. There was also my 16-year-old sister, Eui Moo, and a few other young women in the family. That night my mother called a family meeting in the factory backroom and announced that for everyone's sake they must disperse because 20-some people could not survive in such a large group; therefore, every nuclear family should take care of itself. Mother said she would evacuate the Hurhs to Onyang, and for the Eums she suggested Jinchon, the native town of the Eum family. The two cities were less than 30 miles from the milling factory. So my mother, three sisters and brother evacuated to Onyang where relatives on my father's side had settled down several centuries ago. Mom rented a two-room house on the outskirts of town and prayed every day for my safety. Such was the story told by my elder sister, In Moo.

Too soon the day came for us to part again. Mom wept and so did my siblings. Corporal Chang came on time, and we left Onyang for Seoul where we picked up supplies and then headed back to the frontline. My platoon was in good shape during my absence, thanks to my master sergeant and Captain Lee. Captain Lee was fascinated to hear about my family's refugee experience and said he would like to see my family sometime. What a sympathetic man Captain Lee was, I thought.

The rest of the summer of 1951 on the eastern front was uneventful. I suspected both sides in the war decided that they would like a cease-fire as soon as possible. The lull gave me time to read some of the books I had bought at a secondhand market, for example, *The Story of Philosophy* by Will Durant. But of course, by "philosophy," he meant only Western philosophy. The book was boring but better than nothing. Can you imagine the luxury of reading *Worldly Philosophers* on the frontline?

6. THE FRONTLINE AND FORT SILL

A month passed without any hostility from either side, giving me leisure, serenity — and boredom. My mood changed one day when the company commander asked, "Lieutenant Hurh, how would you like to go to America for some advanced training courses?"

I was taken by surprise. "Are you kidding me, sir?" I responded. He explained that the division commander was soliciting the names of infantry and artillery officers who could be recommended for advanced training courses at the Field Artillery School at Fort Sill, Oklahoma. He asked me again if I was interested. Naturally, my answer was an enthusiastic, "Yes, sir!" My boredom was over.

So I was nominated along with Lieutenant Kim, the company executive, and Lieutenant Choi, the director of the Fire Direction Center. I felt really flattered because I was the most junior among those selected peers. However, I thought I didn't have any chance at all to be selected, but at least I might have an opportunity to see my mother again in Seoul because every candidate had to leave the front and go to Daegu through Seoul for the selection process — whether for an exam or an interview. What a God-given opportunity!

A few days later, I ordered my master sergeant to assemble all the platoon soldiers. I informed them that I would be leaving the next day for the ROK Artillery Command Headquarters in Daegu, and told them about my nomination for the advanced training in America. But I stressed the point that I had little chance of being selected and expected to be back with the platoon within a week or so.

I left my platoon early in the morning with Lieutenants Kim and Choi for Seoul where we would catch a military train to Daegu. When we arrived in Seoul, we had a few hours to spare before catching the train at the Seoul railway station. Since my family's store was only three blocks away from the train station, I ventured out to check the store to see if my uncle was back from Daegu. But what a happy coincidence. I found my mother and uncle were both there. We were all astonished and overjoyed by this unexpected reunion. Mother told me that she had been back and forth from Onyang to Seoul many times since I left her a month earlier because she was now in the trading business. She bought fresh farm produce in Onyang, transported it to Seoul, and then sold it in the market. With the money she earned, she then bought some used clothes from the refugees in the Seoul market, took them back to Onyang, and sold them in the local market for a good profit.

"It is hard work, but it has saved our family so far," she said. I was amazed at her courage, stamina, and enterprising skill. When it was my turn to tell her my side of the story, she just could not believe that I might be selected to go to America for advanced training.

I said, "Mom, I don't have much chance so don't get your hopes up." I explained that most of the candidates were my seniors and that I'd probably be back within a week as soon as the selection process was over at the Artillery Command in Daegu. On my return trip from Daegu, I was hoping to spend a couple of days with her in Seoul. However, Mother thought I might be selected, but accepted that whatever fate brings, so it would be. Most of all she was thankful I was alive and safe.

With only about an hour left before I had to be at the train station, Mother asked, "Are you hungry? Let's find some place to eat!" She was always concerned that I had enough to eat. Now Mother was in high spirits, probably because her son might not make it to America but at least he would be safe for a while. Also with a good spirit, I boarded the army train around six in the evening. The train was jampacked, even in the officers' compartment; many people could not find a seat and had to stand. Moreover, it was a long trip—almost 12 hours to travel less than 250 miles. No wonder we were having trouble winning the war.

At six in the morning we arrived in Daegu. Lieutenant Kim was kind enough to invite me to stay at his home in town. The other candidate from our company, Lieutenant Choi, had his home near Daegu where he stayed. Lieutenant Kim's parents were very friendly and so was his sister—and very pretty, I thought. The screening process for the candidates would take at least three days, and so I was grateful to the Kims for their hospitality. Good food, a comfortable bed, and congenial friendship—even today, many decades later, I vividly remember and am forever grateful for their kindness to me.

Every morning for five days while we were in Daegu, Lieutenant Kim and I went to the ROK Artillery Command Headquarters to go through the selection process. We took exams, written and oral, mainly on English proficiency but not much on military tactics or artillery skills. I thought I did okay but not to my satisfaction. Lieutenant Kim, however, was very worried, and Lieutenant Choi did not talk much about his feelings. In any case, we all felt that we should give up our false hope and get back to reality—our buddies on the eastern front. So we decided to leave right away and started packing. At that point, Lieutenant Kim said, "We have to make sure that none of us was chosen. Who knows?" So we all went together to the Command HQ to check the results.

What an awkward surprise! I, the most junior officer of our group, was chosen but not the others. First I felt elated, but soon I felt really bad. I did not know what to say to my comrades. Lieutenants Kim and Choi expressed their congratulations on my success. Was this happening because of some sort of providence or just pure luck? I could not fathom it. We said our farewells.

I checked into the Artillery Command Headquarters on the same day. One hundred artillery officers of all ranks from second lieutenants to full colonels were to be briefed and prepared to attend the Allied Officer Training Course at the U.S. Army Field Artillery School from late September 1951 through mid-March 1952. A similar arrangement was made with the infantry officers — 250 ROK army infantry officers were selected to take part in a six-month training course at Fort Benning, Georgia. (Later I learned that these programs enhanced the military skills of the ROK officers immensely, and the program was repeated yearly eight times thereafter.)

All the chosen candidates stayed at the ROK Artillery Command Headquarters for about a week and were briefed about the trip to the U.S. Interestingly, we were told nothing to prepare us about American culture and society. After a series of security checks and physical exams, we sailed from Pusan to Sasebo, Japan, on September 10, 1951, on a civilian passenger ship. In Sasebo, we were transferred to a huge U.S. military transport ship called the USNS *General John Pope* (about 200,000 tons). For the first time in Korean history, there were 350 Korean officers sailing to the U.S. for advanced training. We were all excited. I was particularly elated to be going abroad. From my childhood I always wanted to experience something different from Korean culture and society. I was told that when I was a child my mother asked me whom I wanted to marry. I replied, "A Japanese girl." Mother asked why, and I said, "They are different, Mom. I like someone who is different from us."

The voyage across the Pacific Ocean was not always pleasant. Most of our officers suffered from seasickness to various degrees. Plus, many could not eat the American food served in the officers' mess because they were hungry for spicy Korean food — especially *kimchi*, a dish they often ate three times a day. But, of course, no such food was available on the ship, although rice was occasionally served with Mexican food. One day when served a Mexican dinner, an officer made a big discovery — Tabasco sauce. This was the peppery taste the Korean officers had been craving. Within a few days the entire ship ran out of Tabasco sauce!

Most of the Korean officers could not get used to American food, although we had a lot of choices at every meal. Unlike the soldiers' chow line, in the officers' dining room on the ship we had sit-down, served meals with an extensive, written menu, but since we were unfamiliar with the menu choices in English, we did not know what to order. For example, at the breakfast table we had a large menu in front of us, but we were at a loss as to what to order. We looked at each other while the ship's waiters patiently waited for our orders. Finally, Major Hong, who sat the head of our table and was supposed to have a good command of English, ordered something. The waiter took the order and turned to the next officer, Lieutenant Kim. It was apparent, however, that Lieutenant Kim was in agony. A moment passed, and he said in loud voice, "Same please!" The waiter replied, "Yes, sir," and turned to Captain Yang. Without any hesitation, he also said, "Same please." The same pattern was repeated seven times. Now my turn came. I was skeptical and ordered on my own: a fried egg, ham and toast. The next three officers repeated my order. What we ended up with at our table were eight orders of melon and muffins, and four orders of fried eggs, ham and toast. At the lunch table, many people wanted to sit next to me.

Korean officers, however, drank tons of Coke which was available from Coke machines in every corner of the ship. Everyone was fascinated by the automated Coke machines — just put a nickel in the slot and watch as a paper cup dropped and coke poured into it, stopping automatically when the cup was filled. No alcoholic beverages were served on the ship, but the PX carried other items, such as candy, cigarettes, lighters, and toiletries. We enjoyed the luxury of eating Hershey chocolate bars and lighting Lucky Strikes with the windproof Zippo lighters. Where did we get our money? Uncle Sam gave each of us 150 U.S. dollars every month as a personal allowance while we were in the training program. This was like a fortune to us since a second lieutenant's Korean monthly pay was equivalent to about 35 U.S. cents. We received the first payment soon after we boarded the ship. I was amazed to watch how the money was distributed. Two American officers paid out the monthly allowance to the Korean officers in cash — one was distributing the money and the other was guarding the money with a loaded

6. The Frontline and Fort Sill

.45 Colt pistol. I wondered who would dare steal the money on a military transport ship in the middle of the Pacific Ocean while everyone was watching.

For all of us, the 15-day sea voyage was a once-in-a-lifetime experience. We watched the endless horizon of the beautiful ocean at sunrise and sunset. We saw all sorts of marine animals — whales, sharks, dolphins, flying fish, and sea gulls. We forgot about our painful experiences on the frontline of the Korean War. I pondered on the beauty of nature and compared it to the life of humans. In my view, human life had been sometimes ugly, cunning, selfish, deceitful, violent, and destructive. By nature all animals can be aggressive when attacked, but humans often imagine their enemies and attack without any provocation. The struggle for existence (the dog eat dog principle) is a normal process among any living things, but I thought humans should be different from animals because they could reason with high intelligence. However, sometimes humans were worse than animals — for example, Hitler's rational and scientifically designed genocide of the Jews in Europe and Japan's systematic massacre of innocent Chinese civilians in Nanjing during World War II. Human beings are thus capable of "creating" or "inventing" their enemies by constructing an ideology of hate, and then deliberately destroying their "imaginary" enemies very methodically by rational planning and a highly developed technology of mass destruction.

On a beautiful, early September morning, I went out on the ship's deck and watched the vast horizon of the Pacific Ocean with its countless deep blue waves. While I was admiring the beauty of nature, I thought I should become a pacifist — peace at all cost to bring love, hope, and happiness to the world. However, I felt I was going in the opposite direction — going for advanced training so as to kill more people more efficiently. But soon I rationalized that by killing the enemy more efficiently I could save my comrades and the country more effectively. What an irony! I was utterly confused. I was almost 19 years old then.

We arrived in San Francisco on September 25, 1951, just a day after my 19th birthday. When the ship approached the harbor, we were awestruck by the scene — the Golden Gate Bridge, the high-rise buildings of San Francisco, and the spectacular view of the Bay area. Everything looked so attractive and peaceful. What a difference from Korea. Americans were so blessed and Koreans seemed to be so condemned, for whatever the reasons. A strange idea came to me that perhaps this difference was caused by American soil being different from Korean soil. I was determined to see and examine the soil as soon as I landed. We landed but I couldn't see the American soil because it was all covered by asphalt. How stupid I was, but I was still a teen-ager. The other officers were even calling me "Baby Lieutenant."

Anyway, San Francisco seemed like a fairyland to us Korean officers. We felt like we were strange visitors from a different planet. And indeed we must have looked rather strange too — like toy soldiers in clown costumes. We were dressed in U.S. Army surplus kaki uniforms that displayed a big black (**S**) mark on the front of the shirts and wore old combat boots, but we topped off our attire with brand-new officers' dress caps. It might be comparable to a gentleman wearing an ill-fitting, secondhand suit with jogging shoes and a silk hat. Moreover, in these strange costumes, 350 Republic of Korea Army officers were ordered to march through the streets of San Francisco as soon as we landed. People in the street applauded, and the media covered the event. The newspaper headline was "Three Hundred and Fifty Republic of Korea Army Officers Visit San Francisco for Advanced Training in Ft. Benning and Ft. Sill." Later I learned that my mother and sisters watched our march in a newsreel at a movie theater in Seoul. At that time no television was available in Korea.

From San Francisco, the artillery officers took the train and rode in Pullman first-class cars to Fort Sill, Oklahoma. Again we were fascinated by the wonderful machines Americans invented — individual sleeper compartments and luxurious dining cars. Everything was new and exciting to us. When the train stopped at the Albuquerque station, an officer shouted, "Look! Look!" as he excitedly pointed out the train window. He looked stunned, and we all rushed to the window thinking there might have been an accident. What we saw was a peaceful and lovely scene: a young American couple hugging and kissing each other on the railway station platform. In Korea, kissing in public was absolutely unthinkable for any sane person in those days. So the scene was quite a "culture shock" to the Korean officers. Another surprise was a sign advertising food, "Hot Dogs — 25 cents." One of the Korean officers said, "Aha, Americans eat dog meat too!" Although I never tried dog meat in my life, some Koreans do love to eat it. Although we eventually found out what hot dogs really were, I have always wondered about the etymological origin of the term "hot dog." Why not hot sausage?

We arrived at Fort Sill on September 27, 1951, with high expectations. To our disappointment, we were housed in several tents. Field tents for the Allied Officers in the United States? To us this was unthinkable, but it happened.

6. THE FRONTLINE AND FORT SILL

We were told that there was a shortage of BOQs (Bachelor Officers Quarters) in Fort Sill. I wondered why the United States Army could not afford decent quarters for the hundred ROK officers they had invited to the United States. However, I knew we should be grateful that at least we were not on the frontline in Korea. A few weeks later we were moved to a BOQ building where two officers shared a room with a common bathroom down the hall. We dined at the Officers Mess Hall nearby.

The daily routine began with classes starting at eight in the morning and ending around five. Each class consisted of 25 Korean officers and was taught by an American instructor with a Korean interpreter. Most of the young officers had a fairly good command of English, but the older officers generally needed a translator. The Allied Officers Course was quite extensive: it covered not only the detailed and advanced training for fire direction and gunnery, but also equipment maintenance for various kinds of field artillery

Classmates of Section #1, Allied Field Artillery Officers Course at Fort Sill, Oklahoma. Hurh stands in the back row, far left. The American instructor, Major Shaw, is sitting in the middle row, fourth from left. Colonel In Wan Chung, Korean leader of the ROK officers at Fort Sill, middle row, third from left. Lt. Ki Yong Lee, front row far left. Lt. Yung Suk Kang, front row, second from left. Fall 1951.

and ammunition, all sorts of military vehicles, and communication devices. Many of us had never learned to drive any type of vehicle, let alone learn about its maintenance. Also totally new to me were the techniques for surveying the field terrain used for positioning howitzer batteries, locating enemy positions, and computing firing data. This all required good math skills in trigonometry and logarithm, but math was not my best subject in high school. The American instructors assigned us a lot of homework daily and tested us every week. The test results were reported to the head of our group, Colonel Chung, who was supposed to help the underachieving officers. The "help" was usually a warning, or advice, or a threat to ship us back to Korea. I was lucky not to get the "help," but sometimes I was very close because of my math scores. We worked day and night in order to avoid "the help." We did not have much free time, except for some weekends. On Saturdays we usually took in a movie at the post theater, drank beer at the officers club, or ate snacks at the PX. Interestingly when we went to a movie, we always had to wear our army neckties or we would be refused admission. I thought the regulation was rather strange.

I was befriended by three fellow officers — Lieutenant Hyo Sung Lee, Lieutenant Ki Yong Lee, and Lieutenant Yung Suk Kang. The Lees (not related to each other) were my classmates at the Artillery School (the 13th class) and Kang was from the 16th class. We all had four months of combat experience on the frontline except for Kang who graduated from the Artillery School just a few days before our departure from Korea. We had a lot in common — all were a similar age, all grew up in Seoul, all were students when the war broke out (high school seniors except for Ki Yong who was a freshmen at the Seoul National University), and all of us hated the war and our army life. We shared a deep-seated resentment against the Communist invaders who had

Lt. Won Moo Hurh at the firing battery area at Fort Sill, Oklahoma. November 1951.

6. The Frontline and Fort Sill

destroyed millions of lives and shattered our life dreams. We felt completely powerless to change our circumstances. This drew us together. While we drank cheap beer (Miller High Life) at the officers club, we talked about what we would possibly do when and if we survived the war and returned to civilian life. We all agreed that we should continue our studies, but as long as we were at war, there was no way out of the army. As the stack of empty Miller High Life cans got as high as a three-foot pyramid on the table, we called it quits and went to bed.

Everyone slept late on Sunday mornings, skipping breakfast. After lunch, it was time for homework in preparation for Monday classes. On Sunday evenings we went to the PX for refreshments. In the PX was a quite attractive female salesclerk with dark hair, beautiful eyes, and a friendly smile. Many Korean officers wanted to have a date with her, but she always said she was busy. One day a young Korean officer wanted to buy a pair of socks. The beautiful clerk asked him the size of his feet, but the officer did

For the first time in our lives, we saw a water tower at Fort Sill. Lieutenant Kang (on the left) and I are laughing about this odd-looking thing behind us. 1951

not know since he had never bought socks in the U.S. before. She said, "It's okay. I can find your sock size by measuring your hand. Let me see your right hand." The officer extended his hand to her. She held his hand and examined it for a while — touching his fingers and palm, and turning it over. The officer was in ecstasy. Finally she selected some socks. They were perfect fit! Bravo! The word soon spread, and the next day there was a long line of Korean officers wanting to buy socks. Culture shock again? Even such a common thing as an American water tower was an object of great curiosity to us Korean officers. We just couldn't figure out what the odd-shaped thing was in the middle of the Fort Sill parking lot.

Many incidents involving culture shock occurred; two were most memorable. One day I entered the common bathroom in our BOQ building. As usual the bathroom had urinals and toilet stalls. I wanted to use the toilet. Usually I didn't have to knock in order to tell if the stall was occupied, as the bottom of the stall door was about two feet above the floor. All I had to do was glance under the door, and if I saw someone's feet, I knew the toilet was occupied. There were three stalls and in one of them I could see no feet. I pulled on the handle of the door to enter, but it seemed to be stuck for some reason. I gave the door a hard yank and forced it open. What I saw was another culture shock; however, this time it was culture shock in reverse. A Korean officer was squatting on top of the toilet seat. He had stepped up on the rim of the seat and then squatted for his business. No wonder I could not see his feet. Apparently he was more comfortable squatting for his defecation, which is typical of many Koreans and other Asians. I apologized. It was an embarrassing moment for both of us.

The next culture shock I experienced was more profound because it dealt with the existential question of one's ontological identity — the question of "who you are" as defined by others from birth. After spending a couple of weekends at the movie theater or at the officers club, I felt bored and decided on the third Saturday morning to take the public bus into a nearby town called Lawton to see the civilian side of American life. My friends were still in deep sleep so I ventured out alone. When I got on the bus through the front door, I found it was quite crowded with people standing in the aisle and squished three or more in the seats. Hoping to find a seat or even better standing room, I waded back to the rear of the bus. To my surprise the back row of seats was unoccupied. I sat down. I wondered why nobody sat here. The only difference between these seats and the others was a sign

6. THE FRONTLINE AND FORT SILL

above them in contrasting black paint on the light blue walls of the bus. It said, "For Colored." I pondered about the meaning of these words. No matter how much I thought, I could not understand why no one sat in these perfectly good seats.

Stop after stop went by, still I was confused. My silent reasoning went something like this: "For" means suitable or acceptable. "Color" means red, blue, green, and so on. So suitable for colors? It doesn't make sense. Wait a minute. "For" could also mean "because." Probably the sign means "don't sit here because it is freshly painted (colored)!" So I thought maybe it was some sort of "wet paint" sign, and I was sitting on the gooey paint. I felt the seat; it was dry. Next I felt the sign printed above the seats; all was dry. I was thoroughly perplexed. Soon after this a black American soldier boarded the bus and sat down next to me. As an officer of the Allied forces, I had enough courage to ask him, "Sergeant."

"Yes, sir." The black soldier could clearly see I wore an Allied officer's uniform.

"Could you tell me what this sign means?" I asked.

"You must be kidding, sir," replied the soldier straight-faced.

"No, I'm not. I've only been in America for a couple of weeks and have never ridden in an American bus before."

"Oh, now I see," responded the black soldier with a grin. "You see, sir, these seats are reserved for colored people."

"Colored people?" I asked.

"Yes, sir. Colored people — like you and like me."

Without too much thinking, I uttered, "How nice! Reserved for me and for you!"

The black sergeant chuckled, "Yes, sir."

I turned in my seat to look out the window at the scenery but couldn't help wondering why on earth a particular section of the bus was reserved for the so-called colored people, and I was one of them. At that time, the concept of "colored people" had never entered my mind, nor the social meaning of "color" as racial segregation. In fact, I had never imagined my skin or anybody's skin as being colored. Since I did not know the social and historical context of the words "For Colored," the sign was totally meaningless to me, although each word was separately translatable.

Thus it was, to my shock, that I discovered my "color" in the United States, and eventually understood the social consequence of such a concept.

As soon as I got off the bus in Lawton, I saw separate public accommodations on the basis of "color"—waiting rooms in the bus station, telephone booths, water fountains, restrooms, restaurants, and hotels. In retrospect, this was in October 1951, about four years before Rosa Parks, a black seamstress, refused to give up her seat for a white person and move to the back of the bus in Montgomery, Alabama.

After this experience, as being neither black nor white, I did not know which accommodation I was supposed to use, so I ignored the rule and used whichever was most convenient—colored and white. People did not seem to mind. Maybe they perceived me as an exception because I was either a foreigner or an army officer, or both. (Had I studied sociology, I certainly would have understood the plight of the so-called "marginal man"—a person caught in the middle between too races. And, of course, I did not have the slightest idea that I would study social sciences in the United States seven years later.)

Upon returning from my adventurous trip, I shared my experience with the Lees and Kang at the happy-hour table in the Officers Club. They were extremely interested in my story and could hardly wait to visit Lawton as

American Sunday School girls happy to meet a Korean officer (me). Taken at the Second Presbyterian Church, Lawton, Oklahoma. 1951.

soon as possible. The following Saturday and the subsequent weekends we visited Lawton regularly where we shopped and dined. For the first time in our lives we each bought a civilian suit, a dress shirt and a necktie. All dressed up, we had our photos taken in a studio and mailed our pictures home to Korea. In the army supply store, we bought brand new winter uniforms and new pairs of dress shoes to match. We now felt quite civilized. We even visited a Presbyterian church in Lawton, thanks to an invitation extended by an American officer who had served on the Korean front and whom we happened to meet in a store in Lawton.

The other guys in our BOQ followed our lead. Many of them went to Lawton every weekend to shop, to eat, to drink, and to meet American civilians. In a sense, we Korean officers were not only trainees at Fort Sill, but also became "cultural ambassadors" for Korea in Lawton. We found that attending church was the best place to interact with civilians because the members welcomed us warmly, especially when the Christmas season approached. Most of us were not Christians, but they still welcomed us wholeheartedly. When the service was over, we had a wonderful time meeting the American families, young and old, and particularly the small children. They reminded us of our own younger sisters and brothers. We missed our families immensely and also missed Korean food, especially *kimchi*. Lawton did not have any Asian stores or restaurants at that time. However, we bought a good supply of the tiny bottles of Tabasco sauce and carried them in our shirt pockets so they would be handy at mealtimes.

The winter weather of 1951 in Oklahoma was tough, but we survived various field-training exercises. There was no communication from the home front. Time went by very quickly at Fort Sill. On March 15, 1952, we all graduated from the Allied Officers Course and were ready to return home to Korea. In retrospect, we learned a lot. We almost had the FM 6-40 (Field Manuel for Field Artillery) memorized by heart. But my most rewarding experiences were my visits to Lawton where I could interact with ordinary American people. I thought they were the friendliest people I had ever met. They were indeed genuine. Genuine in the sense that they were never pretentious. They were simple, honest, hard working, humble and friendly. I thought I discovered the "soul" of the United States of America right there in the Midwest.

On March 18, 1952, we sailed from Seattle to Yokohama, Japan, on a military transport ship similar to the size of the *General John Pope*. We were looking forward to returning to Korea, but we were worried about what new assignments would be waiting for us. When we arrived in the Yokohama harbor, we saw an interesting scene from the deck of the ship. Japanese dockworkers were picking up the cigarette butts that American and Korean soldiers had discarded from the ship. Moreover, some of our Korean officers intentionally dropped new cigarettes, one at a time, onto the dock so that they could watch the Japanese scrambling to pick them up. Many of the Korean officers enjoyed the scene, but I thought it was cruel, regardless of what the Japanese had done to Korean people in the past. Those poor dockworkers were most likely not responsible for the atrocities committed by the Japanese soldiers in Korea and elsewhere. I thought fighting against evil with evil would not make anyone holy.

We were happy to hear that we were allowed to disembark at Yokohama and visit Japan until midnight. Tired of being confined on the ship, we were ready to go anywhere. At that point Lieutenant Kang, one of our Miller High Life group at Fort Sill, suggested that we should go to Tokyo since his brother, Woo-Bang, was a student there and could guide us to a good place to eat in Tokyo. So we took a taxi together from the Yokohama harbor to Tokyo city, about a 45 minute drive. Tokyo was a hustling and bustling city with all sorts of restaurants. We had the best food in our entire journey across the Pacific Ocean — Korean *bulgogi*— in Tokyo.

After the scrumptious dinner with a wonderful reunion of the Kang brothers, we returned to the ship late at night again by taxi. In the morning, an announcement from the purser's office came over the loudspeaker system reporting that a Japanese cabdriver had found a camera that may have belonged to a Korean officer who rode in his cab last night from Tokyo. I checked my cabin and found my camera was missing. I hurried to the purser's office. It was indeed my camera that I inadvertently left in the taxicab. I wanted to thank and reward the taxi driver, but he had already gone. Having watched the poor Japanese dockworkers and some homeless men on the street corners of Yokohama city, I was very much impressed by the cabdriver's honesty and kindness. It would never have happened in Pusan or Seoul, I thought.

In retrospect, only six years had past since Japan was defeated in World War II, but their pace of economic recovery was remarkable. In contrast, Korea, which had been liberated from the yoke of Japanese colonialism, was now divided and in the midst of a bloody, destructive civil war supported

6. The Frontline and Fort Sill

by the Chinese People's Army in the North and the UN Forces in the South. Ironically, however, the Korean War helped the Japanese economy — many military supplies for the ROK army were manufactured in Japan, such as trucks, soldiers' fatigues, shoes, and C-Rations. In fact, without Toyota and Nissan trucks, the ROK heavy mortar companies would have been immobile. Someplace I heard it said that the Korean War brought to Japan an economic miracle. I thought it was not an overstatement.

We sailed the next day for Pusan — the final stretch of our voyage home. It was a nice spring day and the sea was calm. Everyone was out on the deck, enjoying the warm sunshine. Some American officers were also on board, returning from their R&R (rest and recreation) in Japan. One of them asked me if the Korean officers on board had to take some kind of exam upon their return to Korea. I was puzzled by his question. He said, "Look at that! Every one of you Koreans is studying something." He was pointing at a row of Korean officers sitting in deck chairs, absorbed in reading.

I could not help bursting into a big laugh, and said: "Major, do you know what they're reading? Japanese porn books and magazines they bought in Yokohama last night."

The major was amused. "Really? Can they all read Japanese?" I told him that we were the generation of Koreans who went to school when Japanese was the only language allowed to be used in the schools and in public, according to the Japanese colonial policy. Even our own names had to be "Japanized." The major was amazed.

We landed at the Pusan harbor in the early evening of the next day. The harbor looked about the same as when we left six months before — a crowded, noisy, and gloomy place. We were taken to an army placement center — an even gloomier place. It was a temporary housing unit for transient army personnel who were between assignments and was notorious for bad food and lodging. Perhaps we were all spoiled by the "luxurious" accommodations at Fort Sill and on the military transport ship. Moreover, we were anxious and worried about our new assignments — maybe it would be to the frontline again. After two days of deprivation in the temporary housing, we received our assignments.

All of our "Miller-High-Life buddies," except for Kang, received teaching assignments at the ROK Army Artillery School in Kwangju (Gwangju), Korea. Kang had an order to report to the 18th Field Artillery Battalion, the Second ROK Division, located at the central front — the "Iron Triangle"

(Kumwha, Pungang, and Cheulwon) area — one of the most deadly contested war zones during the Korean War. We felt sorry for Kang, but such is the life fate of a soldier. Those who had not yet served on the frontline were all sent to the front this time. Kang and most of his classmates (Artillery OCS, the 16th Class) had never had any combat experience. The Lees and I were ordered to report to the ROK Army Artillery School in Kwanju on April 20, 1952. Kwangju, the capital city of Cholla-Namdo Province, is located about 200 miles southwest of Seoul. The good news was we all had more than ten days of furlough.

On a rather chilly evening in early April, I left Pusan for Seoul by train with a big army duffle bag and a small briefcase. The other guys (Lees) had their own schedules. The train was crowded, and in those days it took 12 to 15 hours to reach Seoul from Pusan. I tried to doze off but could not because of my mixed-up emotions — excitement, anxiety, and worry. The anticipation of meeting family members excited me, but that was soon followed by anxiety about my future. Moreover, I was experiencing an inexplicable feeling of emptiness and hopelessness. I asked myself: "What's next? Who controls the course of my life ahead, if there is one at all?" I felt powerless, like Kafka's hero who became an upside-down beetle through a mysterious metamorphosis. The war stole everything from me, but most of all it took away my dreams for the future. My dreams had long ago been shattered, and the war was still going on. I just felt numb all over my body.

Early in the morning I arrived at the Seoul Metropolitan Station. I picked up my bags and followed the crowd to the gate. I expected no one to greet me since we did not have a phone at home. In front of the station I could not find a taxi, but my duffle bag was too heavy for me to carry to my home. I found a porter with a traditional Korean A-frame who carried my bags on his back, and we walked to the old Soon Wha Dong house near the South Gate (Nam Dae Moon). I hadn't seen the house in more than a year. It looked somewhat smaller and older than I remembered. The black and gray tiled roof had patches of green moss growing on it, and the wooden front door was showing its wear and tear. Nevertheless, I was glad that I at least had a place to call home. I paid the porter and knocked on the front door. At that point, I suddenly recalled our little dog, called "Bahdugi." He used to run to me and jump all over me to lick my face whenever I came home from school. But now there was silence. I wondered what had happened to him.

6. The Frontline and Fort Sill

I knocked on the door again, and my younger sister, Eui Moo, opened the door and cried out, "Oppa (brother)! What a surprise!" I did not say anything, just hugged her. She ran into the house, announcing my arrival. Everyone was there. It looked like they had just finished breakfast. We were all overwhelmed by the joy of reunion, especially my mother — she could hardly contain her elated emotions, shedding tears quietly, and finally saying, "Thank God! Thank you son, for coming home." When I told her the good news that I didn't have to go back to the frontline and would be teaching at the Army Artillery School in Kwangju, Mother looked pleased and couldn't believe my good fortune. As usual she wanted to celebrate the happy occasion with a tasty meal.

That evening we had a big feast and talked into the night. I heard the details of my family's return to Seoul from Onyang. Our Soon Wha Dong house had been broken into and ransacked. It took weeks to clean and repair the house, but Mother was still thankful that at least the house had not been destroyed. Our family store, which had been managed by my uncle before the war, was not damaged either, but a lot of merchandise had been looted. Moreover, the farm equipment business in Seoul at that time was in a rapid decline. Now my mother was thinking of converting the farm equipment store into an ice cream parlor in the summer and a noodle shop in the winter. Whatever she decided, I thought she would succeed because she had been an enterprising woman her entire life. Sadly, I also learned that our little dog, Bahdugi, was killed and eaten by North Korean soldiers. This had been reported to our family by our neighbors who had stayed behind and happened to watch the brutal act.

The ten-day furlough past quickly and I ended up in the ROK Army Artillery School in Kwangju on April 20, 1952. The 200-mile trip from Seoul to Kwangju was not an easy one. The first car of the train was fully armed with machine guns and a rocket launcher. At the midpoint of my journey, a Communist guerrilla attacked the train, and machine gun shots were exchanged, but nothing serious happened. I realized everywhere in Korea was a war zone, and I felt disgusted, rather than afraid. Since the end of Japanese colonial rule in 1945, the Communist guerrillas (largely infiltrators from North Korea but also recruited by the "underground" Communist sympathizers in South Korea) had been a constant threat to South Korea's national security, particularly in the southwestern part of the Korean peninsula.

It took a whole day to reach Kwangju from Seoul. The train stopped and resumed intermittently anywhere at anytime, like the refugee freight train that I took with my mother from the south bank of the Han River to Chonan. Looking out the train window, I started to daydream about the enormous vicissitudes in my life that had taken place since the start of the Korean War. I could not imagine that it had been less than two years ago. So many changes had occurred in my life — I was a refugee fleeing from the North Korean and Chinese armies for several months, I trained at the OCS school for three months, I fought on the eastern front as a forward observer for four months, and I received six months advanced training in Fort Sill, Oklahoma. Such enormous changes in such a short time. I was only 19 but felt like an old man. War makes you old, if it doesn't kill you.

7

Teaching at the ROK Artillery School

AFTER THE LONG RIDE, our train finally pulled into the Kwangju railroad station late in the afternoon. The passengers were mostly ROK army personnel connected with either the infantry or the artillery schools located on the outskirts of Kwangju city. Many were soldiers returning from brief vacations at home, and others were newly assigned enlisted men and officers like myself. While looking for transportation to the ROK artillery school, I ran into my Fort Sill buddies — the Lees (Hyo Sung and Ki Yong). We did not know we had been riding on the same train since each of us rode in a different car. It was a good reunion!

An hour's ride in the back of an army truck brought us to a huge army training compound called "Sang Mu Dae," which looked like a city of mushrooming Quonset huts. (Later I learned that Quonset huts were multipurpose, lightweight, prefabricated buildings manufactured in Quonset Point, Rhode Island, during World War II to house troops and supplies.) The economical, easy-to-assemble huts served numerous functions: sleeping quarters, offices, classrooms, mess halls, restrooms, warehouses — almost anything. At that time there were only two "normal" buildings in the entire compound, the main administration building for the infantry school and a similar one for the artillery school.

By the time we got to the artillery school's administration building in the evening to report our arrival, all of the offices were already closed except the one for the officer-on-duty. The young lieutenant checked us in and ordered his sergeant to take us to a temporary BOQ (Bachelor Officers Quarters) nearby. The BOQ was one of the Quonsets and contained a couple of dozen army cots with some folded blankets on them but nothing else — no pillows nor sheets. The sergeant explained that no officers actually stay more than one night at the compound as virtually all officers lived off-campus, either in Kwangju city or in nearby villages, such as Songjong-Ri, about five miles from the base. The cots were only temporary accommodations for transient officers. Only enlisted men and officer candidates were housed in the Quonset barracks. The sergeant apologized for the poor sleeping arrangements, but said this was the best they could do.

Although we were very tired, we could not sleep very well that night — due not only to the uncomfortable beds but also to some extremely itchy insect bites that we suspected were from bedbugs or lice. The blankets had probably never been washed. We decided to get the hell out of the place as soon as morning came when we could make arrangements for off-campus housing. What a change from Fort Sill!

The morning finally came, and we were pleasantly surprised to find that the vice commandant of the Artillery School was Lieutenant Colonel In Wan Chung who had been our class leader at Fort Sill. He extended us a warm welcome and encouraged us with remarks about how it was now time for us to contribute to our country what we had learned at Fort Sill. He told us our assignments. I was assigned to the Gunnery Department as an instructor for the officer candidates. Lieutenant Hyo Sung Lee was also assigned to be an instructor for the officer candidates but in the Equipment and Weapons Maintenance Department, and Lieutenant Ki Yong Lee was assigned as the commander of a company of the OCS (Officer Candidates School) students. Lieutenant Colonel Chung's assistants showed us around the school compound and briefed us on the details about our offices, accommodations, and supplies. We then made our way to our respective posts.

At my new assignment as a gunnery instructor at ROK Field Artillery School in Kwangju. Lt. Hyo Sung Lee, on left; Lt. Hurh on right. We recently had been promoted to the rank of first lieutenant. April 1952.

7. Teaching at the ROK Artillery School

As expected, the Gunnery Department was housed in one of the Quonset huts. I reported to the department chair, Major Sung Kuk Yun, who was also one of our Fort Sill classmates. With a big smile he greeted me: "Hey baby lieutenant! I heard you were coming to us." After we exchanged a few pleasantries and reminisced over our good old days in Fort Sill, I was briefed on my teaching duties. There were eight gunnery instructors in various ranks — from second lieutenant to captain. The senior officers taught refresher courses for the battery officers, while the junior officers taught mainly the officer candidate courses. The department chair taught only a few advanced courses. Major Yun said my schedule would be very demanding because of the increasing enrollment of OCS students. He laid out my schedule: I was to teach eight 50-minute classes (8 A.M. to noon and 1 to 5 P.M.), Monday through Friday, and four classes on Saturday as well. I would be responsible for teaching everything from surveying techniques and battery adjustment, to fire direction and the forward observer's duties. I was taken aback by the extensive and heavy teaching load, but managed to say, "Well, sir, that's quite a lot. I hope I can do it."

With a strong voice, he responded, "Sure, you can do it. If you can't, we are going to lose the war! You must do it. There is no other way. Now, this is your desk. Ask Sergeant Kim if you need anything." He was pointing at a large desk, just like a college professor's desk.

At that moment, for some unknown reason, my spirit suddenly rose as if I had been given a noble mission to teach the officer candidates how to save the fatherland from the Communists. During my time in the army, it was rare for me to have this feeling of purpose, but now I had high expectations for my new role as a military instructor.

I hated the Communists not only as our national enemy but also because they ruined my youth and stole my hope. They had become my personal enemy. In Korean, there is a word, *haan*, which has no precise English equivalent but roughly refers to a feeling of repressed anger and resentment against one's own fate for which there is no recourse. Many young officers my age suffered from this feeling of *haan* during the Korean War — an utter sense of powerlessness, meaninglessness, and existential alienation, comparable to the feelings depicted by the writings of Friedrich Nietzsche, Franz Kafka, and Erich Remarque. Whether it was about the institutions of slavery, bureaucracy, or war, their literature shared one thing in common — that is, the depiction of "total institutions" created by the collective forces of society and led usually by the powerful. But the powerless are the ones who tend to suffer the most and their suffering is very personal. For example, Remarque's expressed it well in his novel *All Quiet on the Western Front*.

> I am young, I am twenty years old; yet I know nothing of life but despair, death, fear, and fatuous superficiality cast over an abyss of sorrow. I see how peoples are set against one another, and in silence, unknowingly, foolishly, obediently, innocently slay one another. I see the keenest brains of the world invent weapons and words to make it yet more refined and enduring. And all men of my age, here and over there, throughout the whole world, see these things; all my generation is experiencing these things with me. What would our fathers do if we suddenly stood up and came before them and proffered our account? What do they expect of us if a time ever comes when the war is over? Through the years our business has been killing;—it was our first calling in life [1929, 266].

During the Korean War it seemed to me the powerful echelons in both Koreas tended to glorify the war in abstract terms, using words such as patriotism, liberation, unification of the fatherland, fighting for freedom and democracy, and so on; while for the powerless soldiers and junior officers on the front, the war was a matter of one's own life and death — it was very personal. I do not mean in a selfish sense. Many soldiers were willing to sacrifice their lives for each other, but not necessarily for an abstract ideology, such as fighting against communism or for democracy, but for concrete personal reasons — to save their personal friend's life or to take revenge against an enemy who had killed their buddy. The war was very personal for me. It changed the direction of my life, and it stole my dreams. I felt the Communist invasion from North Korea and China was the prime source of my personal *haan*. Sadly today many powerful leaders in the world do not understand the phenomenology of war since they have never experienced the life-and-death situation of soldiers at the frontline and hence do not seem to fathom the very personal aspect of war. These powerful leaders lack the empathetic understanding of those who fought and still are fighting wars in various regions around the world. Their abstract and naïve concepts of war, peace, democracy, freedom, and so on, are in fact the seedbed of ongoing and even escalating international conflicts. So much for my analysis of my life-condition and predicament.

My routine in the Gunnery Department at the ROK Field Artillery School was as follows: from eight in the morning until noon I usually taught trigonometry, logarithm, and their relevance to surveying techniques for

7. Teaching at the ROK Artillery School

positioning howitzers and conducting fire direction. From one in the afternoon until five, I usually took the students out for field exercise based on the morning's lecture. For meals, the instructors joined other officers on the campus in the Officers Mess Hall located in one of the Quonset huts The menu for all meals was predictable; no matter if it were breakfast, lunch, or supper. We would always be greeted by a bowl of rice, a bowl of soup, and if we were lucky, an occasional dish of *kimchi* or a vegetable, such as pickled cucumber. The menu was always the same, except the content of the soup. That at least varied between fish, cabbage, or a mixture of seaweed and soybean mesh.

Around six in the evening, trucks came around to pick us up and deliver us to our lodging. We, the Fort Sill Trio, found a place to stay in Sojong-Ri, about ten miles from the base. It was a small village with a couple of grocery stores, a small inn with a Chinese restaurant, and a busy train station. The lodging place was a Japanese-style farmhouse managed by a middle-aged couple with a two-year-old boy. We borrowed three army cots and several blankets from the Artillery School and settled in a large tatami room of the farmhouse. The landlord did not request any rent, saying they welcomed army officers for their protection. We did not know exactly what he meant, but we assumed they were still afraid of possible North Korean guerrillas in the area.

Therefore, we acquired free accommodations in a rural town. Our problem was boredom — particularly on the weekends. We did a lot of reading, game playing, walking around the town, and writing letters. Sundays were always problematic because we had to eat some place and had no transportation back to the Officers Mess Hall. Therefore, we either ate at the Chinese restaurant in Sojong-Ri village on credit or opened a package of army rations. At that time, the ROK Army paid us the equivalent of about 35 U.S. cents in Korean money every month, but it didn't go too far. A bowl of noodles at the Chinese restaurant cost about five cents and a pack of American cigarettes, Lucky Strike, cost exactly 35 cents. The pay was probably the lowest pay for an army lieutenant in the world. But the Korean Army rationalized that it was adequate because they supplied everything — food, clothing, shoes, cigarettes, and so on. In any case, it was a joke to wait for payday. Often when payday came, my close friends and I would pool our money and go to the local restaurant for a big party. With a party of ten officers, we could have a decent banquet with rice wine for $3.50!

Because of the low pay, it was no wonder corruption in the ROK Army was generally considered normal or inevitable. But at this point my friends and I did not know about this "side income." We knew our government was extremely poor and thought that we should bear the deprivation. One day, when I returned to my office from a day of tiring lectures, I was shocked to find a carton of Lucky Strikes in my desk drawer. Attached to the package was a person's name. I showed it to my colleagues in the department, and they hinted that it could be a bribe from one of my students in the OCS classes. According to my senior instructors, if an OCS student failed a course and could not graduate, he would be demoted to the rank of an enlisted man, a harsh punishment.

I checked this particular student's test grades and found that, indeed, he was failing. I called him to my office and demanded an explanation about the carton of cigarettes in my desk drawer. He was a big guy, and smiling said, "It's just nothing. I thought you'd like to smoke Yankee cigarettes." I was infuriated. Without thinking I jumped up and slapped his face. Since he was tall, I had to jump up high to hit him. I recall I kept saying, "You bastard! What do you think I am? I'm not a corrupted officer. You can't buy me, you son of a bitch!" And I slapped him twice more. (At that time, slapping a soldier was not unusual. In fact, it was considered a necessary measure to discipline soldiers in the ROK Army.) He was shocked, and everyone in the office was surprised but not shocked. At that point, the department head came in. I did not have to explain. He understood the situation immediately. I asked him what I should do with this student. He said simply, "Flunk him." Therefore, I did. Later, however, I felt sorry for the student because I learned that many instructors would have just quietly given him a passing grade. These instructors had an attitude of "what difference does it make." I was depressed and told myself, "Something is awfully wrong here."

My teaching schedule was becoming routine. I spent most of the morning hours in the classroom teaching logarithm and trigonometry, and in the afternoon I took the OCS students to the field to teach surveying techniques or to the firing range for conducting fire. The firing range and the target areas in Kwangju were larger than those of the Artillery School in Jinhae where I was trained a year earlier. But I could not help sensing the tragedy and irony when I saw where we would be firing. The target area again included mostly hills and mountains that were crowded with many graves. I felt sorry again for the deceased and their survivors. Geographically, Korea

7. Teaching at the ROK Artillery School

simply does not have wide-open fields or desert areas that are ideal for shelling practice. Every piece of farming land is precious because nearly 70 percent of the Korean peninsula is covered with hills and mountains. So the only expendable lands are the hillsides, which were both sanctified by the dead and despoiled by target practice.

I taught 44 hours a week, and was perpetually tired and hungry. On a sunny afternoon of a warm spring day, I dozed off in the classroom while giving an exercise for a surveying class. The OCS students were working on their data computation, and I was standing in front of my lectern trying to keep my eyes open, but I drifted off. All of a sudden there was Colonel Chung right in front of my face. I had not notice his coming. With a smiling face, he whispered, "Lieutenant Hurh, are you okay?"

My answer was naturally, "Yes, sir. Sorry, sir. I was too tired." He patted my shoulder and walked out.

The following week at the Officers Mess Hall, I finally snapped from the constant pressure and the miserable conditions. Usually all junior officers (mostly bachelors) ate three meals a day at the Officers Mess and senior officers (mostly married) ate only lunch with us. At lunch, after returning from the hard exercise at the firing range, I was expecting something good to eat, but as usual, we were served a bowl of clear soup and a bowl of rice and nothing else. Looking at the aluminum bowls in front of me, I suddenly had a strong urge to crush them. And I did. The food spilled all over the table and floor. At that point, again, Colonel Chung's face appeared. Quietly he said, "What are you doing, Lieutenant?"

I said, "I am sorry, sir, but I can't eat this."

The other officers seemed to be shocked but also amused. "Come to my office tomorrow morning," the colonel said and left. I did not think he could eat that so-called food either. My bad behavior was contagious. As soon as the colonel left, a couple of other young officers also squashed their bowls.

The next day I apologized to Colonel Chung for what I had done. He accepted my apology and invited me and my buddies (the Lees) to his home for lunch on the following Saturday in Kwangju city. He lived in a one-bedroom apartment with his wife. We were impressed by their modesty, sincerity, kindness, and warm hospitality. I felt very sorry about my immature behavior and asked him to forgive me. He said: "Cheer up, you men are going to be promoted to the rank of first lieutenant soon. Be patient!" I thought quietly to myself, "And how would that change anything?"

Soon the warm spring had gone by and the long hot summer settled into the Kwangju area. There was no summer vacation. Our routine of training the artillery officer candidates continued without any noticeable change. Things were getting really boring. One day in mid-summer my mother wrote that she was planning a business trip to Chinju (about 80 miles east of Kwangju), and on her return trip home she would like to visit me. It was certainly a pleasant surprise. I was looking forward to her visit; it had been over a year since we had last seen each other. She came to Songjong-Ri by train. I was happy to see her, particularly when I found her still looking young and healthy. At the time she was 41.

She checked into a small hotel and came to inspect my lodging and meet my roommates. As I expected, she was not impressed with my humble housing and said the apartment needed a major cleaning. Over dinner at a Chinese restaurant, I asked what was the nature of her business trip. She told me that the farm-equipment store that she had inherited from my father was running in the red. So my mother decided to close it down and open an ice-cream parlor in the summer and a noodle shop in the winter. For planning this business venture, she needed to consult with some of our family friends in Chinju who had already been successful in those lines of business. Since my mother was a very clever, enterprising woman, I did not doubt that she was doing the best for the family. She stayed in Songjong-Ri for two nights and three days. During her stay she cleaned our room until it was spic-and-span, did all of our laundry, and took us out for three delicious dinners in local restaurants. Before her departure, she gave some gifts to our landlord and his wife. They were impressed by her thoughtfulness.

So went the summer, and on September 1, we were all promoted to first lieutenants. However, hardly anything changed — just a 25-cent raise in pay. There was some excitement, however, when we learned that a number of ROK infantry full colonels would come to us for a special artillery-training course. The ROK Army had selected about 20 senior infantry colonels to come to Kwangju for a three-month crash course in artillery training so that the colonels could be reassigned as division artillery commanders with a rank of brigadier general. We did not like this idea at all because we thought it impossible to make an infantry colonel into an artillery general after only three months of concentrated training. The ROK Army had an excuse that the artillery needed more flag-rank officers to deal with the other branches of the armed forces. I did not envy the senior officers who had to teach the

7. Teaching at the ROK Artillery School

infantry colonels. But who could have imagined that one of these candidates for the "super fast-track" artillery general was Park Jung Hee, the general who would lead the coup d'état nine years later in 1961 and take over the presidency of the Republic of Korea.

When the winter of 1952 drew near, a number of changes began to occur. One of my roommates, Ki Yong Lee, married his high school sweetheart and moved out to a better apartment in Kwangju city. Shortly after, the other roommate, Hyo Sung, also moved out to a new apartment to prepare for his upcoming marriage arranged by his parents in Seoul. Certainly, I could not stay alone in that lonely place any longer; neither did I have a fiancée or even a girl friend. Luckily one of my colleagues in the Gunnery Department, Lt. Moon Woo Lee, offered to share his apartment in Kwangju. It was not much of an apartment—just a small *ondol* room for sleeping in a Korean traditional house managed by a young widow with a six-year-old daughter.

One day I heard from one of my Fort Sill buddies, Yung Suk Kang who was now on the frontline, that his parents had arranged a marriage for him and the wedding date was set for sometime in the spring of 1953. He said he was the first son in the family, and his parents wanted to make sure they were going to have an heir. I felt close to Kang, not just because of our friendship at Fort Sill, but I had also visited his home and met his parents. I wondered how he could manage his frontline duties and married life. Probably the best arrangement he could make would be for his wife to find lodging in a town near the frontline and then he could visit her whenever possible. I sensed that he was in a way envious of my teaching position at the Artillery School where officers could arrange to live with their families. I wondered what I could do to help his situation. Then an idea came to me. What if we swapped our positions? I was fed up with my heavy teaching load and my hungry stomach. I needed a change, but how would my return to the frontline affect my mother?

After a few sleepless nights considering the situation, I decided to talk with Colonel Chung, the vice commander of the ROK Army Artillery School. A week later I asked the colonel if it would be possible for me to trade my position with Lieutenant Yong Suk Kang. He was surprised to hear my request since the war was still going on and no "normal" soldier or officer would volunteer to go to the front. At that time the armistice talks at Panmunjom were progressing at a snail's pace, and the battles on the front became fiercer because each side was desperate to gain tactically advantageous ground before the armistice agreement was signed. The armistice agreement was not going to be a peace treaty, but merely a cease-fire agreement. The cease-fire line (the DMZ: Demilitarized Zone) would be determined by the location of the hostile forces when the agreement was signed. Both Colonel Chung and I knew the precarious conditions at the frontline, but he wanted to make sure and asked, "Lieutenant Hurh, are you aware of the dangers at the front?"

"Yes, sir," I answered,

"Then why this request? Just to risk your life for the sake of your friend? Or for some other reason?" The colonel was curious.

I told him that I was burnt-out at the Artillery School because of the perpetual hunger and the tedious routine without any sense of accomplishment or meaning. I desperately needed a change and so did my friend, Lieutenant Kang, albeit for different reasons. In sum, I told Colonel Chung that it would be good for both of us if we could trade our positions.

After a moment of silence, the colonel said in a somber tone, "I will see what I can do. You'll be hearing from me, probably in a month or so." I thanked him and returned to my office with an unsettled feeling. Had I done the right thing? How would my mother react to this situation — her son volunteering to go back to the frontline?

A month passed, an unusually cold and damp December, followed by the arrival of 1953. There was no word from Colonel Chung. Strangely enough I was neither anxious nor disappointed. I felt rather calm and wanted to let my fate run its course as everything was now beyond my control. Maybe it was God's will that I was looking for a more active and direct service to my country.

I tried to pray, but I did not believe in the "utilitarian" efficacy of prayers for one's own personal advantage, such as success, money, or even health and longevity for oneself. That would be too selfish and utilitarian in the sense that God is "utilized" or "mobilized" to serve a human's desires, not the other way around. In my view, I thought we were supposed to serve God, and it is up to God to decide if we could be helped or saved. Since I grew up in a Confucian family, I had no Christian concept of original sin and redemptive suffering. Koreans do have, however, a concept of the Heavenly Lord or the Supreme Being, Hanunim, but I could not imagine making a business-like deal with God for my own self-interest. Simply put, I did not know how to pray. My fate, I decided, was to wait.

7. Teaching at the ROK Artillery School

Another month passed and the stubborn winter started slowly to give way to spring even in the boring training center. My tedious routine of teaching continued until I was called to report to Colonel Chung's office on a sunny afternoon in early March 1953.

Colonel Chung greeted me, "Ah, Lieutenant Hurh, sorry to have kept you waiting for so long. Your request was approved much earlier, but the formal paperwork took a longer time than I expected." The colonel continued with his usual friendly demeanor to tell me that my friend, Lieutenant Kang, was no longer at the front as he had been transferred to the 76th Field Artillery Battalion in a newly created field artillery group and was temporarily assigned as the director of the Fire Direction Center for the battalion. The colonel explained that the ROK Army was expanding its field artillery power by creating several new field artillery groups, and the 76th Field Artillery Battalion was one of them. They would soon move to Seoul for logistic supplies and eventually be deployed at the front.

"So, Lieutenant Hurh, your new assignment is to report to Major Young Jo Cha, the commander of the 76th Field Artillery Battalion by March 24 to replace Lieutenant Kang. When it's done, your friend, Lieutenant Kang will be relieved from his duty there and will report to me to replace you in your teaching position here. Understood?"

"Yes, sir. Thank you, Colonel!" Now Kang would begin a happy family life in Kwangju, and I would have a more purposeful life at the front. "Hope to see you again, Colonel!" With this parting remark, I felt sad all of a sudden. We shook hands, and I left his office. Would we see each other again? I doubted it, and I was right. Colonel Chung was promoted to brigadier general soon after, and much later he served as a finance minister under President Park Chung Hee for the Republic of Korea. We never saw each other again. He was a good commander, a very good man.

In the early morning of March 24, 1953, after 11 months of teaching in the Gunnery Department, I bid farewell to my friends and left Kwangju for the temporary campsite of the 76th Field Artillery Battalion. The department chair was gracious enough to let me use his jeep for moving. Some of the other officers wondered about my "crazy" move to the frontline, but the Lees, my Fort Sill group, understood me very well. They were now looking forward to their reunion with Yong Suk Kang. I also managed to have a reunion with him even though it was very brief. I tried to call him by phone, but no connection was available to the temporary camp. The previous night

"I Will Shoot Them from My Loving Heart"

I wrote to my mother about my transfer to a new unit that would be regrouped in Seoul and eventually sent to the front, and so I would be seeing her within a matter of weeks.

The temporary regroup camp for the 76th Field Artillery Battalion was located in the hilly area about 15 miles north of Songjong-Ri. When I arrived I saw several large tents, a dozen trucks, and a couple of jeeps, but no howitzers or any other heavy equipment. Apparently, the battalion was to be fully equipped at the supply area in Seoul. Following the directions given by a sentry at the checkpoint, I found a tent that had a sign indicating it was the S-3 (operation and training) office.

I entered the tent and saw Young Suk Kang, who looked about the same except he was quite thin and looked older. We hugged and didn't know what to say. Finally he said, "Welcome to nowhere, Won Moo." Then he introduced me to his assistants, Lieutenant Jong Jeun Kim and Lieutenant Ung Jae Lee. The two young men were very likeable; Kim seemed to be a little reserved, whereas Lee was more open with a big smile most of the time. I liked them both. Kang said they were the cream of the crop among their peers — the top of the 29th OCS (Officer Candidates School) class, and he felt sad to leave them. He made me promise I would take care of them. I said I would, and I felt the warmth of human feelings that I had missed for the past year teaching at the Artillery School. Indeed, it felt good to be a "human" again and to be with someone with whom I could share my destiny in personal terms. And I sensed Kang's feelings as well. He would miss them. So life goes on.

Next Kang and I went to report my arrival to Major Cha, a meeting that was less than cordial. Major Cha was a husky, short man in his early-30s. He said he would welcome me wholeheartedly if I were an additional staff member, but not as the replacement of Lieutenant Kang — particularly when the battalion was going through the hectic time of organizing, regrouping, training, and moving to the front. I detected a sense of resentment in his tone of speech as if I used some connection with the higher-ups for arranging the transfer of his most important staff, S-3. (Following the U.S. army organizational model, there were four staff sections in the ROK army: S-1 [personnel], S-2 [intelligence], S-3 [operation and training], and S-4 [quartermaster] on the battalion and regimental levels. On the divisional level and beyond they were called G-1, G-2, G-3, and G-4, respectively. In the ROK artillery battalion, S-3 was also the director of the Fire Direction Center [FDC], and he was the third in command after the battalion commander

7. Teaching at the ROK Artillery School

[usually a lieutenant colonel] and battalion executive [usually a major]. According to the Table of Organization [T/O], the rank of S-3 is a major but due to the lack of qualified officers, young captains or even first lieutenants, [like me] assumed the task, if they were combat experienced and preferably trained at Fort Sill.)

I was ready for a challenge and glad that I had left the Artillery School. The planning of logistics and training of the recruits for a new artillery battalion was not an easy task and came with heavy responsibilities, but I thought it was a God-given task for me to help bring peace to the Korean peninsula.

On the evening of my arrival, Kang took me to his retreat in an old farmhouse where we drank *soju* (a Korean version of vodka) and ate *bulgogi* (barbecued beef) and talked until well past midnight. The next morning Kang left for the Artillery School, and I began my S-3 job of organizing the ROK 76th Field Artillery Battalion. Thus the trading of our positions was complete—simple and painless.

Creating and operating a new field artillery battalion from scratch was, however, a much more complex and demanding task than I had imagined, especially when we were totally dependent on the U.S. Army to supply weapons, ammunition, communication equipment, vehicles, and other supplies. Day and night I worked with advisors from KMAG (the U.S. Military Advisory Group to the Republic of Korea), and dealt with the Tables of Organization (T/O) and Equipment (T/E) almost every day. The T/O and T/E involved roughly 600 men, 18 howitzers, 70 vehicles of all kinds, small arms that ranged from Colt .45 pistols to machine guns, ammunition, various communication equipment, and many other ordnance and quartermaster supplies. Although it was an enormously difficult task, I liked the challenge—I felt like I was creating something useful to end the war so that I could go on to college. While I was at the Artillery School, I felt my life was wasted most of the time, but now organizing a new field artillery battalion gave me a sense of purpose and a glimpse of hope for my future—an honorable discharge from the army and a chance to continue my education.

Thanks to my two smart and hard-working assistants, Lieutenants Kim and Lee, most of the groundwork for moving the battalion to Seoul for logistical supplies and equipment was completed in three weeks. In retrospect, they were indeed the most efficient assistants I had in my entire military service of seven years. Not only were they hard workers but also brilliant in finding alternative solutions to unexpected problems.

8

Back to the Front

ON A SUNNY AFTERNOON in mid–April 1953, our long convoy of trucks loaded with soldiers and their gear arrived at the assembly area and supply depot in Seoul. The place was the campus of Sook Myung Women's University, which was located in the southwest part of Seoul — close to Hyochang Park, about two miles or so from the South Gate (Namdaemun). My mother's house at Soon Wha Dong was just a ten-minute walk from the South Gate. I thought it was a God-given gift for me to be able to visit my family as often as every weekend before our move to the frontline.

My mother and siblings were delighted to see me again, and I was pleased to see they were all healthy and seemed to be doing fine. I was especially impressed to see mother's new business thriving. She had converted my father's farm-equipment store into an ice-cream parlor for the warm season and into a noodle shop during the winter. Her assiduous ability for business enterprise always surprised me. I was thankful that my mother could support the family, but at the same time as the eldest son in the family, I felt ashamed at my inability to help her financially. My monthly salary as a junior officer was so low that it hardly covered my personal toiletry needs. I was lucky to have such an enterprising and independent mother who had been able to support the family single-handedly since my father's death. I also thought myself fortunate that I had not married. I wondered how a young married ROK officer could support a family with such a dismal salary. Would the situation be better if an officer were promoted to a higher rank — say, a colonel or general? It seemed so, but in reality it was not due to adequate salaries but rather because of their increased access to corruption by using their powerful position in the army. At that time, I could not grasp the extent

8. BACK TO THE FRONT

and seriousness of this problem, but as time passed, I began to learn painfully the complex nature of this problem and its grievous consequences.

On the campus ground of Sook Myung Women's' University, we pitched several large army tents for soldiers quarters, kitchen/mess halls, storage spaces, and so forth. Since the university was closed, we used the classrooms for our battalion offices, training sessions, and officer quarters. The Hyo Chang public park served well as a place for parking equipment, for receptions and assemblies, and for field exercises. Except for Sundays, I worked for six weeks with my assistants and the KMAG advisors to prepare requisitions and check the ordnance and logistic supplies we received. As the battalion operations officer (S-3) my work was often tedious and frustrating, but finally my battalion was ready for "on-the-job training" in late May 1953. The brand-new artillery batteries were to be deployed on the front to function as normal battle units, but were supervised by experienced officers, usually the KMAG officers and/or some selected officers from the U.S. artillery units nearby on the front.

Our battalion was assigned to support the ROK Sixth Division that was covering the midwestern section of the defense line — the Kumsong area, about 130 miles northeast of Seoul. Our left flank was defended by the U.S. Army IX Corps and on the right was the U.S. X Corps. So we, the ROK II Corps (consisting of the 3rd, 5th, 6th, and 8th divisions), were situated in the middle. It appeared the area we were assigned was relatively safe due to the presence of the U.S. Army on each side. However, I felt uneasy because I had heard rumors about a massive concentration of the CCF (Chinese Communist Forces) in front of our sector, and the CCF usually attacked the sectors defended mainly by the ROK Army.

Armed with all the supplies received, our convoy of 18 howitzers, 75 vehicles, and some 600 men reached the front just below Kumsong. Kumsong was an enemy occupied small town located about 20 miles northeast of Hwachon Reservoir and seven miles north of the 38th parallel. We deployed our batteries on the southern bank of the Kumsong River and also set up our Battalion FDC (Fire Direction Center) nearby. Luckily we inherited the old fortified gun bunkers from the 27th Field Artillery Battalion that had been built by one of our 105mm howitzer battalions in the 15th ROK Field Artillery Group, which had now moved to the rear for a new assignment elsewhere. The other two battalions — the 77th (105mm) and the 96th (155mm) — also established their battery positions in our vicinity for on-the-job training.

"I Will Shoot Them from My Loving Heart"

Moreover, there was a mobile U.S. self-propelled and armored field artillery battalion (AFA 300th Battalion) deployed in our area. It was sent by the ROK II Corps artillery to help in training the newly established ROK artillery battalions in our sector. (Later I learned that the ROK II Corps artillery was commanded by the former KMAG chief of staff, Brigadier General Richard W. Mayo. In fact, General Mayo was a founding father of the ROK Artillery.) As a result there was a massive concentration of artillery firepower in our sector — a total of 66 howitzers. So if each howitzer fired ten rounds on a single target it would be 660 rounds of high explosive projectiles bursting on the same spot at the same time! I thought the reason for this concentration of firepower was based on the critical nature of the Kumsong front for both sides. Looking at the map, I could see our defense line was protruding far to the north towards Kumsong, creating a 20-mile bulge in our frontline. The enemy wanted, of course, to flatten that bulge for tactical purposes.

After digging in our positions, our battalion sent out our forward observers to the infantry companies who were dug into trenches and bunkers on the mountains in front of us. We conducted the registration fire and readied our fire support. The mountains were quite high — the highest more than 1,000 meters above sea level — and the mountainsides were steep. Through the deep valleys the clear Kumsong River flowed quietly in the evening sun. Night fell and all was quiet on the Kumsong front. I wondered what would become of us. Returning to my bunker at midnight after working with Lieutenants Lee and Kim, I conked out, even though the bunker was damp and cold.

The next morning, however, I was quite elated to meet a visitor from the U.S. 300th Armored Field Artillery (AFA) Battalion nearby. Lieutenant McIntosh was a tall, young man from Urbana/Champaign, Illinois, who came to help our crew in the FDC as an advisor. He was a very friendly fellow and I liked him from the first instance we met. (Unfortunately now, I have forgotten his first name but I remember he went to the University of Illinois in Urbana-Champaign, Illinois.) He taught us various precision firing techniques that I never learned at Fort Sill, such as computing the data for firing illumination shells and for coordinating the Time-On-Target (TOT) operations for a massive concentration of shelling on a single target area by all available weapons at the same time for maximum destruction. This meant, regardless of where the different firing units were located, the projectiles would land at the same place and explode at the same time. The different

8. Back to the Front

At the Kumsong front with the ROK 76th Field Artillery Battalion where I was the director of the battalion's Fire Direction Center — pictured here with battalion commander Major Young Jo Cha (front row, left), Lieutenant Hurh (front row, right). Back row from left to right: Lt. Jung Kyun Shin, A Battery commander; Lt. Jook Hi Kim, B Battery commander; Lt. Byong Joon Min, intelligence officer; and Lt. Keun Hyung Chang, C Battery commander. The sandbagged bunker on the left is the Battalion FDC. Polaroid photograph taken by Lieutenant McIntosh. May 1953.

firing units included everything — from small arms and mortars, to howitzers, naval guns, and the air force. We did one drill for this operation, and it was indeed tremendous in effect.

Through these training exercises, my friendship with Lieutenant McIntosh grew, although we only addressed each other by our last names — Lieutenant McIntosh and Lieutenant Hurh. It's a shame that I never knew his first name. Anyway, he was always good to my FDC crew. One day Lieutenant McIntosh photographed us and all the commanding officers and staff members of our battalion near the FDC bunker with his Polaroid camera.

Visiting our counterparts at the U.S. 300th Armored Field Artillery Battalion compound in the Kumsong valley. From left to right: unidentified American captain, our advisor Lieutenant McIntosh, First Lieutenant Hurh, and Second Lieutenant Hong, communication officer of our ROK 76th Field Artillery Battalion. Photograph taken with Lieutenant McIntosh's Polaroid camera. May 1953.

We were fascinated to see the instant production of the photos on the spot. I have treasured the two photos he gave me. My assistant, Lieutenant Lee, still fondly remembers him to this day. (Lieutenant Lee now lives in Alameda, California.) Thanks to Lieutenant McIntosh's advice, our FDC improved a great deal, particularly our accuracy in hitting the target.

The need for accuracy soon became apparent when the division deputy commander of the ROK Sixth Division, Brigadier General Lee, came to our battalion and proceeded to our OP (forward observation post). He requested that our batteries destroy one of the live enemy artillery bunkers, a distance of about 300 yards from the OP. Perhaps the general was intentionally testing our skill because it was not an easy task, as we had to put our projectiles

8. Back to the Front

precisely into one of the small firing holes of the occupied enemy bunker. It would be a miracle if we hit the target at all. As the director of the FDC, I ordered our best howitzers (the center piece of the B Battery) to do the job. While the division commander was watching the target at the OP with his binoculars, I ordered my forward observer to conduct the fire mission as usual. I then instructed my assistant, Lieutenant Lee, to conduct a fire for effect by firing three rounds of the same lot number projectiles using the same howitzer consecutively for maximum accuracy. That did the job — a great miracle happened. Two of the three rounds went right into the hole and exploded! I could not believe it — precision artillery fire with an unimaginable accuracy.

The general was immensely pleased. So were we, but our achievement took an interesting turn. A few days later, we heard that our sister battalion, the 77th ROK Artillery Battalion, was also paid a similar visit by the division commander to see how precise they could fire; however, their results were not so good. Their American advisor, Major Seiler, wanted to borrow me for a week or two to straighten out their FDC. I thought it was a ridiculous idea. Our achievement in the precision fire was not based on my solo performance ("a one man" show) but the concerted teamwork of many — our FDC crew, our forward observer, and our firing battery. So I warned our battalion commander, Major Cha, that I would play sick in case Major Seiler would come to us with such a lunatic proposition. Indeed the next day Major Seiler came to visit us, and of course, I was sick with sever symptoms of the flu. Our battalion surgeon told the major that my influenza was highly contagious. He left without a word and did not bother us again — I imagine he came to his senses eventually.

Theoretically I was supposed to be the third in command for the battalion after the commander, Major Cha, and the deputy commander (or battalion executive), Captain Pak; however, Major Cha was largely detached from the daily operations of the battalion, and Captain Pak was excused from frontline duties most of the time to conduct the battalion's "*hooseng sa-op*" (public welfare project) in the rear. *Hooseng sa-op* is a euphemism for the business enterprise dealing with civilian use of military equipment and supplies; for example, the illegal use of army vehicles for transporting civilian goods and/or selling army rations for profit in order to supplement the meager salaries of officers and noncommissioned officers. When I first heard about this, I thought it was an abnormal practice limited to certain corrupted units, but eventually I realized that it was a more or less "normal" practice in the ROK army at that time. Some 40 years later, a former ROK Army chief of staff and my boss, General Sun Yup Paik, described this problem in his memoir, *From Pusan to Panmunjom*.

> Another problem facing me was that of the livelihood of my officers. I raised this issue slyly with President Rhee as I was briefing him on a different subject early in my tenure as army chief. "Your Excellency, soldiers' salaries are too low," I said. "I can barely buy enough food for my family on what I make, let alone support my family. The terrible salary we pay our officers fosters graft and corruption. Officers and noncommissioned officers sell rations and use unit vehicles illegally to make money in the private sector, disguising the usage as a '"public welfare project.' Please be aware of this issue" [Paik, 1999, 212].

I never learned about this kind of problem at the Officer Candidate School. Neither did I learn how to handle the situation when my master sergeant reported to me one day that one of the battalion switchboards had been stolen! There was no entry in my Field Manuel on how to tackle such a problem. Using my common sense, I shouted at him: "Fix it man! Get the damn thing back right away by any cost. Don't ask me how! Just do it. It's an order, sergeant!" He was surprised at my burst of anger but not shocked at my order. Later I learned that stealing things among the army units was not unusual, particularly when "rich" American units and newly equipped Korean troops were nearby the camp. In time, I realized that one could buy virtually anything at the Dong Dae Moon "Black Market" in Seoul, including all kinds of military weapons and supplies, even rocket launchers — with the exception of maybe a tank or a 155mm howitzer. Hence, buying an army switchboard would be a piece of cake!

A few days later, my master sergeant reported to me that he had fixed the problem. I just said, "Good job, sergeant!" I did not ask him how he did it. That's the way army life went on the front. Such a question was not only redundant but also very foolish and even taboo. Another lesson I had to learn was how to handle my drunken American military advisor. As mentioned, the U.S. 300th AFA sent us a most efficient advisor, Lieutenant McIntosh, for our FDC; but in addition, we got another advisor, a captain whose name I don't recall, from the KMAG (Korean Military Advisory Group). He was an older, plump man in his 40s, who chewed tobacco all the time. He came to us one night looking disheveled and smelling of alcohol and ordered us to, "Fire battalion ten rounds to celebrate my birthday." This was, of course, ridiculous! I calmly confronted him, saying: "Captain, there are no enemy activities right now, and you have told us repeatedly to save our ammunition. Battalion ten rounds would waste 180 rounds of ammunition for nothing but your birthday celebration." But he insisted. I became furious and shouted, "You SOB. Goodbye!" and left the FDC to find our battalion commander, but I couldn't find him. Soon after, however, I heard the bursting of 180 rounds of our precious ammunition for one drunken American captain's birthday. He must have forced one of my assistants to give the fire command. What an idiotic situation and a waste of the American and South Korean taxpayers' money.

"Saving ammo" has been a cardinal maxim for any soldier, particularly for artillery. I recall a gunnery instructor, Sergeant Wingate, at Fort Sill, who always reported to the Fire Direction Center by yelling on the phone whenever he fired one round of 155mm HE (High Explosive) projectile: "FDC, one Chevrolet on the way!" and he winked at us with a big smile. Observing this, we Korean student officers wondered what he was talking about. The sergeant later explained that each projectile is as precious as a brand new car, in this case a Chevrolet. We were quite impressed by his analogy. By this logic, Capt. SOB wasted 180 Chevrolets!

The humid heat of June 1953 descended slowly on the Kumsong Valley in Korea. There was no major change on the battlefront, except for an occasional exchange of heavy volleys between the enemy's mortars and our howitzers. I sensed we were in a trench-war stalemate — both sides were waiting for the outcome of the cease-fire negotiations at Panmunjom, and yet each side was desperate to gain more advantageous tactical terrain before the armistice whenever they had a chance. The armistice is not, of course, a peace treaty but merely a temporary cease-fire.

My daily routine continued — a registration fire in the early morning, followed by my daily briefing for the battalion commander and his staff on the condition of the battlefront, such as an up-to-date intelligence report and the operational status of our battalion. Usually in the afternoon the firing batteries were inspected and an occasional visit was made to our observation posts. In the evening, work on future operational plans and advanced training of the FDC crew members took place deep into the night, and fire missions were conducted when requested by our forward observers. Usually the night fire mission requests were for illumination and harassment. In general, all was quiet on our front. Lieutenant McIntosh came over every other night, and we shared our experiences at Fort Sill and exchanged our views on the stalemate of the war. He usually brought a pack of Miller High Life with him.

Around mid–June 1953, the enemy attacks on our infantry outposts became more frequent than usual, and by early July we received at least a dozen fire support requests from our forward observers every night. I thought something was going to happen, but no serious events occurred for a week, particularly during the daytime. All was quite again except for an incessant rainfall, day and night — the hot and humid monsoon season had invaded the Kumsong Valley. The mood was gloomy and depressing. One day two battery commanders came to visit me on a boring, hot July afternoon, and we had a couple of beers. Lieutenant Chang, the Charlie Battery commander, came up with the idea of trying to take a fake photo showing him catching

Lull at the Kumsong front. Posing for a "silly" photograph of Lieutenant Chang's one-handed catch of a projectile from a 105mm howitzer! On the left is Lieutenant Kim and I'm in the center. July 1953.

a projectile as it was being shot from a gun barrel. It was a childish idea, but we all needed to enjoy a lull to survive in the stormy killing field.

Moreover, the commander of our 15th ROK artillery group, Colonel Kim, started to inspect our battery compounds every other day for "sanitary" purposes — to get rid of human feces. He was obsessed with the idea that the best way to maintain our soldiers' hygiene was to clean up all the feces in the unit compounds since our soldiers defecated everywhere and did not use the designated latrines. Our soldiers called him as "Ttong Jangoon" meaning the "Shit General." I did understand his concern, but as the commander of a ROK army artillery group weren't there better things he could do on the front than hunt for his soldiers' BM? Every week he held an unannounced spot check, and when he found feces, the battalion commander was severely reprimanded and had to pick up the BM with his hand. The battalion commander then in turn passed down his anger and frustration to his battery commanders and other subordinates ordering them to catch and punish the litterbugs, or more correctly the "shitbugs."

In the army I acquired a superb ability to use four-letter words without any shame or hesitation. The higher the battle stress, the more frequent became the usage of dirty words as a most effective communication device, whether in Korean or English. In fact, I leaned many four-letter words from American soldiers, in addition to the numerous and inconceivably dirty Korean words I picked up from my fellow officers in all ranks. The use of swear words functioned to relieve stress, anger, and anxiety, but also was quite effective to communicate to your comrades under exigent situations, particularly to give orders to your subordinates. The Korean language is never lacking in dirty words. When I came home for the first furlough from the frontline, my mother was genuinely shocked to hear the barbarous words that I uttered without much hesitation. They just came to me naturally. In retrospect, it took me years to cleanse my foul language, both Korean and English.

Rain had been pouring off and on, day and night in the Godforsaken Kumsong Valley for more than a week. Although our battlefront was relatively calm, the muggy, hot monsoon season was quite unbearable and depressing. More depressing was the news that our battalion commander, Major Cha, was going to be replaced by a new commander within a few days. Although I was not particularly fond of Major Cha, I was apprehensive about this sudden change of a commander at a most volatile time on the front. Major Cha did not understand the reason either. A couple of days later Major Cha was transferred to a reserve unit, and a new commander, Major H — (abbreviated for anonymity), came to us. He was a boyish looking, urbane man of about 32 or so. My assistants and I briefed him about the war situation and the status of our battalion. He did not seem to be interested in our war briefing but was excited about meeting people who had grown up in Seoul, such as Lieutenant Lee and me. He spoke with a perfect Seoul accent and behaved like a typical city slicker. Appropriately, we nicknamed him as Major "Gangpe" (City Slicker). This new battalion commander was more interested in what he could do for fun in the Kumsong area, rather than assuming his new responsibilities. We told him there was nothing to "see" or "enjoy" unless he visited Chunchon city about 40 miles south. I was disappointed and concerned about this "city slicker" commander. I was alarmed by a premonition that we were going to face some kind of trouble ahead.

A week passed without much change in the battlefront and the weather conditions. Pouring rain and dense fog with zero visibility alternated day and night — an ominous time to sense the hell of killing or being killed. Well, hell got loose. The Chinese "volunteer" army launched a massive surprise attack against our sector on the evening of July 13, 1953 (the so-called the July Offensive or Battle of Kumsong). Since the visibility was near zero, U.S. air support was impossible, and the low visibility meant our forward observers could not conduct fire missions, particularly at night, even though we shot a few illuminating shells and risked the exposure of our own troops. Nevertheless, we carried on our fire support of the infantry based on the map coordinates reported by our forward observers. We fired continuously all night and so did all the battalions in our field artillery group, including the U.S. 300th Armored Field Artillery Battalion — a total of 84 howitzers. The barrels of our howitzers soon became hot, and the entire Kumsong Valley was filled with a choking smoke, the awful smell of phosphorus, and the deafening roar coming from our howitzers and the exploding enemy shells.

I was so totally immersed in the FDC bunker in conducting fire that I failed to notice our new commander's absence until midnight. I asked my assistants if they had seen our battalion commander, Major H. They had not. I called his office bunker. His aide said he had left this morning for Chunchon city to check our battalion's "public welfare project." I was dumbfounded! I wondered why the major had not told me that he was leaving for Chunchon. I thought of reporting his absence right away to General Kim, our field artillery group commander, but waited, hoping Major City Slicker might show up at any moment. He did not.

The hell of battle continued all night, and morning came. The battlefront was quiet except for sporadic shelling. The weather was still muggy and foggy, but from my FDC bunker I could see our battery compound, littered with ammunition cases and cartridges. We must have fired at least 10,000 rounds during the night. The gun barrels were so red hot that we often had to pour water over them to cool them off. Luckily, our battalion had no casualties, except for an unconfirmed report that Lieutenant Yang, one of our forward observers, was missing.

Major H. had not returned nor had any call come from him. I called Colonel Lee, the director of our artillery group FDC, to report the current status of our battalion. His assistant, Lieutenant Pak answered, saying the colonel would return my call as soon as he could. I had never met Lieutenant Pak, but we communicated by phone almost every day since being deployed on the Kumsong front. We both were called to join the army when we were still high school seniors, and were also trained in the same ROK Army Artillery School in Jinhae — not at the same time but a few weeks apart. So we used to talk to each other not only for our battle operations but also for sharing our personal views and feelings on many others things — like old friends would do. I asked him his personal assessment of the current battle situation. He said simply, "Please review the evacuation plan of your battalion immediately. Our infantry defense line has been broken and they are already starting to pull out. You'll be hearing from us when to evacuate your battalion, but not yet! I have to go. We'll talk later."

I was speechless and wondered to myself, "Oh, my God. What the hell is going on? Where are my commanders? My boss, Major H., and his boss, Colonel Kim?" Over instant coffee for breakfast, I reviewed our contingency plan for a possible retreat. I was glad that we had conducted a field reconnaissance a month before, and our battery commanders were already informed about the location.

All of a sudden, the shrieking sound of incoming enemy shells pierced our ears. Hell was loose again with the tremendous thunder of explosions. The Communist forces were getting close. My intuition told me that we should pull out. It was about 3 P.M., July 14, 1953. I called Lieutenant Pak at the ROK 15th Field Artillery Group FDC. No answer. The telephone was dead. What should I do? I called the S-3 of the other field artillery battalions in our group — the ROK 96th (155mm) and the ROK 77th (105mm) — for their situation and advice. All lines were dead and so were all outside radio contacts. At that point Lieutenant Lee, my assistant, shouted, "Sir the 96th Battalion is pulling out. Can't you see? Look!" I looked out from the FDC bunker window, and my heart sank. Our neighbor, the 96th (155mm) artillery battalion, was moving out, followed by our other neighbor, the 77th (105mm) battalion. I wondered who had given them an evacuation order. Without the order of the artillery group commander, how could they retreat? I imagined the artillery group headquarters must have already evacuated without informing its subordinates.

More enemy shells exploded in our vicinity. I realized I was on my own with my men, but I was undecided what to do. I knew that I was now responsible for the lives of 600 men, 18 howitzers, 75 vehicles, and other equipment. But I was not the commanding officer of our battalion. I had no right to give an order to evacuate! If I gave an evacuation order, I would be violating the military rule of conduct and could be subject to court-martial. I had been trained to follow the line of command; however, no situations comparable to what I was now facing had ever been covered at OCS or during my Fort Sill training. At that point, Lieutenant Lee, who was looking out from the FDC bunker, shouted, "Sir, look! The U.S. 300th AFA Battalion is pulling out!" It was the last artillery unit in our sector except for us.

Finally, I had to follow my common sense. If we tried to hold the line, our artillery battalion would certainly be wiped out, and the loss of men, guns, and equipment would be significant. Wouldn't it be better to evacuate and save my men and artillery to fight at another time and place? I didn't have much choice. I made the decision to pull out. I called my battery commanders with the order to evacuate to the designated regrouping area about ten miles to the south — in the order of A Battery first, leading our convoy, followed by B, C, and the headquarters company. I would be in the last jeep.

But there was a problem — a most disgusting one. The B and C Battery commanders reported to me that they did not have enough 2.5-ton trucks to pull their howitzers. The reason was that the trucks had been sent to Chunchon for the "public welfare project" a month ago by the order of Major Cha, our former commander. My feeling of disgust turned to anger over the military corruption that was jeopardizing the combat effectiveness of our battalion. I forced myself to think more rationally so I could do my best to lead my battalion effectively. I told the commanders of B and C Batteries

8. Back to the Front

that they were going to be accountable if they abandoned any howitzers. I urged them to try any other trucks available for pulling the howitzers, even three-quarter-ton light trucks, and if all efforts failed, they should destroy the howitzers before our retreat. I gave them 30 minutes to report back to me. My mixed feelings of disgust, anger, and sadness now changed to an overwhelming sense of fatigue. Feeling deadly tired, I noticed an eerie silence in the FDC, although we could hear the heavy rain pouring outside. No one spoke inside; no telephone or radio calls, but everyone watched me.

The longest 30 minutes in my life passed. I called the battery commanders, Lieutenants Jook Hi Kim and Keun Hyung Chang. Both indicated that the three-quarter-ton trucks were able to pull the howitzers on a flat road, but they were unsure if the trucks could handle the steep mountain roads. I made a decision to go ahead. I ordered the entire battalion to move to the first regrouping area as planned. We tried to inform our forward observers about our withdrawal, but we could not because of the communication blackout. It's a strange feeling to realize that the entire battalion is being led by very young, junior officers—first and second lieutenants. We were all under the age of 21. I asked myself, "Where the hell are our Battalion Commanders, Major Slicker and his deputy, Captain Pak? Heaven help us!" Rain started pouring again with thunder caused by both nature and human-made high explosives—the former produced rain and the latter shed blood.

Our convoy moved at a snail's pace on the two-lane dirt road that was the only evacuation route to the south for all units in the Kumsong Valley, unless one took the mountain route on foot, which some infantry troops were doing. I had no idea how many units were withdrawing at this time, but at least three ROK infantry divisions (about 60,000 soldiers) and all the ROK artillery battalions in the sector, including the U.S. 300th AFA Battalion—a total of three medium artillery (155mm) battalions and ten light artillery (105mm) battalions. This meant the road was clogged with several hundred howitzers and about a thousand vehicles, including many tanks, plus thousands and thousands of infantry soldiers who were trudging by foot on both sides of the dirt road. Thank God that for some unknown reason, the enemy did not pursue us, although there was some sporadic shelling. (Later I learned that the size of the enemy attacking force was about five CCF armies—equivalent to about 150,000 men.)

The drenching rain still poured down. I felt sorry for the tired, rain-soaked infantry soldiers walking on both sides of the road. The convoy stood still for a half an hour. Everything was quiet except the sound of rain and noise of our vehicle engines running. I was still angry about my battalion commander's absence but also extremely shocked by the incredibly poor operation of the ROK 15th Artillery Group FDC. They had just left their battle station without informing their subordinate units what to do before the communication blackout! When I called Lieutenant Pak, our communication channels were still intact. Had I not ordered my battalion to evacuate, what would have happened to the 600 men in my battalion? I shivered despite the hot and muggy monsoon weather in the Kumsong Valley.

Our convoy halted again. We had barely made five miles in two hours! Now more and more infantry soldiers were on the road in the soaking rain. They looked miserable but kept moving. I felt like we were all sitting ducks. I was thankful, however, that the enemy attack seemed to have subsided, at least for several hours. I wondered why. Eventually the military police came and began directing traffic and checking for strayed soldiers, deserters, and enemy infiltrators. Any suspicious looking men were directed off to the side of the checkpoint where the military police verified their identity and status. Large groups of soldiers were being detained and looked quite miserable and exhausted standing in the rain waiting to be checked out.

The convoy started moving again very slowly. At this pace we would be lucky if we reached our assembly area by 8 P.M. Everyone looked tired, hungry, and depressed. There were many immobilized vehicles stranded on the roadside. Traffic could easily move around the stalled trucks and jeeps, but a broken-down tank meant traffic usually had to stop until help could arrive. Luckily, our battalion had no vehicular problems that I knew of, and we were doubly lucky that it was rainy and North Korea didn't have much of an air force because we would have been easy targets. Since we were under the order of radio silence, I could not call our battery commanders for the status of the two howitzers pulled by the three-quarter-ton trucks.

Dusk was approaching and it was getting darker every minute. Around 8 P.M. we were able to turn off from the main road and proceed to our preselected regrouping area. Since I was in the last vehicle, I could see in the dusk our entire battalion convoy was moving slowly but soundly toward the gentle slope of a small knoll surrounded by small fruit trees. I was so relieved and thankful and even proud that I had made the right decision. All of our men and equipment were safe—except for Lieutenant Yang who was still missing. Probably he was killed or captured by the enemy.

8. Back to the Front

As my jeep turned into the regrouping area, I couldn't believe my eyes — Major H., my battalion commander who had been incommunicado since the enemy attack, was standing in front of his jeep! More shocking were his first words to me, "What took you so long to get here?" A feeling of extreme rage overwhelmed me, and without thinking, my hand automatically reached the holster of my Colt .45 — I just wanted to shoot the bastard.

At that instant an image of my mother's sad face flickered before my eyes as if saying, "Don't do it, son." At that point, Lieutenant Kim, my assistant, standing beside me, yelled at Major H., "Sir, we were waiting for an evacuation order, but all the communication channels broke down. Thanks to Lieutenant Hurh's leadership we luckily evacuated in time to save our battalion." The major's face momentarily became distorted with anger or perhaps with shame. Recovering my self-control, I asked the Major quietly but firmly: "Where were you when we needed you most? Sir! Our battalion commander! What were you doing while we were under the enemy attack?" He started mumbling something inaudible. Without a word, I turned abruptly and left.

We set up a temporary FDC in a tent and finally reestablished our communication with the 15th ROK Field Artillery Group FDC that was located about five miles southwest from us. I talked with Lieutenant Pak at length about the evacuation process. He said that he felt sorry that they had to evacuate suddenly because of an exigency, but he was glad to hear that we made it to the regrouping area. He never elaborated as to what the "exigency" exactly was. According to his information, the CCF accomplished what they wanted — to flatten the Kumsong bulge protruding into their territory, but they had taken tremendous casualties. Probably that's why they stopped pursuing us any further to the south. (Later I learned that the CCF had about 72,100 casualties in the Kumsong battle, while the ROK and UN Forces suffered 29,630 casualties.)

Our immediate objective was to launch a counterattack as soon as possible to recover the 15 miles of territory we had lost during the July 13 offensive because an armistice might be signed at any time. The only way to accomplish this task was to counterattack with reinforced troops with more firepower. (Later I learned that the U.S. Third Infantry Division and the U.S. 187th Airborne Regimental Combat Team from Japan had helped us to counterattack the enemy on July 16.) From the ROK Army side, the Sixth Division, which we had been supporting, was put into reserve, and fresh troops from the eastern front, the ROK 11th Division, took over our front. Our battalion was ordered to support three infantry regiments of the ROK 11th Division.

Our counterattack began right away — the battle was fierce, but by July 20 we had regained about eight miles, half of what we had lost. Now our artillery group was in full swing because one of the best artillery battalions, the ROK 27th Artillery Battalion, had joined our operation. We fired day and night to support our infantry troops; however, we could not advance any further to the north. The enemy appeared determined to keep their defense line by any means. Around July 25 a rumor circulated that the armistice talks at Panmunjom had progressed to the point that both sides had agreed to establish a military demarcation line at the current location of the battlefront. Soon the rumor became a reality.

In the early afternoon of July 27, our artillery group FDC informed us that the armistice agreement papers had been signed at Panmunjom at 10 A.M. on Monday, July 27, 1953, and that the cease-fire would become effective at 10 P.M. on the same day! "So the war will be over tonight?" someone in our FDC shouted. The events unfolded so fast that we did not know how to respond. I mused to myself, "So this is the solution? And for what? Millions of people killed, but nothing has changed except for the destruction of human lives and their dreams."

The mood at the FDC was somber; however, Major H. suddenly appeared in our FDC tent, dancing around and loudly singing. I thought his behavior was utterly idiotic. How in the world could the ROK Army allow him to command an artillery battalion? Then an unusually high number of fire missions was requested by our forward observers. Apparently the enemy wanted to expand their territory as much as possible before the cease-fire. It was 8 P.M. Within two hours the war would be over, but our forward observers reported that the enemy attacks were accelerating, and they needed more and more fire support. Strangely enough, however, our artillery group FDC ordered us to stop firing at 9:50 P.M., not at 10 P.M. as stipulated in the armistice agreement. Time ticked by quickly. We had to cease fire at ten minutes before ten P.M., even though the enemy kept firing and our soldiers were dying. Our forward observers were furious, demanding our fire support. I asked Major H. to call the artillery group commander to give us permission to continue firing until 10 P.M. Major H. ignored my request and only said, "An order is an order." Many soldiers died during those long, miserable ten minutes. How tragic and absurd for anyone to be killed just a few minutes before the cease-fire. Even today I don't understand who made such an arbitrary and idiotic decision to hold fire ten minutes before the cease-fire while the enemy was still firing frantically up to the last second before 10 P.M. It was the longest, agonizing ten minutes in my entire life.

Finally, exactly at 10 P.M., all was quiet on all fronts. The war was over at last — one of the most useless, senseless, and brutal civil wars of the century. A total of about two million soldiers from both sides — South and North and their supporters (the American and UN forces from 15 countries and the Chinese Communist Forces) perished in the war, and more than two million civilian lives in the Korean peninsula were sacrificed in vain. The hellish see-saw war of three years had accomplished nothing — the military demarcation line between the north and south in the beginning and at the end of the war turned out to be virtually the same. Only the name of military demarcation changed — from "the 38th parallel" to "the DMZ" (demilitarized zone). Moreover, the war never ended; it merely halted since there was no victor or loser. No soldiers on either side ever withdrew. I reminded myself that I had been a participant in this senseless war. I felt miserable. But my excuse was I did not have a choice. My FDC crew members were unbelievably quiet and did not celebrate the cease-fire. Although we were quiet, we knew what each other was feeling and thinking — the mixed feeling of relief at having survived this brutal, absurd war, accompanied by an overwhelming sense of anxiety about our own future. Major H. was the exception. He was still dancing around from one tent to the next in our battalion compound. I envied his infantile naiveté. At least he was idiotically happy — and he was our battalion commander — to our shame.

Although we were at first skeptical if the cease-fire would hold, as the days passed we gradually relaxed and enjoyed playing some sport games and visiting the *chuho* (PX) in the evening to drink soju or Korean *mukguli* (rice wine). Now we could sleep in tents on army cots instead of spending the night in bunkers, but the food remained about the same, not very good.

The war was over. I wondered if I could now go home to join my family and eventually go to college. Would the army let me go? What more was there for us to do? However, after a few weeks we were moved to the rear for retraining. About 50 miles to the south, on the bank of Simpori Creek, we established our retraining camp in theory, but in practice there was nothing to do except to clean our weapons, hold firing practice, read old magazines and visit the *chubo* tent in the evenings for beer and snacks. It was also a time for furloughs for the soldiers, who took turns going home for several days at a time. The battalion saved a lot of rice this way for the "public welfare project."

I too went home for a visit and was sadly reminded of Thomas Wolfe's book *You Can't Go Home Again*. How true! To be sure, I was happy to see my family and friends, but essentially I was out of place. Since the age of 18 I had been away from my family except for a few visits. I had no permanent residence and contributed nothing towards my family's support. Since the Korean War everyone had been uprooted and displaced, particularly the young student soldiers who fought and survived the war at the front. The cease-fire, however, did not grant us an immediate honorable discharge from the armed forces, except for those who had access to political influence by virtue of their family's status and power. In fact, many of my Kyunggi High School classmates did not serve in the armed forces at all, or served only for a few months in the rear. These lucky sons of the power elite could now continue or resume their studies for pursuing their career goals. In short, their lives and dreams were not affected by either the war or peace (cease-fire), but definitely my life and my war buddies' lives were deeply affected. It was extremely painful to encounter these privileged guys in the streets of Seoul and to hear their condescending remark, "So I see you are *still* in the army." It sounded like it was my fault that I fought the war for our country and was still in service even after the cease-fire, while these clever guys could afford to go to college because their fathers had money and power. Should I feel insulted and angry? No, I had to accept the fact that I was out of place in all social spaces — the civil society at large in Korea, the circle of old friends, relatives, and even in my own home. My life in the military was not by choice, but now it was my only world. Permanent friendships were not possible because of the constant mobility. It was an existential alienation in which one's life was so disconnected that it became ephemeral and meaningless.

While the war was going on at the front, I was usually too busy to think about the purpose and meaning of life, but now I felt lost as to what to do with my life. I desperately wanted to be out of the army, but I was told that young officers in the company ranks were most unlikely to get honorable discharges in the foreseeable future. Worse yet, according to our battalion S-1 (personnel staff), the ROK Army Headquarters, indicated that those

8. Back to the Front

officers who had advanced training in the U.S. would certainly be kept in the army indefinitely! I was dumbfounded. I had never heard of this before, nor had I signed any document that I wanted to become an army officer for life! I was overcome by an immense rage, but soon the rage gave way to a deep sense of despair. I felt like an innocent prisoner who had received a life sentence.

In the late August afternoon, returning to my unit from a furlough in Seoul, my jeep passed a church located in downtown Seoul. I had a sudden urge to go inside. I told my driver, Sergeant Lee, to park in the church compound. It happened to be one of the old Protestant churches in Korea: Yeong Nak Presbyterian Church. I entered the large, quiet church. No one was inside. I sat on one of the pews and prayed for God's help to set me free from the army. Silence was my answer. I got up and walked up to the front podium where a large ornate table was centered against the back wall. On the table was a large, open Bible that was placed in front of a shiny cross hanging on the wall. Soon I found myself looking at the open pages of the Bible, printed in large Korean characters. A passage caught my eyes: "Come to me, all you who labor and are heavy laden, and I will give you rest. Take my yoke upon you, and learn from me; for I am gentle and lowly in heart, and you will find rest for your souls. For my yoke is easy, and my burden is light" (Matthew 11:28–30). I uttered to myself, "This must be the Lord's answer. How comforting and soothing are these words!" I left the church with an inexplicable sense of security and peace.

When I came out of the church, Sergeant Lee looked at me with a sort of puzzled look, as if he was saying, "I did not know you were a Christian." But without a word he got into the driver's seat. I said, "It's a beautiful church. Let's go. I hope to get back to our unit before dark." I never attended church on my own before, except for several occasions when I was invited to visit a local church in Lawton, Oklahoma, with other Korean officers from Fort Sill in 1951–52. But now I was thinking of visiting the church again on my next furlough.

Upon returning to our unit in Simpori, I conducted a series of battalion field exercises in the vicinity of Hwachon Reservoir for a week. In late July 1953, our battalion became a part of the Sixth ROK Division Artillery Group, and I was reassigned to defend the DMZ (Demilitarized Zone) about ten miles north of the Hwachon Dam. The only way to reach this particular stretch of the DMZ was to follow a narrow dirt road weaving through the gorge between two huge mountains (Taesongsan on the left, Paegamsan on the right). Both mountains were 1,200 meters above sea level, which meant that in the mid-summer afternoon we could hardly see the sun most of the time from the bottom of the deep valley. The temperature in the gorge was unusually cool, almost too cold to dip one's feet in the crystal clear stream running along the side of the dirt road. In this beautiful place, my big problem was to find a level spot to deploy our batteries of howitzers. After a number of unsuccessful searches, we finally found three very small, flat and clear areas for our battery positions, but they were not lined up parallel to the DMZ defense line but perpendicular since the valley itself was perpendicular to the DMZ line.

We set up our FDC on the slope of the mountain and fortified the bunker with sandbags. Within a few days we were ready to give fire support to the ROK Sixth Infantry Division, but essentially we had nothing to do unless the enemy invaded, violating the armistice agreement. It was a strange feeling of paradox when we thought of the war as over but not really over. The two boundary lines — the 38th parallel before the war and the cease-fire line (DMZ) — were both imaginary lines. How absurd to realize that for these imaginary lines four million real people perished

Uneventful weeks passed, except for a visit from the deputy commander of the Sixth ROK Division, Brigadier General Chang Jung Lee. I had never met him face-to-face before, but I remembered when he had visited our OP a couple of months earlier and I had conducted a precision fire, successfully destroying an enemy artillery bunker. At that time he was so pleased that he called me on the phone, saying I had done an excellent job. Well, here in the deep valley we met. The general remembered me. A pleasant, heavy set man of about 40, he greeted me, and I was surprised to recognize his aide, Lieutenant

I am standing near my Fire Direction Center close to the DMZ at the Kumsong front in January 1954. Notice the very steep gorge and high mountains that required difficult, high-angle firing. Even in the summer, the average temperature at night was around 25°F.

8. Back to the Front

A happy moment after the cease-fire. But what comes next? Left to right: Lieutenant Chang, Captain Park, Lieutenant Shin, Lieutenant Kim, and Lieutenant Hurh. Near Hwachon, August 1953.

Kim, who had been one of my students when I was a gunnery instructor in the Field Artillery School in Kwangju in 1952. What a happy encounter, but I did not know then that this chance encounter would later change my assignment, which would be the beginning of my turmoil.

The cool summer in the deep valley at the front gave way quickly to winter weather in early September. We had to use oil stoves for heat in the FDC. At night, a lot of animals were attracted to the warmth of our stoves — foxes, boars, bears, raccoons, and such. Or, maybe, even tigers. Who knows? One night as I was sleeping in my quarters — a small cottage built by my soldiers with the wooden boards from the ammunition boxes — I heard something hitting and scratching the wall of my cottage. I jumped up, took hold of a semi-automatic submachine gun, and was ready to shoot. The more I listened to the noise from the outside, the more it sounded less like an enemy assault and more like some animals attracted to the heat. I went back to sleep.

With the cease-fire, the soldier's life in the mountain valley, or rather gorge, was boring and depressing, particularly in the damp and bone-chilling

"I Will Shoot Them from My Loving Heart"

Standing on a frozen lake near the DMZ, Corporal Lee (my driver and on the left) shows me his big catch—a red fox. January 1954.

cold winter of northern Korea. We had virtually nothing else to do, except for some fox hunting, card playing, and cooking something unusual, such as a wild boar. I thought it might be a good time to visit each battery commander in my battalion and get acquainted with them on a more personal term. We had three batteries: A, B, C,—A Battery was commanded by Lieutenant Jung Kyun Shin. He and I shared the most similar background as we both were born in 1932, grew up in Seoul, joined the army as high school seniors, and graduated from the ROK Artillery School. There were, of course, some differences—we went to different high schools in Seoul and he was commissioned as an officer in February 1951, about two months earlier than I was. In contrast, both commanders of the B Battery and C Battery—Lieutenant Jook Hi Kim and Lieutenant Keun Hyung Chang, respectively—were born in North Korea but fled to South Korea with their families several years before the war. Both were a year older than Lieutenant Shin and me, but they were nevertheless high school seniors when they joined the army. They were also the graduates of ROK Artillery OCS—Kim was commissioned in mid–March and Chang in late April. According to the Table of Organization, the position of the battery commander was supposed to be filled by a captain and the position of battalion operation officer (S-3) was to be filled by a major. But we were all first lieutenants, yearning to go home and pursue our own lives since the war was practically over. I enjoyed my visits with them over lunch where we shared our plights and hopes for a better future. I also liked the meals their cooks prepared. For some reason, the food at the battalion headquarters always tasted awful.

Signs of the infamous, bitter cold weather of North Korea started to appear in October. We were going to be snowed-in in our bunkers for several months with nothing to do except maintain our combat readiness. I felt especially sorry for our forward observers on the snowy mountaintops. I thought again about the "perfect" limbo in which we were caught—in a cease-fire but always being ready to shoot. The days and nights of the dreary winter continued in the deep gorges of Paegamsan Mountain near the DMZ. Christmas and the New Year came and went, but we only knew it by the calendar. Holidays were meaningless at the front. Time passed on in theory, but stood still in reality as the bitter cold winter continued. I wished humans could hibernate like bears since there was nothing we could do to change the situation or even to dream for a change.

Changes came nevertheless—good and bad. Mother Nature eventually brought us nice spring weather — the snow was melting, birds were singing, and the wild flowers began blooming — even in these Godforsaken valleys. There was also a bad change, particularly for me. Major H., our battalion commander, told me that he had received an order from Colonel Kang, the commander of our sixth Division Artillery Group, to transfer me to division headquarters for a new assignment as acting chief operations officer (S-3) of the Sixth Division Artillery. I was shocked and exclaimed, "What do you mean? I've never been consulted for this transfer!" We both knew this new position usually required the rank of lieutenant colonel or at least major. I protested, "I'm just a first lieutenant. What is happening?"

Major H. calmly replied with a forced smile, "You are ordered to report to Colonel Kang within three days. Then you'll find out the details, but I heard that the order actually came from General Lee, the division commander. He must have liked you."

I was crushed. What a twisted fate! I did not want the job, whether high-ranking or not. I just wanted out — out entirely from the military as soon as possible. I did my best to serve my country by doing well as an efficient artillery battalion S-3, and now this was what I got as a reward? An acting S-3 of division artillery? Oh Lord, give me a break!

I did not have a choice, however. An order is an order. I packed and left the 76th Field Artillery Battalion where I had served for more than two years on the front. It was painful to depart from my FDC crew, particularly from my most faithful assistants, Lieutenants Lee and Kim. We shared so much together — a genuine comradeship. They became just like my real brothers. I resented this unexpected change. Oh, I hated army life, every minute of it.

In two weeks, I reported to the division artillery commander, Colonel Kang. He was a middle-aged, nervous man who wore a heavy pair of glasses. He said that my assignment was to replace the former S-3 (the chief operation officer) of the division artillery, Major Park, who was on leave for medical treatment. I asked him about my duties as an acting S-3. He said, "Well, the war is over. But what we need is more rigorous training of our soldiers. Your mission is to plan and execute a comprehensive program for training our soldiers." What a boring task I now had. I was depressed.

For a couple of months I tried my best to accomplish what Col. Kang wanted, but it did not work because of the low morale of our soldiers. Not many soldiers understood that the cease-fire agreement did not mean a peace treaty. All they wanted to do was to go home because they thought the war was over. I wanted to go home too. I never signed a contract that I would serve the army for life. I saw many of my fellow Kyunggi High School friends who had either not served in the armed forces, or if they had, they were discharged after less than a year of service. It was unfair, but I felt powerless to change my life's course.

The spring of 1954 gave way to a boring summer at the ROK Sixth Division Artillery Headquarters. I spent most of my time drawing up the retraining and field exercise programs for the three field artillery battalions in our command. It was a tedious and time-consuming job that involved largely paper work and dull meetings. The only break in my daily routine was to oversee the field exercises on the firing range located north of the Hwachon Reservoir (also called Paro Ho, a huge man-made lake stretching 20 miles east to Yanggu).

Finally in the fall of 1954, a newly appointed S-3 for the division artillery, Major Byung Kwan Kim, came to relive me from the temporary acting S-3 job. At first I was glad, thinking that I might be able to return to my old battalion S-3 job, or better yet, to get an assignment close to a large city so that I could attend some evening courses at a local junior college. None of these wishes were answered. My new assignment was to stay in the same office and help Major Kim as an assistant S-3 of the Sixth Division Artillery! I wanted to scream and run away. I went to Colonel Kang for an alternative assignment but to no avail. I began to feel sick and tired of everything.

However, an order is an order. I helped Major Kim as much as I could, particularly on the training and tactical operation of the artillery battalions in our command since he had just come from the infantry after completing a concentrated artillery-training course at Kwangju. He was originally from North Korea and entered the ROK Army Military Academy about a year before the Korean War broke out. He was one of those very few young cadets who survived the Communists' massive onslaught on June 25, 1950.

Major Kim thus gave me the impression of a tough professional soldier, but as we got to know each other I was deeply impressed by his extensive knowledge of philosophy, literature, art and even psychology. On many evenings after work, we discussed Kant, Hegel, Tolstoy, Freud, and so on. I enjoyed his company as we shared many of the same interests, but the more we talked about these non-military topics, the stronger became my desire to be freed from the yoke of the military, which I thought I had carried long enough — plus the war was already over. I felt I rightfully deserved an honorable discharge. I disclosed these feelings to Major Kim one evening after a few drinks together. He quietly listened and said, "I understand your plight quite well. I wish I could help, but I am as powerless as you are. I think you need a break, a long one."

Another fall was fading away and the first snow fell in late October. I stayed up quite late one night working on the field exercise plans. When I awoke the next morning, I felt sick with flu-like symptoms — aching muscles, a stuffy nose, stiff neck and knees, and a slight fever. I went to the surgeon's office and he gave me the usual flu medicine to lower my fever and ease my pain. After taking two weeks of rest, I felt somewhat better but the stiffness in my knees persisted, and I had some difficulty in walking. After rechecking my condition, the division surgeon told me that I might have developed a mild case of rheumatism and sent me to the nearest army field hospital in Chunchon for evaluation, diagnosis, and therapy. I was surprised to hear that one could develop rheumatism at any age. I was only 22 at the time.

The Chunchon Field Hospital was a compound of tents, like the ones shown in the movie *Mash*. I went through a number of tests, but the diagnosis was more or less the same — rheumatism or rheumatoid arthritis. The doctors did not seem to know what therapy to prescribe for my problem, and a couple of weeks later I was transferred by train to the Capital Army Hospital in Seoul. The situation in the Capital Hospital was strange. The huge medical building (formally the Seoul University Hospital) was teeming with patients; to help relieve the crowded conditions, the hospital told mobile patients with minor illnesses to go home and check in once a week. I wondered why the ROK army could not have just given us a chance for an honorable discharge. After all, we got sick while serving the country, and since the war was now over, I bet most of us would have been happy to go home for good rather than stay in an army hospital that did not seem to care about its patients.

Anyway, I was glad to see my family again, although my mother worried about my rheumatism. Following her friend's advice, we went to a well-known Chinese doctor in Seoul. He was a kindly looking, silver-haired man who took my pulse for a long time, examined my tongue, eyes, arms, knees, and legs and gave me his diagnosis. He thought I had symptoms of neuralgia caused by excessive stress, malnutrition, and exposure to a very damp, cold, and sedentary environment over a long period of time. He asked, "What kind of job have you been doing?"

8. Back to the Front

I told him about my military service on the northern front in the deep Kumsong valleys for the past 18 months. As the chief operations officer of the ROK artillery units, I had worked mainly in the underground operations bunker that had been fortified with sandbags — a damp and cold place most of the time. The old doctor used acupuncture on my knees, inserting silver needles in two or three places around my kneecap. After a minute or so, he removed the needles expertly — no pain and no blood. He gave me sacks of herbal medicine and told me to come back in two weeks. My mother seemed to be relieved at having found the cause of my problem. She put the herbs and water in an earthenware pot and placed it over a hot charcoal briquette fire to boil. Although I disliked the taste of Chinese medicine, I could manage to drink it all down over a number of days.

Time passed quickly and February came. I felt much better at home under Mother's care and the Chinese medicine seemed to work. My knee pain was almost gone, and I looked forward to spring and strolling in the park under the cherry tree blossoms. I almost forgot that I was still in the army as an outpatient at the Capital Army Hospital. When I checked in the hospital one day in mid–February, a medical sergeant told me that I was going to be transferred to the 27th Army Hospital in Daegu the following week. I asked him if I could see the doctor since I was getting much better and possibly they could discharge me from the hospital. However, he said the discharge process was usually done at the Daegu hospital since the ROK Army Headquarters were still in Daegue, about 200 miles southeast of Seoul. This didn't make much sense to me, but I did not argue and reported to the hospital at five in the morning as ordered. About 50 patients were carried on stretchers into the train. I told them I could walk, but they insisted that I should be carried. I didn't argue again. What's the use! Again I felt like I was the upside-down beetle in Kafka's novel — an utterly powerless creature.

In the cars of the train, the patients were put in upper and lower bunks that stretched along the window sides — much like the Pullman sleeper train that I took when I was going to Fort Sill in 1951. I looked around and noticed that most of the patients were mobile, except for a few who were injured in accidents or had severe physical disabilities of unknown causes. Included were some suicide attempters who "unfortunately" survived and needed medical care — both physical and psychological. Again I thought about the war being over, but these soldiers and I were not at peace. One of the patients next to my stretcher was a young infantry lieutenant who had a self-inflicted gunshot wound. He slept, or looked like he was sleeping, most of the time. He told me that he wanted to kill himself but did not succeed — and he would try again.

"The reason?" I asked.

"Simply, I couldn't stand any more," he responded.

I pressed him further, "What do you mean?"

He answered with a faint voice, "I want to be free from this damn army life!" I thought I understood him and very well, indeed. But I had never thought of taking such a drastic step in order to get out of the army.

The train had no schedule for departure or arrival and seemed to travel at will when it felt like it. It took two-and-a-half days to reach Daegu. The Army Hospital was far more advanced then any other hospital I had experienced. They took X-rays of my knees for the first time in my life, administered a number of tests, and examined everything thoroughly. All the results indicated that I was suffering from chronic but mild rheumatoid arthritis in my knees and back. The doctor said that they would keep me in the hospital for a month or so with medical evaluation, treatment, and eventually they would discharge me from the hospital but not from the army. At that time I would have to report to the ROK Army Headquarters in Daegu for my new assignment.

I was put in a huge dormitory-type hospital ward with 20 other patients who were expected to be discharged soon. I had nothing to do except read and stroll around the hospital compound, or with permission I could go out to the city for a few hours a day. On a beautiful, sunny day, I decided to visit downtown Daegu and stop by the ROK Army Headquarters to see if someone in the Artillery Personnel Section might possibly have an idea about my fate if I were to be discharged from the hospital in the near future. It was a gorgeous spring day with cherry trees starting to bloom, and I felt invigorated by the vibrant signs of life around me in the downtown streets, although my face looked pale as I saw my reflection in the shop windows.

At the Army Headquarters, I felt like I was in a maze as I tried to find the right person in the right place to answer my questions. Finally when I entered the office of the Artillery Personnel Section, I was pleasantly surprised to see one of my Fort Sill classmates, Lieutenant Colonel D.H. Shin, working there. Although we did not know each other on personal terms at Fort Sill, it was good to see him again. He was my senior in rank and age, and was a professional officer for life. After exchanging a few pleasantries, I came to

8. Back to the Front

the point of my visit. After listening to my story, he was somewhat understanding and acknowledged that I had been through a lot during the war, but he went on to clearly state that any possibility of my discharge from the army in the near future was absolutely zero since I had had advanced training in Fort Sill. He said, "The ROK Army and the U.S. have heavily invested in you."

I replied in frustration, "But I did not know, Colonel. No one told me, nor did I sign any contract or paper indicating that I should serve the army for life before I went to Fort Sill! Even after Fort Sill, I haven't received any formal notice to that effect."

The colonel calmly replied, "Now you know, Lieutenant. Let's not argue. Neither you nor I can do anything about this." Then he abruptly changed the subject by asking if I would be interested in joining the first ROK antiaircraft artillery unit that was going to be established near the Osan Air Base in a few weeks. In fact, he was thinking of joining the unit himself.

I was flabbergasted and said, "I know nothing about antiaircraft artillery. Do you, Colonel?" He said, "No, but we'll be trained, both here and in the U.S. at Fort Bliss." In his view, he thought it would be a challenge but exciting and worthwhile work for our country. I asked if I could have some time to think about it. He gave me until the next day to make a decision because he needed to process my assignment order right away — otherwise I might be assigned any place, even back to the DMZ front or to any artillery unit of the ROK First Field Army. I thanked him and said I would get back to him and left his office.

I had a sleepless night considering what decision I should make. What other options did I have? None. I did not want to go back to the front, whether the DMZ or any areas under the Field Army Command. Neither did I want to join the AAA (Antiaircraft Artillery) when I knew virtually nothing about it. Would I like to go to Fort Bliss, wherever that is? Suppose I finished the training at Fort Bliss; wouldn't that mean my chance for discharge from the army would be doubly difficult or impossible? I might be stuck in the army for the rest of my life. What a fate! I wondered if there was an army in heaven. Or, maybe in hell? Finally I drifted off to sleep at dawn.

The next morning at the breakfast table I thought about my dilemma again. One tiny advantage of joining the AAA in Osan occurred to me. The

Osan Air Base was located about 40 miles south of Seoul, which meant that I would be able to attend evening or weekend courses at a junior college in Seoul. Thinking about the possibility of finally being able to begin my college studies was quite attractive. I decided my fate and called Lieutenant Colonel Shin. He was pleased to hear my decision to join him and promised to process my assignment papers.

In late April of 1955, I was discharged from the 27th Army Hospital in Daegu and ordered to report to the Tenth AAA Group Headquarters at Osan Air Base on May 25, 1954. Thus my six months of hospital life ended. On the train to Seoul, I felt resigned to my fate, saying to myself "*dwel tero dwe ra*" (whatever comes, so be it).

# 9

Antiaircraft Artillery and Fort Bliss

MOTHER WAS GLAD TO see me home again — healthy and sound. She was even more pleased when I told her that I was going to be assigned to an antiaircraft artillery unit located at the Osan Air Base. She did not have the slightest idea about antiaircraft artillery, but she did know Osan was only 40 miles away from Seoul. Both of us enjoyed our reunion for several weeks — a sort of extended furlough between assignments. The home-cooked meals and the warm company of relatives and friends uplifted my spirit, but most of all I appreciated the freedom to be by myself whenever I needed it. I was tired of army life with its lack of privacy. Moreover, I now had the chance to find out the possibilities of attending evening or weekend courses offered by some junior colleges in Seoul.

Again, time went by too fast. On May 25, 1955, I reported to the Tenth Antiaircraft Artillery (AAA) Headquarters at Osan Air Base (called "K-55" by its airfield designation). The air base took its name from "Osan-ri," a small farming village, located about five miles northeast of the K-55 airfield. The airfield was one of the major U.S. military installations in South Korea, built and operated by the U.S. Air Force during the Korean War. It was first operational in December 1952 and served a crucial role in giving vital air support to the UN ground forces, especially when the Communist forces launched massive attacks on all fronts on the eve of the armistice, July 27, 1953.

When I arrived at the Osan Air Base, after a two-hour bus ride from Seoul, I knew nothing about its historical background. I had never been to the village of Osan or the air base, although I remembered passing it occasionally when I was traveling to the south by train. Express trains normally did not stop at the Osan station. The bus I took stopped almost everywhere including the Osan Air Base. No wonder it took more than two hours to travel a mere 45 miles.

As I got off the bus, I was surprised to see the hustling and bustling activities on the road leading towards the main gate of the air base. Crowded along both sides of the paved road were many shops of all sorts, including bars and cafes particularly designed for American GIs. U.S. soldiers guarded the main gate of the base. I approached the main gate in my ROK army uniform, and the guards waved me through. I asked the guard how to get to the ROK Tenth AAA Group HQ. He replied, "Get on any of the trucks that come every 15 minutes and tell the driver that you're going to the Korean Triple A."

The base covered a huge area. I could not imagine how the U.S. Air Force developed the 9,000-foot runway and other facilities in such a short time — and in the middle of rice paddies. I was impressed. The buildings were a combination of wood structures and Quonset huts and included offices, quarters, mess halls, and officers clubs and such. All were built on the small hills adjacent to the airfield. I could not see any antiaircraft artillery batteries from the top of the truck I was on.

When I got to the Korean Triple A Group Headquarters, I was greeted by a young captain in the S-1 (personnel) office, who told me that I was assigned as a radar officer for the Tenth AAA Group and that I was to go immediately to the newly created ROK AAA (90mm gun) Battery located near the village of Osan and participate in the radar training offered by the American advisors there. So I had to turn around and go back to the village I had just passed through two hours before.

Towards evening I got off the bus at Osan-ri, climbed up the hill nearby, and found the ROK 90mm AAA Battery. I could see the antiaircraft guns on the top of the hill and a couple of big trailers with radar dishes on their roofs. I wondered what I was getting into as a radar officer. I knew nothing about radar and was totally uninterested. I wondered, "Is this what I get after two years of bloody service on the front?"

A tall, friendly looking ROK army major came out of the trailer and greeted me, saying "Lieutenant Hurh, welcome to the Radar Club! I am Major Pak." Major Pak was a career officer and the chief of radar operations for our AAA Group. So he was theoretically my boss, at least for now. We lived in two different worlds and were separated not only by rank and job title but also by our life-philosophy — he wanted to stay in the army for life, whereas I wanted out of it.

For a couple of months, Major Pak and I learned the operation of SCR-584 radar, vintage World War II equipment. It used an automatic tracking system so the direction and range information on the target was instantly converted to firing data, which in turn could direct and lay the guns automatically by electronic cables. All the gunners had to do was load the guns and fire. So the major function of the AAA radar officer was roughly equivalent to the mission of the field artillery forward observer — detect and track the enemy target and deliver accurate information for fire direction. For this job, not much tactical strategy was required, but it did need a great deal of mechanical dexterity and a lot of patience. The training sessions seemed at first quite interesting but soon became tiresome and boring because of the repetitive nature of the work, day after day, in the confining space of the trailer. In retrospect, we thought at the time the 90mm gun with the SCR-584 we had inherited from the U.S. Army, was the most advanced antiaircraft weapon not knowing the U.S. had already developed a surface-to-air guided missile system (the Nike Ajax in 1953 and later the Nike Hercules).

Fortunately, however, unlike the assignment on the frontline, every officer in the ROK AAA group had weekends off, except for an occasional on-duty weekend. Most weekends I went home and attended an evening course, Economics 101, at a junior college (Kukjae Daehak) in Seoul. Since the Korean people had suffered from Japanese colonial oppression, the Korean War, poverty, and social dislocation, I was very much interested in studying the economic and political development of Korea. Although it was hectic to take such a "crash" course by commuting, I felt a purpose in life when I was learning something creative and productive, rather than destructive. I still had a faint hope that one day I might be able to graduate from college somewhere.

Finally, the boring eight weeks of radar training ended with a field exercise near the Inchon harbor for tracking and shooting dummy targets in the bright summer sky above the Yellow Sea. Upon returning to the Tenth AAA Group Headquarters at the Osan Air base, I was a bit surprised to hear that Lieutenant Colonel D. H. Shin (my Fort Sill classmate who had arranged my transfer to radar) had already arrived at the air base from Daegu to become the commander of our AAA group. When I entered his office in one of the Quonsets to report my return, he seemed quite pleased to see me and asked how I liked the radar training. I told him the truth that it was a tedious and boring mechanical job. I asked him what my next assignment would be. "Ah, that's just what I wanted to talk about. Major Park can handle the radar job by himself. Where we need your help is in the overall planning and operation of the new AAA batteries, such as the 40mm automatic gun batteries. I want you to work with Major Choi in S-3 (Operations Staff)." I felt like I was born to be a S-3 for my entire life.

Life at the Osan (K-55) Air Base was a new experience for me as a Korean AAA officer. As mentioned, the base was built and operated by the U.S. Air Force. Shortly before I was there, the main user was the 58th Fighter-Bomber Wing of the U.S. Fifth Air Force, and later the 314th Air Division. I heard that U.S. antiaircraft artillery batteries, particularly the 40mm automatic guns, were also deployed within the K-55 compound, as well as 90mm M3 guns in the contiguous areas before the armistice in 1953. But after the cease-fire, the need for the AAA had declined. So we inherited almost everything from the U.S. AAA—weapons, equipment, offices, and officers quarters with showers and toilets. Moreover, we were allowed to enjoy U.S. Air Force Officers Club privileges. For the first time in my life I learned how to play pool. But I often felt sorry for the American officers when the Korean officers monopolized the entire set of pool tables. Moreover, some of our Korean officers bought bottles of major-brand whisky, such as Johnny Walker or I. W. Harper at the officers club and then sold them on the Korean black market for profit. I also recall how the Korean officers liked the American lunch at the club very much, particularly enjoying the ham-and-fried-egg sandwich as a change from Korean food.

The Osan Air Base was thus a self-contained "city" in the middle of rice paddies and scattered farming villages. No civilians were allowed to enter the base except for the air base service workers who had to check in every morning and then check out in the evening at the main gate. Hence married Korean AAA officers who wanted to bring their families had to find a place to live in nearby towns and commute to the base every working day. The nearest town was Seojong-ri, about two miles south of the air base. Since most of us were bachelors, we often went to Seoul for the weekend. I thought it was an ideal situation for attending Saturday classes in Seoul. Eventually, however, I found that the reality of commuting every weekend to Seoul was much harsher than I had imagined. But I carried on.

9. ANTIAIRCRAFT ARTILLERY AND FORT BLISS

At the base, I did mostly paperwork, prepared briefings, and organized meetings for developing the Tenth ROK Antiaircraft Artillery Group to the size of a brigade. I never had a chance to see the SCR-584 radar again or the 90mm guns. I knew so little about the actual operation of antiaircraft artillery, but here I was working to establish an AAA brigade! I thought something was not quite right because I was wasting their resources and they were also wasting my time. Why couldn't the army replace me with an eager career officer and train him in the U.S. for the new ROK AAA Brigade? They would be happy and so would I.

Instead, I was promoted to the rank of captain with some other officers on September 1, 1955. The promotion was not based on a particular merit but merely on the length of service in rank, usually four years of service as a first lieutenant. I was expecting it and was not impressed. I just wanted out.

After several month of the same routine of trying to build the new ROK AAA Brigade, I received a notice about an opportunity to study English in preparation for the possibility of going to America to attend an Associate Antiaircraft Artillery Battery Officer Course at the U.S. Army Antiaircraft Artillery and Guided Missile School in Fort Bliss, Texas. Was this another strange fate in my life? After much thought, I decided to interpret my life-fate in positive terms. I reasoned to myself, "Since it looks like I am destined to serve in the army for life, why not brush up my English, see a different part of the U.S., and maybe become one of the first ROK army specialists in the guided missile program." In retrospect, it was a foolish thought, but I desperately needed to look forward to something. I signed up.

The six-month English course for the ROK officers began on March 19, 1956, at the Army Adjutant School in Daegu. There were 25 infantry and ten artillery officers in the class. I was pleasantly surprised to see Captain Sung Choi, my Kyunggi High School classmate, in our midst. I did not know he too had graduated from the Combined Army Officer Candidate School and was commissioned as an artillery officer several months earlier than I was. So we were in the "same boat" again.

The instructors were Korean army officers whose specialization was to translate/interpret English to Korean and vice versa. We called them "the interpretation officers (*tongyok jangkyo*)." The course was intensive in the sense that it included four hours of lecture and another four hours of lab practice five days a week. The lab gave us a chance to listen and practice

English conversations through audiotapes and was one of the most advanced modern language labs in Korea at that time. Every week we were given a test and repeatedly warned that we could not be sent to the U.S. if we failed the final oral English exam given by the American advisors. The major reason for requiring such a rigorous English course was that the ROK army had discontinued the practice of sending Korean interpreters with the ROK officers for training in the U.S.—like the program in which I had participated with 99 other Korean officers at Fort Sill five years earlier in 1951–52. This time the Korean officers going to the U.S. would be in the same training classes with other American officers.

Strangely, the Adjutant School did not have any lodging for us, although we were allowed to eat in their officers' mess hall. So everyone had to find a place to stay for six months. After a frustrating search together with Captains Sung Choi and Yu Kap Kim (whom I had met at the AAA Headquarters), we rented a room in an old traditional Korean house near the Adjutant School.

The days passed quickly, especially weekdays with their heavy load of class work. On weekends we did some sightseeing around Daegu and Kyongju, the ancient capital of the Silla Kingdom. Attending weekend courses in Seoul for me was now impossible because it was about 200 miles to Seoul and the train ride took more than 12 hours. Captain Choi, however, went to Seoul at least once a month and brought back some tasty *kimchi* (pickled cabbage) and *kochujang* (hot spicy bean mash) to spice up our bland food at the officers mess hall.

As a whole, however, we were bored at Daegu—there was nothing to do besides study. One day an idea came to me about how to use these wasted days. I had had a problem of maintaining hygiene for my penis for many years, particularly at the front as the excessive foreskin caused frequent infections and needed to be cut off (circumcised). One day I read in the local Daegu newspaper that a private health clinic would do the job in 30 minutes at a very reasonable price. I consulted with Captain Choi, and he agreed I should have it done. Early one evening I went to the clinic that was located in the doctor's home. The skinny Korean doctor examined my vital organ and said, "Yes, you need an operation, otherwise, you might lose your thing." I told him to do it right away. He began the procedure with the help of a nurse, who happened to be his wife. But in the middle of the surgery, the power failed and the lights went out. In shock I cried out, "Oh God, what is going to happen now?" It wasn't unusual for the power to go out at that

9. Antiaircraft Artillery and Fort Bliss

time in Korea, but why did it have to happen at this critical time? The doctor calmly told his wife to bring some candles. So under candlelight, they finished my adult circumcision. It was very painful for three weeks, but eventually I recovered from the pain. Although the doctor said he removed the stitches, he must have missed a few as they came out many years later. Nevertheless, the surgery was a success, and thereafter I never had another infection.

Finally, the six months of English lessons came to an end, and a panel of American advisors interviewed us individually to test our oral proficiency in American English. Those who passed the test would be sent to the U.S. military schools in a couple of weeks, and those who failed would return to their former unit as soon as possible. The interview took place in an army tent for some unknown reason. Everyone seemed to become tense while waiting his turn to be tested. But I felt rather calm because it was a not a big deal for me to go to Fort Bliss anyway. I thought I would be really nervous if the test were a scholarship competition for entering one of the best colleges in the United States! While I was waiting, I found myself daydreaming about studying the social sciences at an Ivy League college. Wouldn't it be nice if they set me free from army life altogether? At that moment I heard, "Captain Won Moo Hurh! It's your turn." An American sergeant gestured me to come into the tent.

Three U.S. Army officers were sitting behind a large table — a somber looking middle-aged lieutenant colonel in the middle, a friendly looking major on one side, and a clean-cut but very serious looking captain on the other side. All were looking at me intently, as I stood before them. No handshakes were offered and I wasn't offered a seat. In fact, there was no chair on my side of the table. I felt like I was in a court-marshal. So I smiled, and said: "Good morning, gentlemen." The colonel smiled back, and started to ask me questions. The questions focused on my military experience, particularly on the application of the Fort Sill training to my job at the frontline during the war as the director of the FDC of the ROK 76th Field Artillery Battalion. I told them the effectiveness of training, particularly stressing the importance of the registration fire and calibration of howitzers. However, I emphasized that there was a need to teach the field artillery battalion S-3 how to fire high-angle fire, VT (variable-time) fuse ammunitions, and illumination shells, and to engage in the TOT (time on target) assault missions. One of the panelists, the friendly looking major, asked me, "Captain, what would you be looking forward to if you go to Fort Bliss?" I said I would like to learn about the Nike guided missile. The panelists looked at each other — and said nothing. The colonel said, "Well, that's all, Captain Hurh." I was surprised by the sudden ending of the interview, and yet felt relieved at the same time. I thought I probably failed the test. So be it. The entire interview lasted only about 15 minutes.

The next day the test results were announced. I passed. Captain Yu Kap Kim, our roommate, also passed, but my friend, Sung Choi, failed. I was saddened and shocked because he was such a brilliant fellow in everything, not only in academics but also in sports; he was one of the most celebrated baseball players at Kyunggi High. His father was a prominent lawyer in Seoul but had been abducted by the North Korean Communists in 1950, and the family never heard from him again. I recall visiting Sung's home when I was in Seoul and meeting his mother who was gentle and loving, just like my own mother. I wondered why Captain Choi failed the exam. Choi himself could not figure out the reason either. He spoke better conversational English than I did. Before he came to the Adjutant School to learn English, he served as an aide to General Jae Hung Yu, the chief of staff of the First ROK Army. That meant he had gotten acquainted with many American generals and their aides. Then, why? No one knew. Naturally in the army there is no appeal or questioning of test results.

My dear friend Sung Choi went back to his unit, and I was ordered to report to the Inchon harbor authority to embark on a U.S. military transport ship on October 2, 1956. The ROK Army thoughtfully provided a bus to transport the U.S. bound Korean officers and their family members who would like to see them off at the Inchon harbor (about 25 miles from Seoul). My mother, who was sitting next to me in the bus, expressed her mixed feelings about my trip because she worried that this additional training in the U.S. would prolong my military service and delay any chance for a college education. I told her that I had the same fear, but probably it wouldn't make any difference. With no "*bback*" (the Korean word for power, connection and influence), I could never be liberated from the army anyway. She sighed, looking out the bus window, and said, "How I wish your father were here!"

When we arrived at the Inchon harbor, I was surprised to see we were a relatively small group of only about 50 Korean officers waiting to board a LST (Landing Ship Tank) that would take us to a large military transport ship anchored a mile away. Inchon had never been a good port for ships because of its shallow waterfront.

9. Antiaircraft Artillery and Fort Bliss

The Korean officers bid farewell to their families and friends, took the LST, and boarded the large military transport ship to sail to Sasebo, Japan. On board I found that there were eight Korean officers who had the same destination — Fort Bliss, Texas. As we became acquainted with each other, it turned out that I happened to be the only one in the group who had been to America before (Fort Sill). They expected me to help them to reach Fort Bliss upon arrival in San Francisco.

The voyage from Inchon to San Francisco via Sasebo, Japan, took almost three weeks. Unlike the 1951 voyage, I noticed a lot of American officers' families with young children on board, which made it feel more like a vacation cruise liner; the atmosphere was quite pleasant and the time quickly passed. I met many American and Korean officers on board who were from various branches of the army, marines, and even the navy. From San Francisco we took a train, riding in a Pullman car, and arrived in El Paso, Texas, on October 24, 1956.

A friendly captain met us at the train station and escorted us to the U.S. Army Antiaircraft Artillery and Guided Missile School in Fort Bliss. We were impressed by the vastness of the school compound and the surrounding landscape — a desert-like dry terrain with strange rocks and huge cactuses. Interestingly, we could see some distant mountain ridges to the south and thought they must be near the banks of the Rio Grande, which defines the border between the U.S. and Mexico. Later we found out that the border city of Juarez, Mexico, was only 12 miles away from Fort Bliss.

As we approached the main gate of the Fort Bliss base, we were impressed to see a huge replica of the Nike surface-to-air guided missile displayed near the gate entrance. We were excited over the possibility of learning about a new antiaircraft weapons system beyond the old World War II leftovers, such as the 90mm and 40mm guns. We also passed a replica of the "old" Fort Bliss, which was originally built in the mid–19th century to guard El Paso from Apache and Comanche Indian raids

Our escort led us to a large building called Hinman Hall, the U.S. Army Antiaircraft Artillery and Guided Missile School Headquarters. Another friendly captain gave us a brief orientation to the base, the course schedule, and took us to our quarters. I was surprised to see the plush accommodations — single rooms with attractive furniture and a bathroom for every two rooms! According to the captain, our quarters used to house the WAC officers, but happened to be available for the Allied officers. Lucky for us!

The first Allied officers group to study at the U.S. Antiaircraft Artillery and Guided Missile School at Fort Bliss, Texas. I am in the middle row, second from right. Included are officers from Japan, Thailand, and Korea. 1957.

The classes started a week after our arrival. But I was disappointed. Most of the classes dealt with field-artillery fire direction and gunnery. The course essentially was a repetition of what I had learned in Fort Sill in 1951. The only exception was the extensive training on motor vehicle maintenance. I just wondered why in the world I had to relearn field artillery gunnery at the antiaircraft artillery school? We did not even touch any old World War II vintage antiaircraft weapons, such as the 90mm M3 guns or 40mm automatic weapons. The courses on guided missiles were included in our printed schedule, but all Allied officers were to be "excused" — that meant the missile classes were classified. While our American classmates were attending the highly classified course, we non–Americans (the so-called Allied officers) had free time. Some, including myself, were disappointed at being excluded from studying the new field of guided missiles, but others were glad for the free time. In our Allied officers group, there were two Japanese, one Thai, and eight Korean officers.

9. Antiaircraft Artillery and Fort Bliss

For me our Fort Bliss training was a waste of time. I passed every single test in the course with an A+. The other guys, particularly the American classmates, felt jealous. They wondered how I could always receive perfect scores on every test and thought I was cheating. What nonsense. They should have known that I was a Fort Sill graduate and later a gunnery instructor at ROK Artillery School. What rubbish to spend time and money on me to rehash the old field-artillery techniques that I had already mastered, taught, and practiced on the front during the Korean War as the chief operations officer of a field artillery battalion. In fact, we Korean Allied officers learned nothing new in this so-called AAA Battery Officers Course, No. 3.

In retrospect, it is my conjecture that probably the U.S. Army planned to teach the ROK artillery officers the antiaircraft artillery weapons and gunnery, except the guided missiles, but because of the cease-fire in 1953 and with the overwhelming superiority of the U.S. Air Force and the guided missile systems deployed in the Far East, they might have thought it was no longer necessary to upgrade the ROK antiaircraft artillery. But why had we ROK officers been invited to Fort Bliss for the "antiaircraft" artillery training in the first place? Moreover, I heard from my old frontline buddy, Captain Jung Kyun Shin, that he would follow in my footsteps by joining the second wave of ROK officers scheduled to arrive at Fort Bliss around the time of our group's (the first wave's) graduation. So a second wave of ROK officers were coming to take the same course I took. It didn't make any sense.

Anyway, we graduated from the course, officially titled *Associate Antiaircraft Artillery Battery Officer Course — Class 3,* with 44 other American officers in the Hinman Hall Auditorium, at 1500 hours, Friday, March 8, 1957 — and learned not one thing about antiaircraft artillery. I happened to keep the announcement of the graduation exercises. The commandant of the U.S. Army AAA and Guided Missile School at Fort Bliss was at that time Major General Daniel A. O'Connor.

Just a couple of days before our departure from Fort Bliss, my old-time buddy, Captain Jung Kyun Shin, and his group arrived at Fort Bliss. I was so pleased to see Jung Kyun. Over a few bottles of Falstaff beer at the officers club, we spent hours filling in the three-year vacuum created by my departure from the old 76th Field Artillery Battalion on the Kumsong front where he was the A Battery commander and I was the battalion S-3 (the chief operations officer). I never would have imagined we would meet again in Texas!

Finally, our four-month sojourn at Fort Bliss was over. The Korean officers were instructed to report to Fort Lewis in Tacoma, Washington, by March 12, and scheduled to sail from Seattle by a military transport ship to Inchon, Korea, on March 25. So we stayed in Tacoma for almost two weeks. Not having much to do, I visited Seattle University and inquired if I might have a chance to study there. A very friendly lady at the Registrar's Office said that all I needed was to have proper credentials and immigration papers. She told me the first step was to apply for admission and handed me a thick application packet filled with information and forms. I took the packet, but soon realized that even if I were admitted I would not be able to attend Seattle University. First of all, the army would not let me out. Second, without an American citizen's sponsorship, I could not obtain a visa to the U.S. Third, how could I finance the college tuition, room and board, and other costs? I thought it was just a futile dream, but I kept the application packet just in case.

In a depressed mood, I boarded the Korea-bound military transport ship on a foggy March morning. The voyage on the Pacific was more or less the same as before, except for a chance to get acquainted with a Greek officer, Lieutenant Christos Orfanides, who was assigned to the Greek detachment of the UN forces in Korea. I did not know we still had some UN contingents stationed in South Korea in 1957 — almost four years after the cease-fire.

On April 14, I arrived in Inchon harbor, received my new assignment order, and headed home for a ten-day vacation. With two other officers, I was assigned to the ROK Army Antiaircraft Artillery School in Seojong-ri, located about two miles south of the Osan Air Base, but I was ordered to report to the First ROK Army Antiaircraft Artillery Brigade Headquarters at the Osan Air Base. I was rather surprised at the assignment because I had never heard of the ROK AAA School or the existence of the First ROK AAA Brigade. They must have been developed while I was at Fort Bliss. The Tenth ROK AAA Group Headquarters was the only Korean army unit in the Osan Air Base while I was there before my departure to Fort Bliss.

After the ten-day vacation at home in Seoul, I went to the Osan Air Base by a local bus. There the other Fort Bliss graduates and I met Brigadier General Lee and his staff members, who briefed us on the recent changes and reorganization of the ROK Army Antiaircraft Artillery units. The ROK Antiaircraft Artillery School was one of the newly created units that had been developing at Seojong-ri about two miles south of the Osan base. We were assigned to help develop the unit's training curriculum. It was a big disappointment for us, however, when we found out the status of the so-

9. Antiaircraft Artillery and Fort Bliss

called ROK AAA School. We were approaching Seojong-ri when our jeep driver pointed out several large army tents pitched on the hilly eastside of the town and said, "Sir, that's the AAA School in progress." We climbed the hill and reached one of the tents with its posted sign "S-1, Personnel Office." There we met a very short major waiting for us, who was the commandant of the AAA School. His last name was Choi, a common Korean name, but we later called him Major "Jui," which means "mouse" in Korean. So "Major Mouse" welcomed us. He said he was from the infantry but now was committed to train AAA soldiers. I thought it was ludicrous. It seems no one in the Korean Army knew anything about the antiaircraft artillery!

In retrospect, it was a joke that we three officers from Fort Bliss were assigned to plan a training curriculum to teach AAA Gunnery. How could we plan and teach anything we never learned? So all of our officers taught our AAA soldiers only about field-artillery gunnery as usual and nothing about antiaircraft artillery. When I brought up this problem to Major Mouse, he said, "At this point in time, there is nothing we can do about it. Be patient. Everything needs time." He thought we could use 90mm antiaircraft guns as field artillery pieces and that our noncommissioned officers could also teach 40mm antiaircraft automatic weapons. I was simply dumbfounded.

Time passed with these ridiculous duties. We worked in the tents on the hill during the day and came home to the dingy room we rented in Seojong-ri. After seven years in the army I had advanced to the rank of captain, yet my living accommodations were still primitive. I was depressed and wondered if I could go on with this routine anymore. One day I read in the newspaper and later heard an announcement on the radio that the Korean Ministry of Education would hold a national competition for selecting Korean honor scholarship students to send to college in the U.S. I thought to myself, "Perhaps this might be my God-given chance to continue my studies."

I applied for the competition that required a series of exams to be given on July 5, 1957. I was not sure how to prepare for the exams. I thought I might be asked questions related to my prospective field of study — in English, of course. Since my interest at that time was the political economy of Korea, I was reading various American magazines, such as *Time, Newsweek, Reader's Digest*, and related Korean sources. One day an article written in English caught my eye with the title "The Spirit of American Democracy." (Unfortunately I cannot recall where I found that article and have recently tried to find it, but without success.) I read the article with keen interest because it dealt with the separation of powers, and yet it stressed the functional interdependence among the three branches of the American government — the legislative, the judicial, and the executive. I thought that was the soul of American democracy — *e pluribus unum* ("out of many, one"). That meant also the ethnic diversity of the American people from all over the world would unite together in the spirit of American democracy — "equality for all."

The exam date for the international scholarship was approaching, but I told no one, including my mother, about it because I was afraid of my possible failure. I had never failed an exam in my life. God had helped me, I thought. However, I felt some anxiety when I sat down to take the written test in a room with many other applicants. The test dealt mainly with English comprehension and grammar, and with the applicant's major area of study. My specialty was political science. I was astounded at the final and most important question on the test: "Write an essay on the topic American Democracy in three pages." What a coincidence! Well, it was a piece of cake for me, thanks to the article I had read not long ago, "The Spirit of American Democracy." I wrote four pages for the essay in 30 minutes.

After the test, I tried not to dwell on it, as I was still afraid of my failure. I heard a rumor that there were about 2,000 applicants. If true, I thought my chances were nil. Anyway I tried my best. That's life. A couple of weeks later, I received a letter from the committee chair of the Study Abroad Ministry of Education indicating that I had passed the exam! I could hardly believe my eyes. I felt that God did care about me after all. I shared the good news first with my mother. She was overjoyed, but asked if the army would let me out. That, indeed, was the million-dollar question. I told her, "I don't know, Mom. I'll cross that bridge when I am close to it — it's a long journey and this is my first step." She sighed.

I did not have to break the news to my friends. The national media did it for me in the following days. Nearly all the newspapers in Seoul announced the names of the 21 Honor Scholarship candidates who were selected. Many people sent me congratulatory messages and asked me what school I was going to and when. It was another good question for which I had no answer. The letter from the Ministry of Education contained a formal certificate, with a big seal, stating that I passed the qualification examination for studying abroad. No other details were in the letter. A few days later, when I asked

9. Antiaircraft Artillery and Fort Bliss

the Ministry of Education about the details, I was told that it would take several months for the committee to decide who was going to what school and when. They needed to work with the prospective American colleges and universities for various scholarship possibilities for each selected candidate. Mrs. Charlotte D. Meinecke, the U.S. advisor to the Committee on Study Abroad, was the chief coordinator for this task. I thought the process might take almost a year to make 21 scholarship arrangements for the selected candidates.

The initial excitement had slowly waned as time passed, and the dull routine continued at the AAA School. In early August, Captain Shin, my old buddy, returned from Fort Bliss, and we rented a better apartment together on the second floor of a Japanese-style house overlooking the market place in Seojong-ri. I told Shin about my luck of passing the national scholarship exam for studying abroad. His reaction was similar to my mother's, and he asked, "What good is it if you can't leave the army?"

I replied, "How about my requesting a long leave of absence, giving them a promise to return?"

My buddy laughed loudly and said, "Impossible — not even probable, unless you have some clout in the ROK Army Headquarters."

That gave me an idea. Perhaps I could find some clout if I were transferred to army headquarters. I went to Seoul on the following weekend. My plan was to contact my old Kyunggi High School friend, Captain Sung Choi, who had been serving many generals as an aide-de-camp in the First ROK Army Headquarters and later in the Office of the Army Joint Chiefs of Staff. After many unsuccessful tries, I finally contacted him. I told Sung about my problem and asked him if he could help me transfer to the ROK Army Headquarters in Seoul. Surprisingly he said, "I can't promise you, but I'll give it a try." He explained there might be a good chance for me to work in the Office of the Secretary for the General Staff (SGS) at the ROK Army Headquarters. Since General Sun Yup Paik's appointment as the new ROK Army chief of staff in May 1957, a lot of personnel changes were taking place, and his assistant secretary, Colonel Kwan Young Kang, was looking for a couple of young operations officers for the SGS, preferably from the artillery branch. Sung said he would put in a good word for me.

A couple of weeks passed but no word came from either Sung or the ROK Army HQ. I was almost ready to give up, but then, in early September 1957, the First ROK Army AAA Brigade Commander, Brigadier General

"I Will Shoot Them from My Loving Heart"

Lee, called me to his office. I wondered what was happening. General Lee did not look happy but not angry either. The first words he said were, "Captain Hurh, you are transferred to the Army Headquarters by the order of the ROK Army chief of staff, General Paik. He wants you to report to his chief secretary, Major General Hyung Tae Moon, as soon as possible. You can leave us today, if you wish. No paperwork is necessary — the Army HQ will take care of it. Good luck!" I thanked him and left the AAA for good. For the first time in my life I felt the astonishing power of clout in the bureaucratic organization. It's fascinating but scary.

10

Serving the Top Brass

THE REPUBLIC OF KOREA Army Headquarters was located in the southern part of Seoul near the Han River. The large compound of red brick buildings was originally built and occupied by the Japanese Imperial Army, but at the end of World War II, the occupancy changed to the U.S. Eighth Army and changed again later to the Republic of Korea Army. I was assigned to the office called the SGS (Secretariat for the General Staff) located on the first floor of the Central Administration Building near the front gate. The "General Staff" meant the four major branches of staff members (G1–personnel, G2–intelligence, G3–operations and training, and G4–logistics) serving the ROK Army chief of staff, General Sun Yup Paik. General Paik was the first four-star general in the ROK Army who became the ROK Army chief of staff for the second time in May 1957. His first tour as army chief had been from July 1952 to February 1954. General Paik was one of the most respected and decorated generals in the ROK Army. I had never met him in person, although we were fighting the war on the same eastern front in the spring and summer of 1951—he as the commander of ROK I Corps, but I merely as a forward observer for a heavy mortar company in the ROK 11th Division under his I Corps command. He was then a major general and I was a second lieutenant.

The four-star general's office was located on the second floor of the Central Administration Building of ROK Army Headquarters, and I, Captain Hurh, was to work in a first floor office of the same building with other members of the SGS. Major General Hyung Tae Moon headed the SGS office and his deputy was Colonel Kwan Young Kang. Both of them had worked with General Paik very closely for many years. The former served as the G-3 (operations staff) and the latter as the chief secretary for General Paik while he was the commander of the ROK First Field Army prior to his appointment as army chief. I was quite impressed to see how an interpersonal network operated and impacted one's job assignment. I began to learn a sociological lesson, so to speak: Ability is a necessary but not a sufficient condition to produce job mobility. One needs an opportune chance and good personal connections in addition to one's ability and effort. In retrospect, I learned, indeed, a hard lesson in the ROK Army—"Find or create chances where your ability would work best for you in the long run. If not, accept it as fate." It's easier said then done.

On the sunny morning of September 10, 1957, I passed through the MP guarded main gate of the ROK Army Headquarters and within a five-minute walk reached the Central Administration Building, again guarded by two MPs. I was directed to the main SGS office on the first floor where I was supposed to report my arrival for duty to Colonel Kang, the deputy secretary of the ROK Army chief of staff. When I entered the office, I was rather surprised to see a quite large open-spaced office with about 15 officers at their desks. It looked like a busy newspaper editorial office. At the center of the office, I recognized an artillery colonel—a very cold and nervous-looking man. He was Colonel Kwan Young Kang, a man I had never met before. I saluted him and extended my hand. There was no smile on his face as he shook my hand.

Colonel Kang then led me to the office of General Hyung Tae Moon to report my arrival. Major General Moon was a middle-aged, genteel-mannered man with a big smile who spoke with the heavy accent of Jolla Province (southwestern Korea). "Welcome to the SGS!" He looked like a kind grandpa rather than a major general of the army. His office was also large with an assistant, Major Nam, and two female secretaries. I was then introduced to the staff members of the SGS in the main office: the administrative secretary (Major H. J. Shin) and his staff, the conference and ceremony coordinators (Captains Kee Ju Lee and Hei Chu Kim), and the citation officer (Major T.H. Ku) and his staff.

All of these people looked friendly, and I felt quite at ease with them, except for Colonel Kang. He said I was going to be the transportation coordinator for the SGS. The SGS had three L-19 airplanes (a Cessna type of light plane) and ten jeeps at its disposal, and I was responsible for coordinating their use mainly by high-ranking generals and their guests. But eventually I

10. Serving the Top Brass

leaned that my tasks were not always so clear-cut. When things got busy, everyone had to pitch in wherever it was needed. My artillery training wasn't much help in this office. I had to learn the maze of army bureaucracy by swimming through its intricate channels. For example, what would you do if a member of the ROK National Assembly called you for an airplane to visit a place that had nothing to do with the ROK Army? Or how about an army general who asks for a jeep to transport his family for a private trip? I was tired of going through these hurdles and begged Colonel Kang to change my job assignment. Surprisingly, he understood my plight and changed my duty to citation officer. This job was easy and psychologically rewarding. What I had to do was type appreciation letters in English in the name of General Sun Yup Paik to meritorious American and UN Force officers for their distinguished services to the Republic of Korea and mail them with the appropriate citation plaques or arrange for special presentation ceremonies in the office of General Paik, the chief of staff, ROK Army.

The staff members in the SGS helped each other very well. One day I was asked to fill in for our conference coordinator, Captain Hei Chu Kim, who was absent because of a cold. I was amazed to experience how tedious and complicated Captain Kim's job was when I had to arrange the seat assignments for the generals in the upstairs conference room. There were more than 150 generals and their seats had to be arranged according to their rank, date of promotion, length of service, and so on. And of course, everything had to be up-to-date. If the seating was wrong, there would be trouble as the generals were extremely sensitive to status.

Anyway, I was content with my job of handling citations, but I was given an additional assignment — to manage Colonel Kang's steel office cabinet. I was ordered to sit next to Colonel Kang, and his steel cabinet was located right behind my desk. I was to arrange Colonel Kang's things in order, such as his paper files, office supplies, documents, and mysterious packages. Quite frequently some of Colonel Kang's visitors — usually civilians — left small packages, about ten by six inches. I was told by the colonel to keep them in the steel cabinet and to give them to his jeep driver at the end of the day. I wondered what was inside, but decided it was none of my business.

I was more concerned about my aimless army life. I appreciated the chance to attend evening courses at a local junior college in Seoul, but I was anxious to know what was happening regarding my winning the national scholarship competition to study in the U.S. As I got to know my fellow officers at the SGS more closely, I discovered that Captain Hei Chu Kim, who worked in the Conference and Ceremony Section, was in the same boat with me. He also was one of the winners of the national scholarship for study in the U.S.! We felt fortunate to have found each other so we could face our common problems and fate together. In retrospect, we didn't have the slightest idea that our common fate would make us close friends for the next 21 years.

Hei Chu Kim was the son of a Presbyterian minister, a refugee from North Korea, and had been a student at Dae Gwang High School in Seoul. When the Korean War broke out, he joined the ROK Army as a communication (interpretation) officer. He had an excellent command of English. His wife, Hyung Ja Paik, was a music student at Ehwa Women's University. They were married just a year before I was assigned to the SGS, ROK Army Headquarters.

Hei Chu and I shared a common plight — mainly how to deal with the problem of getting an honorable discharge from the ROK Army so that we could go to school in the U.S. as honor scholarship students, as recommended by the Korean Ministry of Education. First, we needed an admission letter from our prospective college or university to initiate the tedious bureaucratic process. We inquired about this by calling the Ministry of Education, but nobody knew what was going on. We almost gave up our dream of studying in the U.S., thinking it was just like a futile bubble in the vast ocean, as Buddhists would say.

Moreover, when the year turned to 1958, our SGS office became busier than ever because of the volatile conditions in Vietnam. On a Sunday in late March, I was on weekend duty as the officer at the SGS. Around 3 P.M., I received a call from an official at Kimpo Airport reporting that 25 Vietnamese officers had just arrived and were looking for a representative from the ROK Army Headquarters to receive them. The airport official said that the ROK Army chief of staff had invited them to Korea, but no one was there to greet them! I was shocked. I was never informed about their arrival. Apparently, someone goofed — either from the Vietnamese or the Korean side. I immediately called Colonel Kang's residence, but no one answered. It was the same case with General Moon (secretary to the general staff, ROK Army Headquarters). It seems they were all out for a picnic on a sunny spring day to enjoy the cherry blossoms.

10. Serving the Top Brass

I had to make a decision instantly. I ordered the commander of the ROK Army HQ Company to arrange a lodging place for the 25 officers and to provide transportation (an army bus) immediately. Within half an hour, I left for Kimpo Airport in my jeep, accompanied by the bus that was to pick up the Vietnamese officers. The airport was about 20 miles away, but it usually took 30 to 40 minutes to get there. Upon arrival, I could feel the Vietnamese officers' disappointment. I imagined that they expected a ceremonious welcome when they stepped off the plane. Instead, after a long, confusing wait, a lowly captain in a jeep greeted them with an army bus. I sensed they felt they were not welcome. In spite of my forced, big smile, the leader of the visiting group, a middle-aged colonel, didn't look very happy to see me. I apologized for my delayed reception and escorted everyone to the bus. Later I was told by Colonel Kang that it was not our mistake — the Vietnamese officers had mistakenly arrived a day early. But who knows? I could not believe either party.

Anyway, I was proud of my impromptu accomplishment. I successfully escorted them to a decent accommodation without any major problems and pleasantly reported the outcome to my boss, General Moon, at his residence in the evening. At first he was shocked to hear of the Vietnamese officers untimely arrival but immensely relieved to learn that I had taken care of everything as the officer of the day is expected to do. He repeatedly thanked me and said what a wonderful job I had done. However, that night I could not make contact with my immediate supervisor, Colonel Kang. The next morning when Colonel Kang learned of the event, he just asked: "Did the Vietnamese colonel ride with you in your jeep or in the bus with the other junior officers?"

I replied, "In the bus, of course."

He said, "No, that's not right. He should have been in your jeep."

I was surprised but later admitted my oversight. You have to honor the ranks in the army — a cardinal rule in any army. So went my stupid army life, and I was indeed getting sick and tired of it. I couldn't help wondering what had happened to my honor scholarship to study in the U.S.

Eventually fate began to turn in my favor. In early April 1958, I received a letter from Glen Rankin, director of admissions at Monmouth College in Illinois, notifying me that I had been awarded a full tuition scholarship; however, I had to meet other expenses, such as room and board. He enclosed the so-called I-20 Form that I had to fill out to apply for a student visa at the Consular Section of the U.S. Embassy in Seoul as soon as possible. Registration for the fall semester would begin September 15, 1958, and I should arrive in Monmouth not later than that date. The first part of Rankin's letter did not pose much of a problem. My mother was willing to support me for my room and board, but the second part of the letter was a big problem for me because the I-20 Form required documentation of my sponsorship by a U.S. citizen. The sponsor had to sign an affidavit guaranteeing that I would not become a public charge during my stay in the U.S. This meant I had to find an American citizen who would be willing to post a bond, if necessary, should I become a public charge by violating the civil and/or criminal laws during my sojourn in the United States of America.

My friend at the SGS Office, Hei Chu Kim, received a similar letter from the University of North Dakota in Grand Forks. We did not know how to tackle this seemingly impossible task of finding a sponsor, but one thing was clear to us that each of us had to do it in his own way and damn quick. The clock started ticking, but I had no idea where to begin. I wrote to some of the American officers in the U.S whom I had met on the front or at Fort Bliss, but as I expected, there was no reply. I don't blame them — who would like to assume such a heavy responsibility for sponsoring someone you just happened to have met under the accidental circumstances of war?

As the days passed without any progress, I felt increasingly helpless. To make my situation worse, I had to spend a week in the Capital Army Hospital for an appendectomy and another week for home rest. Watching my demoralized status at the hospital and at home, my mother lamented one day: "How I wish your father was with us so he could help you by pulling some political strings to find an American sponsor." She thought that one of his many Korean friends might have known some Americans willing to sponsor a ROK Army officer who had been competitively selected by the Ministry of Education as an honor scholarship student for study abroad. Her voice was softly trailing off and tears were welling in her eyes. I could not stand looking at her any longer. I looked down. At that moment she exclaimed loudly, "Why couldn't I think of it before? I better talk to Mr. Sang Jin Yun, your father's best friend." Mr. Yun had been very active in working for Mr. Kwan Shik Min's successful election campaign for a seat in the Korean National Assembly. Now, as a member of the National Assembly, Mr. Min might be able to help me in someway to find an American sponsor. Mom decided to phone Mrs. Yun because in Korea it would not be appropriate

10. Serving the Top Brass

for her to ask a favor directly of someone's husband. However, she needed to find their phone number because they had recently moved to the East Gate area. With this positive possibility, Mother gave me a smile, a sweet smile that I hadn't seen for a while.

Many years ago the Yuns were our next-door neighbors while I was in elementary school. In fact my siblings and I grew up together with their children as playmates in the same neighborhood. Mr. Yun was in a similar business (farm equipment) as my father. I can still recall them often coming home together late in the evening after work and after a "happy hour," and coming to me to check on my progress in writing Chinese calligraphy. Yun was an avid connoisseur of Chinese calligraphy.

The following morning Mother was in a very happy mood when she told me to get ready to meet with Mr. Yun at his newly acquired home near Seoul's East Gate. She had made contact with the Yuns, and he said he would do his best to help me. Mr. Yun asked me to come to his house in the evening and bring my resume and the documents related to my honor scholarship and any other relevant papers.

We were excited to see Mr. Yun. The last time we saw him was at my father's funeral in August 1946—12 years ago. In those 12 years so much had happened. But most of all, the Korean War disconnected us from everyone and everything. However, my mother and Mrs. Yun managed to reconnect again after the war.

Mr. and Mrs. Yun greeted us in their living room. Both of them showed little sign of aging except for some gray hairs—they must have been in their 60s then. Over tea and cake we talked for a couple of hours. After listening to my problem in detail, Mr. Yun decided to contact his friend in the National Assembly, Kwan Shik Min, for help and promised to let me know the outcome within a couple of weeks or so. We expressed our heartfelt gratitude and left the Yuns. Mother was elated, and I felt hopeful.

A week passed and then another, but no news came from Mr. Yun. Finally in the third week, Mr. Yun brought us the good news that his National Assembly–member friend had found a potential American sponsor for me— Mr. Johnstone, a former vice president of Merck & Co. whom Mr. Min had met while on his official tour in the U.S. a year before. Mr. Yun said: "You're very lucky. After learning you are one of the Kyunggi High graduates as written in your resume, Mr. Min went an extra mile to help you out. Did you know that Mr. Min is also a Kyunggi alumnus?" I did not, but later I found out that he graduated from Kyunggi High in 1937 — fourteen years before my class of 1951. Again I was reminded that personal connection is the *sine qua non* for social mobility, particularly in Korea at that time. Who you know was often more important than what you know for improving your life chances.

I do not recall in detail, but Hei Chu Kim also found an American sponsor — probably through church networks since he and his wife were very active in the Presbyterian Church. So Hei Chu and I were slowly jumping over one hurdle after another, and almost everything was taken care of except for the passport and visa applications for studying abroad. But we had one more tremendous hurdle to overcome. We had to leave the army first. Hei Chu and I filed applications at the G-1 (personnel) office at the ROK Army Headquarters for honorable discharges so we could study in America as national honor scholarship students. About three weeks later, we were called into the G-1 section office for an interview. A fat colonel asked us what would be our major areas of study at our prospective colleges in the U.S. Hei Chu said sociology at the University of North Dakota, and I said economics at Monmouth College. Hearing this, the SOB colonel (I forgot his name but we called him Colonel SOB thereafter anyway) suddenly stood up from his chair and shouted at us: "You mean you are going to study a civilian subject for your private knowledge? You are still army officers. Unless you plan to study military subjects, we cannot allow you to go abroad! Your application is denied!" We were dumbfounded. I said, "Sir, that's why we would like to be discharged from the army. We are not pursuing any military knowledge or skills. We have served the ROK army for more than seven years, and the war is now over. We did more than our share of military service for our fatherland. Now we would like to leave the army and pursue our own academic interests. There are many ways to serve our country besides the army, sir!"

We left the SOB colonel's office with a sour taste in our mouths. Now what should we do? We decided to meet with our boss, General Moon, and ask for his help. The next morning we pleaded our case to General Moon and appealed for his influence over the G-1 office's decision. The general was very sympathetic about our plight and promised he would try his best to find a solution. A couple of weeks later the general called us in and said he and the G-1 general (not Colonel SOB) found a compromise — to grant us a leave of absence with pay for a year to study whatever subjects we wished in the U.S.! The leave of absence would be effective on August 1, 1958.

10. Serving the Top Brass

A paid leave of absence for a year to attend a college in the U.S.? Then what would happen after a year? I thought it was crazy. Plus, the "paid" leave of absence was practically a joke as our monthly salary at the time was about 30 dollars or less. Well, we did not have much choice but to get going and thought eventually we would cross the one-year bridge when we got to it. Many things could happen within a year, we hoped. We knew there was no other option available for us to take than to accept our fate and the one-year leave of absence.

Having overcome a series of barriers, now things moved along quite rapidly. Hei Chu and I were relieved from our duty at the ROK Army Headquarters on August 1 and received our visas from the U.S. Embassy in Seoul. We made our reservations to depart from Kimpo Airport by a propeller-driven Pan American Airways plane for the United States on September 13, 1958. Our immediate families and close friends came to the airport to see us off on a sunny fall afternoon. At that time Kimpo Airport consisted of just one runway and a temporarily built passenger terminal that resembled an army field office. We boarded the plane by a mobile stairway, and when we got in our seats we could see our family members and friends through the plane window. My eyes were drawn to my mother's face, and I could see Hei Chu's eyes were fixed on his wife, Hyung Ja. As the plane started moving, the crowd of family and friends remaining behind began to wave their hands. Tears started welling in my eyes. I could see through the plane window my mother and Hyung Ja were wiping their tears with handkerchiefs.

I wondered if this adventure was worth it at all. When could I finish my studies and return? Four years, eight years? Or would we have to come back next year when our leave of absence expired? The sorrow of departure from my loving family and the extreme anxiety about an unknown future did not last long. It soon gave way to an exhilarated feeling of liberation as soon as the Korean peninsula disappeared from my sight. A feeling of relief overwhelmed me.

So Hei Chu and I were free at last to study in America in 1958 — at least for a year we thought. To our happy surprise, however, in the following year we received an official document (Defense Ministry Order No. 312) in the mail from the Ministry of National Defense, Republic of Korea, indicating that we were honorably discharged from the Republic of Korea Army as of July 31, 1959! Receiving the news, I could have danced in the street and sung in the rain all night long in Monmouth, Illinois, and probably Hei Chu

Farewell party before my departure for Monmouth College in the United States. My Kyunggi High School classmates treat me at a Chinese restaurant. I'm sitting at the head of the table. August 1958.

could have done likewise in Grand Forks, North Dakota. After all, God knew our sacrifice — seven long years in the prime of our lives consumed by the army. We just needed patience.

God seemed to help us even after our discharge. Hei Chu finished his study with a Ph.D. in sociology at the New School for Social Research in New York, and I finished my Ph.D. in sociology and ethnology at the University of Heidelberg in Germany. Later we both somehow ended up as professors in the same Department of Sociology and Anthropology at Western Illinois University in Macomb, Illinois. What an incredible coincidence! Or was it God's providence? Deo gratias!

Epilogue

Now I am a 78-year-old retired professor trying to sort out my past memories for future generations so that I can send them a message that war is an institution of senseless killing invented by Homo sapiens, whether it is an offensive or a defensive war. In fact, in modern warfare the difference between "offense" and "defense" is very murky — the two concepts are often tautological. Think of the recent popular euphemisms — "preemptive strike" or "regime change!" They simply mean, "we are invading your country because you might attack us in the near future. So, in order to defend ourselves, we have to attack you now before you attack us." And further, "we want to replace your head of state at our will, so that you could become more like one of us."

Hence, a group of people can create their own imaginary enemy based on their perception of a threat from the other group, whether it is real or just imagined. Compared to other living creatures, humans are rather good at this image construction thanks to their superb cognitive faculty of using abstract symbols, such as language, writing systems, scientific technology, and most of all, religion and ideology. An ideology is one's subjective idea or image about objective reality; it's not necessarily an objective reality itself. It is the picture of reality in one's mind, but the picture is also a collective product of a social group whose values one has internalized. According to my readings in anthropology, ethnology, and sociobiology (e.g., Desmond Morris, Robert Ardrey, Edward Wilson), animals also attack other groups of animals (usually inter-species aggression, rather than intra-species aggression) for food and/or defending their offspring and territory, but a deliberate preemptive attack against an "imaginary future enemy" without actual provocation and a perception of imminent danger is very rare.

Furthermore, another ubiquity among all human groups — whether "civilized" nations or "primitive" tribes — is to invoke the name of their group's most Sacred Almighty (e.g. God, Allah, Kami, T'ien, Hannun-nim, Manitou, and so on) for justifying the destruction of their enemies as a "holy" mission. One does not have to hunt far for historical evidence, such as the Crusades or the *kamikaze* fighters, to understand the unimaginably dreadful nature, extent, and consequence of glorifying war as a holy mission given by the Almighty. Recently, the entire world could see vividly on the TV screen the glaring example of carnage in Iraq and Afghanistan being generated by a war between Islamic fundamentalism and Christian ethnocentrism.

When I started writing this epilogue, my eye was caught by the title "GOD & WAR," printed on the cover of *Newsweek* for May 7, 2007. I found the following passages by Evan Thomas and Andrew Romano in their article, "In God They Trust," most insightful:

> Still, faith in "American exceptionalism"—and God's alleged recognition in the eyes of some that we are indeed exceptional—has inspired our leaders to wage wars that, with the benefit of hindsight, seem anything but just. Believing, as Bush put it last Fourth of July, that "freedom is the gift of God," the president has made it his mission, and America's to spread liberty and democracy far and wide—by force of arms, if necessary [*Newsweek*, May 7, 2007, 36].

I shudder whenever I hear some U.S. leaders saying words like "liberation" or "spreading democracy" when what is really meant is "invasion" or "conquest" of another sovereign nation they don't like. When Premier Kim Il-sung, the North Korean dictator, invaded South Korea in 1950, he used similar words for justifying his invasion by claiming that his People's Army had a historically righteous mission to "liberate" (*haebang*) South Korea from Syngman Rhee's regime so that the divided Korean peninsula could be unified into one Korea under the banner of the "Democratic" (*minju*) People's Republic of Korea, i.e. North Korea!

In my view, there is no such thing as a "holy" or a "righteous" war in and of itself. All I know and feel through my own war experience is that war in general is the most diabolic manifestation of the human predicament. **Simply put, war is hell.** You cannot imagine its atrocities unless you *personally* experience it. For those who are in combat at the front, war is not an abstract institution of political games but a serious existential reality of one's own life or death.

Hence, war is very personal. If you are at the front, confronting a life-and-death situation, many abstract concepts, such as patriotism, fighting for freedom, democracy, the fatherland, to save the world, and so on, simply disappear. What remains in you is a cardinal desire to keep yourself alive and to save your comrades near you, even at the cost of your own life. By saving your buddies, you are also going to be saved. During the Korean War, I observed that soldiers fought primarily for each other and not for an abstract collective ideology. The morale of the soldiers at the front is thus heavily dependent on their very concrete existential reality — their close personal ties with comrades in arms for mutual survival — rather than on their devotion to an abstract ideology of war.

Frankly speaking, what I observed and experienced during the Korean War was that most of the soldiers and officers, including myself, fought in the war because: (1) there was no other option available to us than to join the armed forces — military service has always been compulsory for all eligible young men in Korea then and now; (2) we did not want to die in the battlefield; (3) we wanted to save our families; (4) we wanted to save our comrades and take revenge against those who killed our comrades and our families; (5) we wanted to end the war so that we could go back home to our families as soon as possible; and lastly (6) we wanted to eradicate the Communist invaders who ruined the lives of millions including our own. And that was exactly how I felt on the battlefields of the Korean peninsula during 1950–53.

How about other wars before the Korean War, for example, World War II? A monumental social psychological study was done on the attitudes and adjustment of American soldiers during World War II. The study was published under the title *The American Soldier: Adjustment During Army Life* (1949), edited by a prominent sociologist, Samuel Stouffer, and his associates. The book happened to deal with a most relevant question: what motivated American soldiers to fight during World War II? By conducting and analyzing more than 600,000 interviews with soldiers during and after World War II, Stouffer's research team concluded in general that the American soldiers kept fighting for two major reasons: (1) to get it over so that they could go home; and (2) their strong personal ties with their comrades in arms (buddies). These are indeed very personal reasons (family and friends) — not the ideological justification or the professed national aims of the war at all. They fought the war mainly for their own primary group, to use a sociological term — that is a small, face-to-face, intimate social group, such as the family, close friends, and comrades in arms. Even the German *Wehrmacht* soldiers under Hitler fought not primarily for their *Vaterland* (fatherland) or the *Führer* but for their primary group ties, according to another well-known study done by two military sociologists, Edward Shils and Morris Janowitz (Shils and Janowitz 1948, 280–315).

Also I learned from various studies done on the German army during World War II that German troops were organized based on their soldiers' geographic origins — where the soldiers came from: such as the Mannheim Company, Heidelberg Battalion, Frankfurt Regiment, and so forth. In fact, the Japanese Imperial Army had a similar way of troop composition mainly based on the soldiers' native towns/cities, such as Nara Company or Kyoto Battalion. They all knew that their soldiers' combat effectiveness would be greatly enhanced by the soldiers' feelings of group solidarity when they came from the same hometown or region — again primary-group ties.

During the Korean War, the primary group ties among South Korean soldiers were forged by their common urgency for defending their families and buddies. Moreover, for the young officers of my cohort — the "baby lieutenants" aged 18 to 19 — there was an additional deeply felt common bond among us because we were all high school seniors or college freshmen. Unlike our superiors, our life goals were set elsewhere rather than becoming a general or a colonel in the armed forces. Most of us never wanted to become professional army officers for life, but had to make a choice between two options when the war broke out — whether to become a private first-class enlisted man by conscription or to become a second lieutenant by taking the three month "express training course" at the Officer Candidate School. It was not much of a choice. Thus we shared a common life fate (*Lebensschicksal*) — the "*somo jangkyo*," the officers *to be consumed* on the battlefields right after their commission.

We also felt we were special in the sense that we were pure and innocent and even naive — free from corruption, unlike some of our senior professional officers. We felt we were some sort of sacrificial lambs, fighting the war for their glory. They were the career officers out for money and power, but we were largely "drafted" officers to be consumed as infantry platoon leaders or artillery forward observers at the battlefront. We felt our youth was literally "consumed" by the war. For that, we resented the war and hated the Communists who caused the war. I felt lucky to have survived the war, but I deeply resented the war that wasted the prime seven years of my life. This feeling of resentment was the common bond among the company-grade officers during the Korean War, particularly the graduates of the Army Comprehensive

School of Officer Candidates (Yukgun Jonghab Hagkyo) whose casualty rate was 60 percent — the highest rate among any officers' group in Korea at that time. But we accepted that as fate, and we kept fighting — for each other.

How about the wars after the Korean War, such as in Vietnam and Iraq? The story was more or less the same. A prominent military sociologist at Northwestern University, Charles Moskos, studied the American soldiers who fought in the Vietnam War and arrived at the same conclusion that soldiers fight primarily because of the close personal bonds with their fellow soldiers (Moskos, 1970). Moreover, he advanced a hypothesis that the intense primary group ties among soldiers at the front might not necessarily come purely from their "buddy relationships," but rather from their *own survival instinct*, that is — by saving your comrades, you are going to be also saved because they are going to save you when you are in danger. In short, they are mutually interdependent for their survival at the battlefront. Thus, it has eventually become clear to me that ideology alone is not a necessary and sufficient cause as a strong combat motivation for soldiers, but the primary-group cohesion among soldiers is. Empirical studies done on the major wars in the past century have consistently confirmed it.

A most recent study on the combat motivation of soldiers in the Iraq War in 2003 also identified the strong social cohesion and personal bonds between soldiers as the prime cause for U.S. soldiers to fight. However, it also claims to have found that ideological factors, such as freedom, democracy, and liberty, also played a crucial role in motivating American soldiers to fight in Iraq. However, the study suffers from some serious methodological problems as indicated below.

The study in question, *Why They Fight: Combat Motivation in the Iraq War*, was conducted in Iraq by a team of researchers headed by Dr. Leonard Wong, associate research professor at the U.S. Army War College's Strategic Studies Institute, right after Operation Iraq Freedom took place from March 20 to May 1, 2003. Their research monograph concludes: "Soldiers still fight for each other. In a professional army, however, soldiers are also sophisticated enough to grasp the moral reasons for fighting" (Wong et al. 2003, 23). The report suggests that this is a result of the transformation of the army from a fledgling, all-volunteer experiment to a truly professional force (Wong et al. 2003, viii). In other words, this study reconfirms not only the classic findings on the critical importance of social cohesion and emotional bonds between soldiers in combat motivation but also advances a new and surprising finding: unlike the soldiers in the past wars (World War II, Korean War, and Viet Nam war), the U.S. soldiers in the Iraq War indicated that the ideological factor was also a crucial factor in their combat motivation. Even more surprising is that the research team came up with a serendipitous hypothesis: the significance of ideological factors in combat motivation of the U.S. soldiers in the Iraq War might have derived from the transformation of the U.S. army from a conscript army to an all-volunteer army in 1973. In the researchers' own words:

> The findings showed that U.S. soldiers continue to fight because of the bonds of trust between soldiers. They also fight, however, because of the trust established with the Army as an institution. Our soldiers are professionals and are the culmination of 30 years of an all-volunteer force [Wong et al. 2003, 25].

The conclusion may have some significant implications for researchers and policy makers, but their attribution of ideological factors in soldiers' combat motivation to the transformation from a conscript army to a professional army still remains as an untested research hypothesis. Although Wong's team did an interesting exploratory study, the ideology hypothesis in combat motivation needs to be tested by a more comprehensive sociological survey with a rigorous methodology. The most serious problems of Wong and his associates' study include: (1) their inadequate sample size and sampling procedure and (2) premature conclusions based on their small exploratory analysis of interview data collected from accidental or convenient samples without due consideration of the problems of statistical validity and the timing of conducting the survey during the course of the Iraq war.

According to their report, the research team obtained their survey data by interviewing three distinct groups of samples: (1) 30 Iraqi Regular Army soldiers; (2) 40 U.S. troops—16 marines and 26 infantry soldiers; and (3) "over a dozen members of the media embedded in U.S. Army ground units" (Wong et al. 2003, 6). The first and last groups were selected for a comparative analysis, according to the research report. They did not elaborate, however, how these samples were selected—random, purposive, or just accidental (convenient) samples. Thus, even just for an exploratory study, a sample of 40 respondents seems extremely inadequate for examining about 120,000 U.S. soldiers who participated in Operation Iraqi Freedom. The same is true for examining the relationship between an all-volunteer army and the ideological factor in combat motivation. Moreover, the timing of the interviews could have significantly influenced the American soldiers' responses.

Epilogue

The research team does not indicate in their report the exact dates of their interviews, but their report was released in July 2003 when most of the U.S. and British troops were still basking in the jubilation of their "mission accomplished" in toppling Saddam Hussein's regime. For that matter, the entire world seemed to be mesmerized by witnessing the "shock and awe" invasion of Iraq by the Coalition Forces that brought the swift fall of Baghdad in only three weeks. I could not believe my eyes when I watched the TV news video showing a huge crowd of Iraqis cheering as a large statue of Saddam toppled to the ground. It was also quite an upsetting scene to witness the beginning of the demise of one sovereign nation by a surprise attack from another nation without an immediate provocation or a formal declaration of war.

Now, seven years have passed since our initial "victory" in Iraq — the fall of Saddam Hussein and his regime — yet today our troops are still fighting there and have extended further into Afghanistan. I wonder if Wong's research team has replicated a similar kind of survey since then. If they did the study now, would they reach the same conclusion on the American soldiers' combat motivation in Iraq as they did in their summer 2003 survey? So far, I have not seen any published report by Wong or his team on such a follow-up study.

In my view, war makers tend to glorify war by evoking God or God-given ideology; however, they rarely fight on the battlefield themselves. But soldiers do. They fight not only for their own lives but also for their comrades. For them, war is hell. For war makers, war is an opportune chance for enhancing their political expediency as self-appointed leaders for accomplishing their "God-given holy mission." Interestingly, during the Bush administration none of the U.S. top leaders had ever served their "beloved" country on the battlefield — and none of their children had either.

In closing, I would like to thank my comrades in arms — the ROK (Republic of Korea) Army soldiers under my command and my fellow "baby lieutenants" or "consumptive officers" — who sacrificed their dreams of youth and their young lives to save their comrades, family, and country during a brutal and senseless civil war. I am also deeply grateful for my comrades in arms from the UN forces, particularly the U.S. soldiers and officers who fought with me in the trenches and bunkers in the Godforsaken mountains and valleys at the Kumsong front. I still fondly remember the name of a young American artillery officer from the U.S. 300th Armored Field Artillery

(AFA) Battalion, Lieutenant McIntosh (I forgot his first name but I recall he was originally from Urbana/Champaign, Illinois), who, as my advisor, helped me in saving the lives of 600 men, 18 howitzers, and 75 vehicles of our ROK 76th Field Artillery Battalion on the eve of the July Offensive (July 13, 1953), just two weeks before the armistice. In fact, without the help of the U.S. Armed Forces, the entire ROK Armed Forces would never have survived the war at all.

I also thank my family for their unceasing love and patience to keep me alive and sane. My mother, widowed at age 34, who sacrificed her life to raise her five children without getting any help from her first son who was always absent from home during his seven years of military service. In Korea the oldest son should take care of everything when his parents are getting old. I feel very sorry for failing in my filial duty and immensely thankful for her sacrifice, particularly during the Korean War. I also regret that I did not have much time together with my siblings to get to know them better. I used to make an excuse — "It's the stupid war! You see? I hope you will understand. I have no control over it!" But how sorry I am, for I could have done better.

My loving wife of 48 years, Gloria, also told me in the early years of our marriage that I was often having nightmares and sometimes almost punched her with my fist in sleep. Many nights I had bad dreams of the Korean War — for example, I dreamt our troops were enveloped by the enemy and I had to fight in hand-to-hand combat. In my sleep I screamed, tossed around, and tried to hit something in an attempt to save myself from the enemy. When my wife woke me up, I was covered with a cold sweat. The last nightmare about the war was a year ago. Would that mean my PTSD (Post-Traumatic Stress Disorder) from the Korea War lasted more than 50 years? I just can't believe it.

The Korean War gave me, however, an invaluable lesson: respect life, any life — even of your enemy, imagined or real.

Appendix:
ROK Infantry and Artillery

Table of Organization, ROK Infantry and Field Artillery (1950–1953)
(A rough sketch for the general reader)

Infantry (Strength) Echelon of Units (From high/large to low/small)		*Field Artillery* (Fire capacity to support infantry)
Corps (2–3 Divisions)	40–50,000	Corps Artillery Group (6–12 Battalions)
Division (2–3 Regiments)	10–20,000	Division Artillery Group (3–4 Battalions)
Regiment (2–3 Battalions)	2–3,000	Artillery Battalions (1–2)
Battalion (2–3 Companies)	200–600	Artillery Battalions (1)
Company (2–3 Platoons)	60–200	Artillery Batteries (2–3)
Platoon (2–3 squads)	30–40	Artillery Battery (1)

Composition of a ROK Field Artillery Battalion (1950–1953)

Battalion Headquarters	Battalion Commander (Lt. Colonel or Major)
	Battalion Executive (Major or Captain)
	Battalion Staff: (Captain or 1st Lt.)
	Personnel (S-1)
	Intelligence (S-2)
	Operations & Training (S-3)
	Fire Direction Center (Director: Captain)
	Ordnance & Logistics (S-4)
Three Howitzer Batteries	3 Battery Commanders (Captain or 1st Lt.)
	Battery Executives (1st Lt. or Master Sergeant)
	Forward Observers (2nd Lt. and Corporals)
	Firing Detail/Gunners (Corporals and Sergeants)

APPENDIX: ROK INFANTRY AND ARTILLERY

Major Artillery Weapons available for the ROK Field Artillery (1950–53)

Mostly the ROK used U.S. 105mm howitzers in the early phase of the Korean War. Later they were supplemented by the U.S. 155mm howitzers and the 4.2-inch mortars. All of these weapons were World War II vintage. A typical ROK field artillery battalion was equipped with 18 105mm howitzers (6 howitzers for each battery).

References

Ardrey, Robert. (1961). *African Genesis*. New York: Atheneum.
———. 1966. *Territorial Imperative*. New York: Atheneum.
Choe, Jong Chul. (2006). 금관가야왕국 (*Geum Gwan Gaya Kingdom*). Seoul: Miraebooks.
Ilyon (Kwan Ji Kim). (1281–83). *Samguk Yusa—Garakki* [Memorabilia of Three Kingdoms, vol. 2, History of Garak]. Ilyon was a Buddhist monk (1206–1289). Kwan Ji Kim was his secular name. This is the original edition written in classic Chinese. Translated edition is below.
———. (1997). *Samguk Yusa* [Legend and History of the Three Kingdoms of Ancient Korea or Memorabilia of the Three Kingdoms]. Translated by Ha Tae-Hung and Grafton K. Mintz. Seoul: Yonsei University Press.
Korean War Veterans Association (전우회). (1995). "Combat Codes" (전훈). P. 4 in *The 6.25 Korean War and the Army Comprehensive School* (in Korean). Seoul: Sam Kwang Publishing. ("6.25 Korean War" is the term used in Korea to refer to the war. "6.25" stands for June 25th, the date the Korean War began.)
Kwon, Byung-Rin. (1990). "Kimhae: Proud Heir of the Kaya Legacy." *Seoul: The Monthly Magazine of Korea Illustrated* (October): 38–47.
Lee, Jong-gi. (1987). 가락국의영광 (The Glory of Garak Kingdom). Kimhae: Research Institute on Garak (Gaya) History.
Morris, Desmond. (1967). *The Naked Ape*. New York: Dell.
Moskos, Charles C. (1970). *The American Enlisted Man: The Rank and File in Today's Military*. New York: Russell Sage Foundation.
Paik, Sun Yup. (1999). *From Pusan to Panmunjom*. Dulles, VA: Brassey's.
Remarque, Erich Maria. (1929). *Im Westen Nichts Neues* (All Quiet on the Western Front). Boston: Little, Brown.
Shils, Edward A., and Morris Janowitz. (1948). "Cohesion and Disintegration in Wehrmacht in World War II." *Public Opinion Quarterly* 12 (Summer):280–315.
Stouffer, Samuel, E.A. Suchman, L.C. DeVinny, Arthur A. Lumsdaine, Marion Harper Lumsdaine, Robin M. Williams Jr., M. Brewster Smith, Irving L. Janis,

Shirley A. Star, and Leonard S. Cottrell Jr. (1949). *The American Soldier*. 2 vols. Princeton, NJ: Princeton University Press.

Thomas, Evan, and Andrew Romano. (2007). "In God They Trust." *Newsweek*, May 7, 35–36.

Weems, C.N., ed. (1962). *Hulbert's History of Korea*. 2 vols. New York: Hillary House.

Wilson, Edward O. (1975). *Sociobiology: The New Synthesis*. Cambridge, MA: Harvard University Press.

Wong, Leonard, Thomas A. Kolditz, Raymond A. Millen, and Terrence M. Potter. July (2003). *Why They Fight: Combat Motivation in the Iraq War*. Carlisle, PA: Strategic Studies Institute (SSI), U.S. Army War College. http://www.strategicstudiesinstitute.army.mil/pdffiles/PUB179.pdf

Yangchon Hurh Family Genealogy. (c. 1927). Preface vol., 1–2.

Index

*Numbers in **bold italics** indicate pages with illustrations.*

All Quiet on the Western Front 10–11, 70, 104
Allied Field Artillery Officers Course (Fort Sill) 88, *89*, *90*, 95
Amaterasu Omikami (sun goddess) 22
The American Soldier: Adjustment During Army Life 173
antiaircraft artillery (AAA) 143–153, *154*, 155–160
Ardrey, Robert 171
Armistice 71, 77–78, 109–110, 121, 129–130, 134, 145, 148
Army Artillery School (ROK) 5–6, 56–58, *63*, 97, 99, *102*, 103, 105–108
Army Comprehensive School 5, 55, 58–62, 181

B-29 Bomber 53
basa seoktap 18
Battle of Kumsong 124–130
Buddhism 18, 24, 77

Cairo Declaration 30
cease-fire 78, 110, 121, 130–131, 134, *135*, 137, 138
Cha, Maj. Young Jo 111, 112, *117*, 119, 123, 124, 126
Chang, Cpl. 79, 80, 82
Chang, Lt. Keun Hyung *117*, *122*, 127, *135*, 137

Chinese calligraphy 20–23
Chinese Communist Forces (CCF) 43, 69, 115, 131
Chinese medicine 32, 141; herbalist 3
Cho, Lt. Chang Ho *63*
Cho, Pvt. 67
Choen Ja Mun 20
Choi, Capt. Sung 150, 152, 159
Choi, Lt. 70, 83, 84
Choi, Maj. 148, 157
Chonan *x*, 79, 99
Christianity 76–77, 95, 110, 133, 172
chubo (PX) 58, 131
Chung, Col. In Wan *89*, 90, 102, 107, 109, 110, 111
Chung, Kwang Jo 62
Combat Code viii, 60, 181
comfort women 23, 70
Complete Collection of World Literatures 77
Confucius (Confucianism) 14, 24, 33, 77, 80
corruption 106, 114, 119–120, 126
cultural ambassadors in Lawton, Oklahoma *94*, 95
culture shock 86, 88–90, *91*, 94

Daegu *x*, 50–59
Democratic People's Republic of Korea (North Korea) 34
dirty words 123

INDEX

disciplinary measures in the ROK Army 60, 106
DMZ (Demilitarized Zone) *x*, 110, 131, 133–*134*, *136*, 137, 143
Durant, Will 82

Eum, Myung Sum 12, 13

Fighting Cannons 41
fire for effect 62, 72
For Colored 93–94
Fort Bliss 149, 151, 153, *154*, 155, 156
Fort Lewis 156
Fort Sill 65–100, 101, 103, 109, 111, 113, 116, 121, 142, 143
From Pusan to Panmunjom 120
funerals, Korean traditional 33

Gapyong 37, 38
Gaya (or Garak) Kingdom 14–16, 18
General John Pope 85, 95
The Glory of Garak Kingdom 18
GOD & WAR 172

H., Maj. 125, 129, 130, 131, 138
Hakto Hogukdae 34
Han, Lt. Yang Shin 8, 9, 10, 60, *63*, 65
Han River 26, 36–37, 40, 45, 49, 52, 79, 99, 161
hangul (Korean alphabet) 21
Hirohito (Japanese Emperor) 30
The History of Three Kingdoms see *Samguk Yusa*
Hong, Capt. Jong Chul 59, 60, *63*
Hong, Maj. 86
Hong, 2nd Lt. *118*
Hulbert's History of Korea 16
Hurh, Bang Ja 14, 44
Hurh, Bu Yong 12, 13, 14
Hurh, Eui Moo 14, *33*, 44, 82, 99
Hurh, Gloria ix, 178
Hurh, Queen Hwang-ok 14–18; tomb *18*
Hurh, In Moo 14, *33*, 44, 82
Hurh, Jun 12
Hurh, Paul ix

Hurh, Soonja *33*
Hurh, Won Moo 25, *33*, *63*, *81*, 89, 90, *91*, 94, 102, 117, *118*, 122, *134*, *135*, *136*, *154*, *170*
Hurh, Yong Moo 14, *33*, 44
Hurh, Yoon Seong 80
Hurh family genealogy 15–19
Hussein, Saddam 177

In gwa ungbo (the cause-effect principle) 64
Iron Triangle 97–98

Janowitz, Morris 174
Japanese Occupation of Korea: annexation of Korea 12; colonial policy 22–23; schools 22, 31; swordsmanship (*Kendo*) 30; World War II conditions 28–29; World War II surrender 31
Jeonhun (Combat Code) viii, 60, 181
Johnstone, Mr. 167

Kafka, Franz 103
Kang, Col. Kwan Young 138, 139, 159, 161, 162, 163, 164, 165
Kang, Woo-Bang 96
Kang, Lt. Yung Suk *89*, 90, *91*, 94, 96, 97, 109–112
Kim, Maj. Byung Kwan 54, 139, 140
Kim, Lt. Chang Joon 53, *63*, 64
Kim, Col. 123
Kim, 1st Lt. 59
Kim, Gen. 124
Kim, Geon Bae 54
Kim, Capt. Hei Chu 162, 163, 164, 166, 168, 169, 170
Kim, Hyung Ja 169
Kim, Il-sung 34, 39, 172
Kim, Cpl. Ju Sik 75
Kim, King Suro 14–18
Kim, Lt. (3 different Individuals) 72; a different Lt. Kim 83–86; a different Lt. Kim *122*
Kim, Lt. Jong Jeun 112, 113, 116, 138
Kim, Lt. Jook Hi *117*, 127, *135*, 137, 138
Kim, Pvt. 67

INDEX

Kim, Sgt. 103
Kim, Capt. Yu Kap 150, 152
Kim Hae (capital of Gaya Kingdom) 14, 17, 18
Ku, Maj. T.H. 162
Kumsong front 115–116, *117–118*, 119–121, *122*, 123–131
Kyunggi High School 28–30, 34–35, 37, 42, 59, 132, 139, 149, 159, 167, *170*

Lawton, Oklahoma 92, 94–95, 133
Lee, Brig. Gen. 156, 159–160
Lee, Brig. Gen. Chang Jung 118, 134, 138, 156, 159–160
Lee, Capt. Kee Ju 162
Lee, Capt. Keum Yeol 71, 76, 78, 79, 82
Lee, Col. 125
Lee, Cpl.(2 different individuals) 67; a different Cpl. Lee *136*
Lee, Gen. 138
Lee, Lt. Hyo Suk *63*, 73
Lee, Lt. Hyo Sung 90, 94, 98, 101, *102*
Lee, Lt. Ki Yong *89*, 90, 94, 98, 101, 102, 109
Lee, Kimo 50
Lee, Lt. Moon Woo 109
Lee, Myung Sang 59
Lee, 2nd Lt. 59
Lee, Sgt. 133
Lee, Lt. Ung Jai (also spelled Jae) ix, 112, 113, 116, 118, 119, 126, 138

MacArthur, Gen. Douglas 40, 41
marginal man 94
Mayo, Brig. Gen. Richard W. 116
McIntosh, Lt. 117, *118*, 120, 121, 178
Meinecke, Charlotte D. 159
Min, Lt. Byong Joon *117*
Min, Kwan Shik 166, 167
Min, Queen 12
Moon, Maj. Gen. Hyung Tae 160, 161, 162, 164, 165, 168
Moriyama, Tomoyuki (Japanese name of Won Moo Hurh) 22, 28
Morris, Desmond 171

Moskos, Charles 175

Nakdong River 5
Natzume, Soseki 243
Nietzsche, Friedrich 103
Nomujas (drafted laborers) 6–7
North Korean invasion (June 25, 1950) 35–36
North Korean People's Army 37, 39–41, 43, 49, 52, 74, 99, 172

O'Connor, Maj. Gen. Daniel A. 155
Orfanides, Lt. Christos 156
Osan Air Base 142–147

Paik, Hyung Ja 164
Paik, Gen. Sun Yup 120, 159, 160, 161, 162, 163
Pak, Capt. (also spelled as Park) 119, *135*
Pak, Lt. 125, 127, 128, 129
Pak, Maj. 146, 147
Panmunjom *x*, 109–120, 130, 181
Park, Capt. 65, 66
Park, Pres. Chung Hee 111
Park, Maj. 138, 148
People's Court 36–37, 40
public welfare project 119, 124, 126, 132; *see also* corruption
Pusan Perimeter 52–53

Quonset huts 101

Rankin, Glen 165, 166
recapture of Seoul (Sept. 15, 1950) 40–41
refugees 5, 44–48, 50–51
Remarque, Erich Maria 10, 103
Republic of Korea Army's Combat Code *see Jeonhun*
Rhee, Pres. Syngman 34, 36, 41, 172
The Romance of the Three Kingdoms see *Sam Gugji or San Kuo Chih Yen-Ie*
Romano, Andrew 172

Sam Gugji or San Kuo Chih Yen-Ie 22

Samguk Yusa 15–16
Seiler, Maj. 119
Sekai Bungaku Jenshu see *Complete Collection of World Literatures*
shamanism 24
Shaw, Maj. **89**
Shils, Edward 174
Shin, Lt. Col. D.H. 142, 144, 147
Shin, Maj. H.J. 162
Shin, Lt. Jung Kyun **117**, **135**, 137, 142, 144, 155; as Brig. Gen. ix; as Capt. 158
The 6–25 Korean War and the Army Comprehensive School 60
Slicker, Maj. 127
The Story of Philosophy 82
Stouffer, Samuel 173
stupa 18
Sung, Hyo 109

Taoism 24
target practice 61, 106–107
Tatakau Kaho see *Fighting Cannons*
38th parallel *x*, 30

Thomas, Evan 172
time-on-target (TOT) 116
Tolstoy, Leo 23, 69

U.S. 300th AFA (Armored Field Artillery) Battalion 120, 124, 126

Western literature 24
Why They Fight: Combat Motivation in the Iraq War 175
Wilson, Edward 171
Wingate, Sgt. 121
Wolfe, Thomas 132
Wong, Dr. Leonard 175
Worldly Philosophers 82

Yagyuk Gangsik 58
Yang, Capt. 86
Yang, Lt. 125, 128
Yang Cheon Hurh Si Saebo 19
You Can't Go Home Again 132
Yu, Gen. Jae Hung 152
Yun, Sang Jin 166, 167
Yun, Maj. Sung Kuk 103

www.ingramcontent.com/pod-product-compliance
Ingram Content Group UK Ltd.
Pitfield, Milton Keynes, MK11 3LW, UK
UKHW042011140426
5217IPUK00015B/1107

9 780786 465033